MCC
MASTERCLASS

MCC
MASTERCLASS

THE NEW MCC
COACHING BOOK

TONY LEWIS

WEIDENFELD AND NICOLSON · LONDON

First published in Great Britain 1994
by Weidenfeld and Nicolson
The Orion Publishing Group Ltd
Orion House,
5 Upper St Martin's Lane
London WC2H 9EA

ISBN 0 297 81431 1

Design by Harry Green

Filmset by Selwood Systems, Midsomer Norton
Printed in Great Britain by Butler & Tanner Ltd, Frome
and London

NOTE ON THE ILLUSTRATIONS

The majority of the photographs in this book are the work
of Patrick Eagar, and for this reason he is not credited in
the individual captions. The MCC, the authors, and the
publishers would, however, like to express their
appreciation of his help in the preparation of the book and
are grateful to be able to reproduce so many fine studies
of the game and its players.

Acknowledgements are due to certain other
individuals: to David Dunbar for the picture of Peter May
taken by his father, Jim Dunbar; to Clive Radley for his
help on several technical photographs; to Jim Ruston for
a photograph of R.C. 'Jack' Russell; and to Richard Wilson
for valuable assistance with reasearch.

Acknowledgements must also be made to various firms
and agencies: to All-Sport (UK) Ltd; to A & C. Black
(Publishers) Ltd for three photographs by Sylvio Dukov
from *Skilful Cricket* by Bob Woolmer: to John Fairfax Pty
Ltd for the *Sydney Morning Herald* 1928 picture of
Hammond and Oldfield; to the Hulton–Deutsch
Collection Limited: and to the Sport & General Press
Agency Ltd.

The diagrams have been drawn by Technical Arts
Services; and the special technical photographs were
taken by Jon Stewart.

Acknowledgements are also due to Phil Lockyer of the
Arundel Castle Cricket Foundation for help on 'Coaching
Young Cricketers'.

FOREWORD

MCC is deeply grateful to all those who have worked so single-mindedly to help to produce this exciting new coaching book and the videos that back it up. To read this litany of famous names is to conjure up some of the greatest moments in Test cricket over the past thirty years. It is a significant commentary on the role of MCC in world cricket and to the spirit of the game at the highest level that the great masters of the game in our time should have come together to pass on the benefit of their wisdom and expertise to a younger band of cricketers and indeed to generations unborn.

The precepts the experts uphold are not transient precepts and deep thought and much hard work has gone into their presentation. It is our hope that this book will become an indispensable bible to cricketers all over the world, and in organising its production Tony Lewis and Peter Walker are underlining the responsibility MCC has never shirked in its desire to see the true principles of good cricket flourish. May all who benefit from this publication remember that cricket is a game played not just with head and hand and eye, but also, and perhaps above all, with the heart and all of us who love the game are custodians of its spirit.

Dennis Silk.

President, MCC

CONTENTS

PREFACE

The first edition of *The MCC Cricket Coaching Book* was published in 1952. Then, and through its many revisions, the aim was to view the game's techniques, to assist coaches and to appeal to cricketers, young or old, who wanted to check their game against the accepted orthodoxies.

MCC Masterclass moves away from that approach to one which is presaged in the title – essays of instruction, advice and experience composed by masters of the game. To complement their written word, teaching videos have been made. Cricket skills can be presented successfully in book form as we will show but the visual possibilities of learning have moved on. Television is a superb propagator of international cricket and it is appropriate that some of those cricketers who have thrilled many nations in Test matches should become the most attractive teachers.

Indeed these 'Masters' have been chosen because they have a famed understanding of their art and craft and are the finest teachers in the game. Their style is personal and direct, the language of master to pupil or sometimes of the fatherly figure who can come up with a technical suggestion which will suit you. Imagine a university supervision by an expert who talks, cajoles, demonstrates and lays out his whole thesis before you for debate.

As the author, I found it an enriching experience to bring their cricket intelligence to you in book form. Although I had my own wide experience on which to draw as a player, writer and broadcaster, I was constantly surprised by rare bits of insight. I was impressed by the depth of thinking which these most successful cricketers put into their game.

'Keep it simple, mate,' Dennis Lillee advised me, and I have. This is a book which simply explains how to play cricket. It omits much that was in the book it has replaced. There are no chapters on grounds and pitches, Group Coaching or non-turf pitches. Fitness for Cricket is limited to personal advice from the masters within their chapters, and all advice on fitness is directly related to the skills of the game. Advice on equipment comes as and when the teaching turns that way.

In short, *MCC Masterclass* is an attempt to present tuition in simple, expert words. All eleven masters confess to have been blinkered and dedicated to practice when they were young. This new MCC coaching book is therefore a highly focused tutorial for all cricketers.

As in my previous work for MCC, the bicentennial book, *Double Century: The Story of MCC and Cricket*, my editor has been John Bright-Holmes, a man of words and the way to use them, who also loves the game of cricket. He has embraced the fresh version of Masterclass. Our partnership has always been a happy one and we have both appreciated the energetic back-up and attention to detail of my secretary Siân Thomas.

I hope that *MCC Masterclass* will be both vivid and personal, attached only to the playing of cricket. It ignores the wide undergrowth of theory which tends to grow around the great game and enmesh it in confusion. MCC's contribution is simple – each essay comes essentially, as the old record company used to advertise, from His Master's Voice.

Presentation new: truths old.

TONY LEWIS

Llantrisant
Mid Glamorgan
February 1994

THE SPIRIT OF THE GAME

BY TONY LEWIS

Cricket famously incorporates a code of behaviour not written in the Laws of the game, so much so that the saying 'It isn't cricket' has been handed down as a general accusation of cheating, sharp practice or poor behaviour.

There is much in the game which calls for honesty and good sportsmanship, for respect for the umpire whatever his decision, and for your opponents. Cricket in the eighteenth century was sometimes believed to be a substitute for duelling, and certainly there are confrontations between individuals within a match which are like skirmishes within a battle. When winning becomes too important, when the participants believe themselves engaged in war not recreation, then the temptation to indulge in gamesmanship and unfair play is obvious.

Each one of the Masters whose advice and experience fill this book, emphasises the enjoyment of playing cricket. 'Above all, enjoy it,' writes Richie Benaud. The unwritten code centres on respect for your opponent which ensures that the match is played aggressively with a will to win, but at the same time in a spirit of harmony and good temper.

Regrettably cricket's reputation as a tutor of good sportsmanship is flawed. International cricket has been beset by the problems of players who pressurise umpires, illegally tamper with the ball, bombard batsmen with abusive language and conduct themselves without the sense of chivalry once so admired. It is well worth reproducing the stricture of Mr Harry Altham and Sir George Allen, co-authors of the previous *MCC Cricket Coaching Book*, even though their language may now appear dated: 'A cricket team should feel that they are playing with, as well as against, their opponents. The home side should remember that they are hosts, the visitors that they are guests, and both should realise that the true greatness of the game lies in combat and comradeship combined.'

Going for victory is everything in a cricket match. A model to study is the 1960–1 series between Australia and West Indies when the captains, Richie Benaud and Sir Frank Worrell, broke the pattern of dull, defensive cricket around the world by blasting each other with every attacking gambit in the book. A brilliant series resulted – no prisoners taken and a beer together at close of play, every day.

The governing bodies of cricket, however, have had to tax themselves with devising punishments and remedies for the game's blemishes. MCC's Cricket Sub-Committee is made up of the highest calibre of former Test player and administrator and its agenda has included many discussions on Fair and Unfair Play (Law 42). Similarly the Boards of Control around the world have been forced to ask – how can the spirit be returned to cricket? How can cricket again represent integrity?

Cricket Clubs and organisations have a responsibility to preserve the sportsmanship historically locked within the game of cricket. It can be argued cogently that behaviour on the field simply mirrors the society outside it, but it is also probable that the rules and regulations of cricket breed confrontation and allow space for sharp practice. This is why the focus should fall upon the captains. The role of the captain must not be underestimated and Boards of Control have found it worth saying publicly –

each captain, in conjunction with his manager/coach, is responsible for the way his players conduct themselves before, throughout and immediately after the match. It is the captain's duty to prevent threats and verbal abuse and he has a responsibility to take immediate action whenever it occurs. It is the captain's responsibility to see that there is strong, mutual respect between players and umpires but, in any case, no verbal abuse should ever be directed at an umpire.

Captains should stop their fielders running at an umpire with their appeal in order to affect his decision, and no fielders should leap about congratulating a catcher before the umpire has actually said that it is 'out'. The captain, of course, should see that his team does not participate in acts of sharp practice.

So now we can see how important captaincy can be at every level. Schoolmasters must select their captains well but it would be a mistake to choose him because he is an obvious disciple of the moral code of cricket. In order to carry with him the whole of his team the captain must have their respect as a player. In a perfect world captains should know the Laws, understand the game, know exactly how to treat each different player and also perform well his own skills.

You will read how our Master-captains crystallise the requirements of a captain to a simple requirement, but you must also be aware of how his role is crucial to the spirit in which the game is played.

And without apology I return for a conclusion to the original Altham-Allen text. 'Nor does any other game expose a player to a more varied or exacting trial. It can be a lonely and formidable experience to walk out, perhaps after a long wait, to bat at the crisis of a match, possibly to face a fast bowler on a lively pitch, or a spinner on a turning one: formidable too to stand under a high catch knowing that to miss it may cost the game. Bowler and fielder alike may often towards the end of a hard day have to "steel their hearts" for a final effort.

'There are also the less obvious but more insidious trials of failure and success: the greatest players will have spells when nothing will go right; then comes the test of still keeping cheerful and finding some consolation in the success of others: and if fortune smiles for a time and the game seems easy, the true cricketer will remember to keep a modest mind.'

DENNIS LILLEE

BISHAN BEDI

RAY ILLINGWORTH

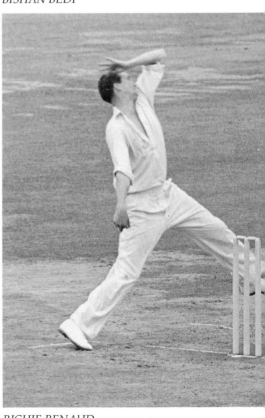

RICHIE BENAUD

RICHARD HADLEE

1
BOWLING

DENNIS LILLEE

RICHARD HADLEE

RAY ILLINGWORTH

RICHIE BENAUD

BISHAN BEDI

FAST BOWLING

DENNIS LILLEE

'All I ever wanted to do was to run in a long way and bowl fast,' I wrote in my book *The Art of Fast Bowling* (1978). 'To do that for prolonged spells meant that a high degree of physical fitness was required, a fact that I appreciated mainly through the coaching of my grandfather, Len Halifax, and even in my days as a junior I was always prepared to shoulder the wheel and do all the hard work that goes with the search for stamina.'

Basic actions

Let me now start with questions. Do you have the enthusiasm to bowl fast? Then go out and try it.

Can you bowl fast? Does your body say 'Yes' or 'No' to you? Listen to the message from your body. Even though you have been watching the great fast bowlers and have been inspired to try to join them – just as I was inspired as a boy by Wesley Hall, the West Indian – do not go any further if your body is uncomfortable bowling fast. On the other hand, if you have a natural aptitude then go for it. Do not even consider at this stage the skills and variations which go to make a very good bowler, just go out to the nets with one word in your mind – fast. Fast is not medium-fast: it is truly fast. Go for speed. Bowl the fastest you can bowl.

I believe that fast bowling is a natural act but, as experience of play builds up, say in school, coaching helps to refine the run-up and action, to rationalise the body movements and, by increasing the skills, to mature the cricketer. To many batsmen, fast bowlers are a mental and physical threat. Just think how destructive, therefore, is a fast bowler who has the cricket intelligence to analyse and improve his performance with sound techniques.

You must have a vision of how you want to look and feel about your action. You can actually feel the control in your run-up and the surge of acceleration towards the stumps. Aim to be running at your fastest about four strides from the delivery: that means you can arrive at the crease well balanced with your head still. With proper balance you can then launch yourself into the delivery, getting the front arm up high in preparation for a powerful follow-through. If you have the desire to bowl fast, the physical ability, and the understanding of what you are trying to achieve, then you can aim for the top.

But do not be put off by people telling you that there is a 'right' way to bowl. I was one who was always trying to be classical but I did share a most successful partnership in the Australian team of the 1970s with Jeff Thomson. He slung the ball down, and quickly too. He used to veer out as he arrived at the crease to make room for the right arm to whip over from behind his back; he used to catapult the ball down the other end. Different actions: similar results.

Kit

Your kit is important. When I was bowling at my best I liked a higher cut boot for ankle support but one that was light in weight. I liked them with a wedge or chip of rubber in the heel and a good spread of sprigs or spikes, about four in the heel, and eight or nine in the front. Because I played so much I had my boots made with orthopaedic advice and, if you are going to be a serious fast bowler, you should

Lillee's partner during the 1970s – Jeff Thomson: 'he slung the ball down and quickly too'.

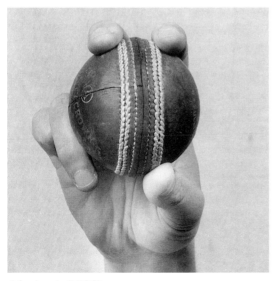

A basic grip (MCC)

work out exactly what boot you need and get it specially fitted for your foot.

Fundamentals

The fundamentals of a good bowling action are:

1. A correct grip;
2. A smooth and economical run-up;
3. An easy, rhythmical and well-balanced delivery, making full use of height and body;
4. A deliberate and fluent follow-through.

Grip

Hold the ball in the fingers, not in the palm of the hand. This way you have control of the ball. Think of the fingers as the final extension of the wrist and hand because the fingers impart the whip effect which gives the ball 'life' off the pitch.

Run-up

Do not run further than is necessary. There has to be a gauge inside you which tells you what is your optimum speed. Do not charge in. The run-up should be long enough for you to build up your speed stride by stride so that you peak about three or four strides before the delivery. Then you have to hold the speed right through your action into the follow-through. Do not race in from the start; gradually get faster, otherwise you have wasted valuable energy. As well as speed you must think rhythm and balance.

How do you know how far to run? Take a friend with you on to the field, make a mark on the turf, and run in without wickets or crease to bowl your fastest ball in any direction. This will be a natural run because you do not have to worry about arriving at a crease. Your friend will note where you let the ball go and measure back to the mark in ordinary walking paces.

Let us say it is 24 paces. Next you go to the practice pitch and place your toe on the

A left-arm quick bowler whose action and follow-through Lillee admired – Alan Davidson (Sport & General)

bowling crease, facing back to the start of your run. You then walk back the 24 paces just as if you are walking down the street. Do not force it; do not stretch out the paces; do not go through your run-up backwards (as I have seen some bowlers try to do). The only regular measurement is the smallish step we take when we walk naturally. Make your mark at the end of your run.

I recommend the smoothest possible approach to the wicket. Rhythm is sometimes elusive but you must concentrate on it. Listen to your coach. Sometimes stutters in the run-up go unnoticed by the young bowler himself.

If you are struggling to find a regular rhythm try this exercise: go into an empty field with no obstacles nearby and, from a marked point, do a full run-up with your eyes closed. Imagine you are an old steam engine. Walk two or three paces, start to jog, and gradually build up to about three-quarter speed, thinking of the sound and action of a steam train as you are running. I have used this method many, many times and it works wonders in bringing out

smoothness, or, if you are having no-ball problems, use this same technique utilising the open field, a friend marking out the run-up, as you perform it, eyes closed as described.

It is important to watch good fast bowlers in action. I used to admire the run-up of Wes Hall and the delivery action of Australia's Alan Davidson. I had to go to the grounds to see these two at work but young cricketers these days have a golden opportunity to study the best in the world on television.

Sideways-on or front-on?

For fast bowling you can use one of two actions. Either you are side-on or front-on. You still have to adhere to the rules for swinging the ball, grip and follow-through in particular, but fast bowling and swing can work with either of these actions. With the side-on action, you turn to 'load up' the body and then pivot and follow through. With the front-on action you keep your feet pointing towards the target,

The follow-through is an essential part of a bowler's action – Alec Bedser (Hulton-Deutsch)

Dennis Lillee, 1972. 'The spring is cocked': weight well back and body sideways, head perfectly poised

and therefore your body too, and run through once you land on the front foot, not pivot.

Make sure you are not over-coached. What we do not want is a mixed action – feet going forwards, shoulders turning to leg or the other way around. Make sure you feel comfortable: you have to *feel* fast bowling. So the first exercise is this – run up and see if you can bowl fast. That is the first test.

The follow-through is the most important part of the action. If you see a fast or medium-fast bowler pull up after bowling within three yards or so he is not getting the best out of himself. Do you ever see a sprinter hit the tape and stop dead? Look at this picture of Alec Bedser, of Surrey and England, whose splendid follow-through is based on a firm front leg.

The follow-through is the natural extension of your action.

So, I repeat, there are two basic actions, the sideways-on action, as used by Dennis Lillee, and the open, chest-on action as demonstrated by Malcolm Marshall of the West Indies who, I must remind those who have never coached 'front-on' bowling, took 376 Test wickets.

The sideways action

The sideways action is the classic one. To my mind it is the ultimate. Imagine you are the batsman. What do you see? You see an accelerating bowler, head still and menacing, presenting you with a twist of the body, strong thrust of the leading arm high in the air, followed by the windmill action of the bowling arm rushing through at near maximum height before letting go the ball. When you are batting you know when a bowler is going to arrive at the crease balanced and ready to explode. You can see it in his rhythm.

If you are the bowler, to get that sideways feeling, imagine you are a cartwheel turning or a tyre rolling forward. It needs a conscious effort to be side-on at the crease, especially when you take a long, accelerating run to the

POSITION 1   POSITION 2   POSITION 3

stumps. It is difficult to twist your body into the side-on position at high speed but you have to if you want to be a fast bowler.

Let me break down the bowling action into five positions, but remember that none of these positions is fixed, there are no static positions. Think of the illustrations more as high-speed photographs. A bowler never holds any of the positions, he just passes through them.

The following descriptions assume that a right-hand fast bowler is bowling to a right-handed batsman

POSITION 1

Position 1 occurs just after a jump off the left foot and while the body is in the air. The shoulders are sideways, pointing down the pitch. The right leg is passing in front of the left: it crosses in front. The right foot is turning so that it will land parallel to the bowling crease. The left arm is bent and ready to swing upwards: the right hand is about level with the face.

POSITION 2

Position 2 occurs on landing. The body has completed a half-turn so that the left shoulder and hips are pointing down the pitch. The right foot has landed *parallel* to the crease, which is important to ensure a full sideways turn of the body; the body lands in a rock-like position; the front arm, though not rigid, is extended upwards as high as possible and the bowler is looking down the pitch from behind it. The weight is on the back foot and the body is leaning away from the batsman with the front leg raised high and bent slightly. The right arm (bowling arm) is about to swing forward and down past the chest at the start of the delivery swing. The spring is cocked ready for release and the delivery stride now takes place, led by the front arm which is thrown out and down in the direction of the batsman. As the front arm goes down so the bowling arm straightens and comes over like a cartwheel.

POSITION 3

The weight is about to be transferred from the back foot to the front foot which has not yet reached the ground. The left shoulder and arm

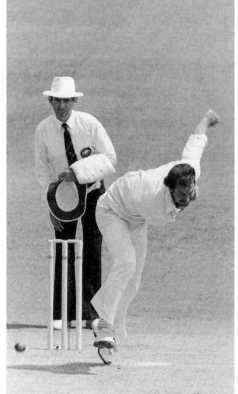

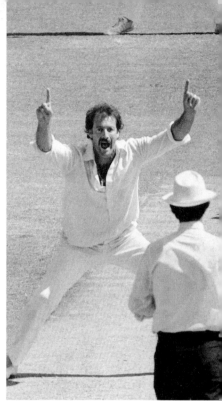

POSITION 4 POSITION 5 *Perth 1982*

are still pointing down the pitch, the back is arched and the head is looking along this leading arm. The left foot will land flat and in line with the back foot which points naturally towards the middle-and-leg stump.

Do not worry about the length of stride except to be sure that you have a firm base for bowling and are comfortable with it. Too short a stride may result in the weight being transferred too soon. Too long a stride will result in loss of height and possibly balance.

This is the moment when the left leg becomes a crucial member of the perfect sideways action. It will give slightly when it lands and the weight comes over on to it, but it must straighten promptly because it is the firm pillar for the pivot.

The pivot will start around the left leg and then, as the full weight is taken on this leg, it will continue around the whole left side. The hips will come through and then the shoulders come over the top. The continuing swing of the left arm down and backwards, tucked in to the left side, together with the upward swing of

the right arm will bring the left shoulder below the right at the instant of delivery.

The bowling action is a mechanism. The slightest mistiming of a part of this body-action can kill the speed and accuracy of the fast bowler or, indeed, of any bowler.

POSITION 4

This is the split second when the ball is released. The full weight of the body will be over the front leg. The bowler will release the ball with the left side firm and from the greatest possible height. The head will be over or slightly in front of the front foot and the eyes will be looking down the pitch.

POSITION 5

Once the bowling arm has completed its action the right shoulder will be pointing down the pitch and the bowler will be looking at the batsman over this shoulder. The front arm will have completed a full circle and the bowling arm will have been carried past the hips close to the body on the left-hand side.

19

The front-on action of Malcolm Marshall

The follow-through continues on to the right foot as the hips complete almost a 180° turn from the original side-on position. In these final strides the bowler must not turn away too sharply to the off side, but at the same time he must be careful not to run down the pitch.

The front-on action

The front-on, or chest-on, bowler does not place his back foot parallel with the bowling crease. Rather his back foot points down the pitch. He does not gather his body and rock back. Instead he runs through smoothly, usually without much of a jump. His left shoulder goes up high but he looks at the batsman from inside the front arm. He never throws his shoulders into the sideways position. Otherwise action and follow-through are the same.

Feel easy about bowling sideways-on or chest-on but never mix the two. I have seen boys with the foot position of chest-on and the shoulder position for side-on. That strains the back and destroys speed, rhythm, and swing. I have also seen the opposite, the feet in sideways position and the body above in a front-on position. Both mixtures are an invitation to back trouble. There are many other variations of the mixed action but all spell long-term problems.

Through research it is now established that the position of the back foot at delivery almost always determines if one is naturally a side-on or a front-on bowler. Make up your mind. Be one or the other. No mixed actions. And do not let any coach make you feel that you have a second-rate action because it is front-on.

I cannot emphasise too much how essential is the follow-through. I have always seen it as the act of thrusting the top part of the body through a vigorous arc at the point of releasing the ball. In my coaching experience I have seen bowlers transformed once they start concentrating on the follow-through. They suddenly find themselves bowling a yard or two faster, and the wicketkeeper has to stand further back as the ball begins to hit his gloves harder. Exaggerate the follow-through action if you like. At one stage in my career my fingers used to touch the ground after delivering the ball. Following through is habit. It is very difficult sometimes to persuade a young bowler that he is losing half of his speed by staying upright after releasing the ball.

You follow through down the pitch as the body goes through the natural motion of slowing down. Again you must think about the rhythm which gives a fast bowler a long life in the game and helps prevent injury. Stopping too soon loses you that rhythm and puts a strain on the body, especially the legs. Your follow-through needs to take you away off the pitch in an arc, as quickly as is comfortable. The line of the arc is important, because if you run into the 'danger area' in front of the stumps you will attract an umpire's warning for running on the pitch.

SWING AND CUT

DENNIS LILLEE AND RICHARD HADLEE

The theory of swing is this: as the ball travels through the air, so the air 'splits' on the seam. The differing airflow exerts different pressures on each side of the ball – and thus causes the ball to swing. The ball will swing more consistently if one side of it is more shiny than the other because the air on the shiny side flows past relatively undisturbed but the airflow on the rougher side and on the seam becomes turbulent. This is why bowlers persist in shining the ball on their clothing however old it is. The slower the ball is bowled the more chance there is of it swinging because it will be more susceptible to the change in pressure.

Outswinger

Probably the most difficult ball for the batsman to play is the outswinger, the ball which swings in the air away from the batsman towards the slips. Fast bowlers expect to swing the new ball when it is still shiny and the seam is firm and prominent, and opening bowlers who can command outswing may well take vital wickets for their side.

Every bowler has to work out the exact grip which suits his own action best but both of our Masters, Dennis Lillee and Richard Hadlee, agree with the following nine points:

1. The seam is upright but angled slightly in the direction of the intended swing, i.e. towards first slip.
2. Hold the ball loosely with the tips of the first two fingers close together on each side of the seam and with the thumb under the seam of the ball. With the ball angled, however, the fingers will be slightly across the seam.

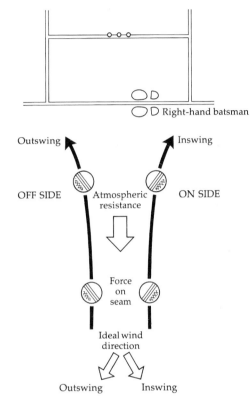

Explanation of swing bowling

Grip for outswinger. On delivery it is angled towards first or second slip (MCC)

3. The shiny side of the ball should be on the outside, the side opposite to the way you want it to swing.

4. When you release the ball the seam must be vertical and angled in the direction of the intended swing.

5. You will need to experiment to know exactly where you should place your fingers and thumb and you must choose exactly what suits you. For example, although we say that the thumb should be directly underneath, on the seam, it is more wise for you to be comfortable and have the certainty that, when you release the ball, the seam goes down the pitch *upright*. It is of no use following a coaching book slavishly if the ball is not going towards the batsman with the seam upright.

6. In this respect the position of the wrist is crucial. At the moment of delivery the wrist locks, and the bowler must feel that his two fingers each side of the seam stay behind the ball as long as possible.

7. The ideal action for bowling the outswinger is the classical sideways-on action where the right foot lands parallel to the bowling crease, the shoulders turn towards the on side and the front foot is placed slightly across the line of direction, i.e. towards the on side.

   It is easier to bowl the outswinger from close to the stumps. In the follow-through the bowling arm cuts across the body and finishes down the left side of the body.

   It is also possible to bowl outswing with an open-chested action. To do this with control you will have to experiment with the wrist position and work out your own individual technique.

8. It is important to be able to select and hit a target with the outswinger, but it is no use having the ball swing early in its flight. The idea is to draw the batsman into a drive or a forward defensive stroke and then, once he has committed his bat to a line of flight, the ball swings late away, finds the outside edge of the bat, and flies to the slips for a catch.

9. When you are back at the start of your run, consider what your intention is. If the batsman has driven you successfully once or twice, maybe you will want to drop in a short one to make him less certain of the length and drive him on to the back foot, but your overall strategy is to draw him forward into the late swing.

Inswing

1. Inswing is most effective when the ball swings late in its flight. Again, the ball is held loosely with the tips of the first two

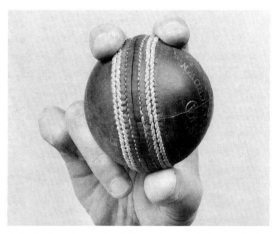

Grip for inswinger. On delivery it is angled towards fine leg. (MCC)

fingers and angled slightly in the direction of the intended swing, i.e. to fine-leg. The first and second fingers will lie on top of the ball, one on each side of the seam. The first finger usually lies alongside the seam and the second on the outside of the seam.

2. As the shiny side of the ball is held on the opposite side to the direction of swing, the shiny side is on the left-hand side as the bowler views it.

3. For inswing, at the moment of delivery, the front foot may be placed slightly wider than for the outswinger because room has to be created for the bowling arm to follow through down past the right-hand side of the body, not across it as for the outswinger. The inswing bowler is usually a little open-chested at the moment when he releases the ball. Again the wrist firmly locks and the fingers stay behind the ball for as long as possible.

4. It is easier to bowl the inswinger from wide of the crease but this rather signals the intention to the batsman, and it also creates a sharp angle of approach to the wicket which may persuade the umpire to give the batsman the benefit of the doubt in marginal lbw decisions.

5. Inswing bowlers will expect to get catches close on the leg side and will usually position a backward short-leg and short square-leg. The line of attack will be on or about off-stump, which, with a full length and the ball swinging in late, aims to draw the batsman into a firm forward stroke.

Imran Khan was a genuinely fast bowler who developed remarkable control of the inswinger. His line would sometimes be wide of off-stump by a foot and a half. Some deliveries would swing in late and sharply, others he could send straight on. This presented the batsman, every ball, with the agonising problem of which deliveries to prepare to play and which to leave alone.

Very good batsmen who were his victims said that Imran could swing the ball inwards so late that the effect was of a fast off-break bowler, drawing them forward and making the ball dip in between bat and pad to hit the stumps.

So as well as looking for catches on the leg side the inswing bowler is seeking wickets outside off-stump.

Cutters

OFF-CUTTER

The off-cutter is delivered with an action similar to that used to bowl an outswinger, and can be used as a variation to it (see page 21).

Imran Khan – a genuinely fast bowler who developed remarkable control of the inswinger. He could swing the ball inwards so late that the effect was of a fast off-break bowler

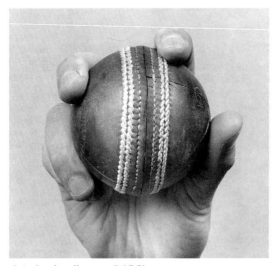

Grip for the off-cutter (MCC)

Grip for the leg-cutter (MCC)

The fingers pull across the seam at the instant of delivery, to impart fast spin, rather than being kept behind the ball as for the outswinger.

Many Test-class bowlers bowl an off-cutter with a similar grip as for the off-break (see top of page). In other words it *is* a fast off-break. The seam points to fine-leg and the index finger does all the spinning work. However, this off-spin hand action is much easier for the batsman to detect.

Another grip places the first two fingers closer together on top of the seam: the seam points straight or towards fine-leg; the thumb is directly opposite the fingers, under the seam, with the inside of the thumb pressed against it.

At the instant of delivery the first finger pulls down and across the seam while the hand rotates in a clockwise direction. This action can be strengthened if the bowling hand follows through across the body, to finish close to the left side as for the outswinger.

LEG-CUTTER

The leg-cutter is used to describe a technique closely allied to that of the inswinger but, by pulling the fingers across the seam of the ball at the moment of delivery, leg spin is imparted to the ball.

The ball is held between the first and second fingers, with the second finger pressing firmly on the outside edge of the seam and the first comfortably spaced from it on the smooth surface. The thumb is underneath on the side of the seam.

At the moment of delivery the second finger pulls down on the seam, the thumb pushes and the wrist rotates so that the palm of the hand faces inwards (palm facing the leg side), thus causing the ball to spin from leg. The arm must be kept high in the delivery and there must be a full follow-through.

One of the greatest bowlers of the leg-cutter, Alec Bedser, held the ball with a similar grip but also with the fingers across the seam. The delivery is then like a fast leg-break.

The leg-cutter must be bowled to a full length and the line of attack should be the middle or middle-and-leg stumps. Alec Bedser proved that it was possible to bowl both the inswinger and the leg-cutter without obvious change of arm action. The inswinger ducked in late to the batsman and the leg-cutter pitched in line with the stumps and cut away towards the off.

FOCUS ON YOUR TARGET

DENNIS LILLEE

You need thought as well as physical timing and ball speed. You need a target. Fast bowlers should attack the off stump. If batsmen are slow to move they are never quite certain where they are standing in relation to the off stump. Keep the ball well up to the bat even if the batsman drives the ball for runs. You are aiming to make the ball swing or move off the seam and the batsman is most vulnerable when he is looking to play a firm stroke.

I used to aim for the base of the off stump and the ball would land on a good length, neither overpitched nor too short. If I wanted to test the batsman around his body – but still on a good length – I would shift my target to the base of the middle-and-leg stumps. Some days I would find that I was dropping the ball too short, so I moved my target up the stump to the middle or to the top. Alternatively you can over-pitch and take a fresh aim for the front crease or a mark on the pitch. But whatever you do, do not change your action or the mode of your delivery as you seek your length on the day. Keep blasting away with a full follow-through, otherwise you will simply be putting the ball on a spot and that is useless.

Most important of all, when you get back to the start of your run-up, observe your target and concentrate. Focus. Never set off without a clear definition in your mind of where you hope the ball to go and what you would like it to do.

HOW TO START

I am often asked how I started bowling fast. First of all I loved cricket and fast bowling excited me. I was spellbound by the long run-up of Wes Hall, and by Fred Trueman of England and the left-hander Alan Davidson. When I saw them run in I thought that I too would do it one day. On the school playground I ran in and bowled as fast as I could at my mates. At that stage I gave no thought to my action.

There were no videos then, but I went to the textbooks and I took notice of the rec-ommended foot-placements. I watched where the arms should go and how I should follow through. Then I would take the book out on to the lawn in the back garden and try to put the theory into action. Then, back in the house, just to make sure I was doing it correctly, I spent hours in front of the mirror looking at my action.

Good advice at this stage is to take a view of your action in the mirror and outdoors, and also get your action videoed. It is a priceless advantage we never had in my day.

As a young fast bowler I held the ball for outswing and inswing and just bowled as fast as possible with no regard to action refinement. Early in my Test career I developed stress frac-tures in my back which forced me to make a closer assessment of my action, its strengths and possible weaknesses.

I knew I could be fast. That I had established. Now I began to look for swing and cut and other variations and the use of the bouncer and yorker. All of this, once I had changed my technique from the mixed action, I had unknowingly developed.

So let me complete my initial advice:

1. Find out if you can bowl fast and go out and do it;
2. Learn about the recommended actions and work on the one that suits you, side-on or front-on;

3. By practice, learn more and more skills;
4. By experience, learn how to conserve your energy and vary your approach.

Essential to all this, is fitness and stamina. And remember you are a fast bowler, nothing less.

Fitness and exercises

In the old days fitness was just a matter of bowling yourself fit or running on the roads. Nowadays we have cross-training which can include bike-riding, long-distance running, sprint work, swimming-pool work-out, and many types of aerobic programmes. Strength training is included specifically for the building up of stomach muscles, side and leg muscles, and the back, arms and chest.

It is most important that you are directed in training by an expert who completely understands what body strengths and flexibility you need to bowl fast and can create a programme of work which suits them. That is what cross-training means – relevant exercises to bolster the strengths required for a particular pursuit.

I always considered stretching as the best insurance policy. There is a static stretch. Follow that with a mobile stretch. Never push too hard, never bounce into the stretches, but ease the body through the lines along which you will be asking it to move swiftly when you begin bowling.

But please note too that, after a game, you should stretch down. After your work the muscles shorten: lengthen them again when you get back in the dressing-room. Have a hot bath or spa or massage and then follow it with a cold bath or shower. That gets the tensions out of your body.

I recommend to bowlers that they follow their cricket with a swim for fifteen minutes, because a swim helps to stop the stiffening of the body muscles. Do not do this only every few days. It has to be a regular practice.

Do not overdo net practice. We used to bowl in practice nets five nights a week. Now we do three nights and fill in the rest of the time at our cross-training. Three-quarters to one hour flat out each night in the nets is sufficient for a fast bowler.

Aggression

Aggression is important as far as I, as a fast bowler, am concerned, but I look at my mother and father and I do not see aggression in them. I guess it comes from a will to win. I always think that I want to win and there is this batsman, some twenty-two yards away, standing in my light. I want to make sure that he is walking off to the pavilion as soon as possible. It is not a personal thing. If the words begin to fly then it is up to the umpires to step in. They have a big role to play.

The batsmen I respected most were the ones who were prepared to take me on: in other words they were always looking to attack me. Clearly they are taking a greater risk than the batsman who is simply sitting there, waiting and trying to wear you down. Each team needs a dour defender in order that the fine players can attack you: players such as Greg Chappell, Viv Richards, Barry Richards, Garfield Sobers, Rohan Kanhai, Clive Lloyd, Roy Fredericks, Tony Greig, Ian Botham, David Gower and Allan Lamb. There are many others but this list serves to make the point: in the end the batsmen I respected hit the ball somewhere and got me worried. They were ready with their shots and looked to get on top. They were the rare guys and I really respected them.

Incidentally, do not be worried about taking your batting coaching from a bowler. Part of the bowler's vital intelligence is to 'read' batsmen, to look for his strengths and weakness. I used to watch his feet movements: which position he gets into before I have let the ball go, whether he goes right back and right forward or shuffles about the crease. How does

Dennis Lillee: 'I cannot emphasise too much how essential is the follow-through'.

he hold the bat? Which is his strong hand? Watch where his head goes. How still is he, etc.?

Yes, indeed, a bowler can make a top-class batting coach, but I do not recommend it the other way around. To bowl fast, let me say again, you have to *feel* you are a fast bowler. No batsman who hasn't bowled fast can possibly know about that.

Bouncer

The bouncer is aimed to force the batsman on to the back foot: you want him to be surprised and hurried, to make a mistake either in hooking the ball, fending it off, ducking or swaying out of the way. You are trying to create a mistake.

The secret to bowling successful bouncers is timing, when to bowl it, how quickly and along what line. You must know how a particular batsman will respond. If he is a compulsive hooker then a foot above his head means he is having to pull the ball down – a very difficult exercise. You have a real chance of getting him out. If he is one who likes to get his body right behind the ball and the elbow up straight in a textbook backward defensive stroke you need to make the ball climb up from about chest high so that he cannot get on top of it or meet it without having it bouncing out to gully or

27

to one of the short-legs. (See photographs of Dexter, page 111, and Gooch, page 132.)

The bouncer can soften up a batsman. Maybe he is not too courageous and maybe, having been scared back on to his stumps one ball, he is on the way back next ball just when you are sending in a full-length delivery, perhaps the yorker which can race underneath the bat as it lands close to the base of the stumps.

On the other hand, if the batsman deals with the bouncer well I might pack it away. I remember Ian Chappell telling me many years ago about Andy Roberts, the West Indian fast bowler. Ian asked Andy why he never bowled bouncers at him. Andy replied that he had seen Ian handle the ball well and so decided not to waste an effort in that direction again. As far as Andy was concerned the bouncer was never right for Ian. Other bowlers' opinions on that subject differed, and they felt they had a chance with Ian with the short bouncer.

Having said that, Andy Roberts was a most dangerous bowler of bouncers because he would feed you one you could hit and then send down another which looked similar but which was much faster. Do not ignore, therefore, the possibility of varying the speed and trajectory of your bouncers.

Preparing for an important match

I have asked you to bowl as fast as you feel comfortable and to graft on the many skills as your career develops, but there is a matter of temperament which makes the successful player. I am often asked if I followed any special routine before an important match. My answer was to keep to exactly the same routine before a big game: do not make it extra special and therefore a tense occasion by stepping outside your normal pattern of living. If you normally cut the lawn on the Saturday morning before a club game, then still do it when it is the last match of the season for the League title or to win the cup.

Do not sit on a couch and think about the game because you will have run through the problems before they arise. They may never arise. Do the normal thing.

Of course you will be nervous. I was nervous right from the moment I woke up on the morning of a big match, but I felt all right as soon as I started doing things around the house. The next time I was nervous was in the car driving to the ground; then, as soon as I was chatting to my mates in the team, I recovered. We were now sharing the experience.

I was nervous again some five or ten minutes before going out to take the new ball, loosening up in the dressing-room. I was on my own again; the use of the new ball is always crucial and it was all down to me, or that is how I felt it. Then, just before I bowled the first ball, a wave of nerves would sweep all over me and the first ball would be bowled and I was helped by the word 'work'. Australians use it more than the England players. Work suggests a hard stint of concentration and imagination and a top performance. The word 'play' does not convey what is required of an opening bowler in a big match. Once I was working, I was all right.

Practice

Final thoughts. Never just go through the motions or exercise. Practise like you would play a match and always rehearse two different run-ups, the full one for fast bowling, and a shorter one. You never know when you might need the shorter one. Sometimes you are tired but the captain still wants more. Sometimes on slow surfaces a cutback in speed can give you more movement in the air.

Certainly towards the end of their careers some of the finest Test bowlers cut down their speed to get more swing and cut and more control. Michael Holding was one. Richard Hadlee and Malcolm Marshall were other greats who also succeeded in doing this.

FAST AND MEDIUM-FAST BOWLING

RICHARD HADLEE

Medium-fast bowlers are called up for accuracy, so you need to be able to make a batsman struggle hard for freedom of stroke. Medium-fast bowlers are able to swing the ball more consistently than the faster men and they need the skill to pitch the ball regularly on the seam.

So when I decided to cut back from being a fast bowler with a long run-up to a medium-fast bowler I needed to master that special combination of accuracy and attacking skills because the best batsmen love nothing better than to bat against a bowler who is not fast enough to make them hurry, who bowls loose deliveries, and who does not move the ball in the air or off the pitch.

Hitting the ground hard

But – and let me assert the most important truth of our trade – a medium-fast bowler who believes he is on a mechanical, intellectual job of work will be hammered to all parts of the field. You still need aggression. Every bowler does, whatever his speed or style.

Always be sure that the ball is hitting the wicketkeeper's gloves hard. You do not need a long run-up to make a batsman hurry in his stroke. With good timing throughout your action, and a strong wrist and finger movement, you can make sure that the ball hits the ground hard and that any unsafe batting technique is quickly exploited.

Be medium-fast – but be aggressive.

Self-image

We all communicate different messages but, if I tell you how I want to be seen as a cricketer, then it may help you to define your own strengths and demonstrate them, to identify your flaws and repair them.

I convey an image of aggression and confidence with a determination to win whatever discomforts I have to endure along the way. I want people to understand that I am always playing the game to the best of my ability, often inspiring team-mates to bigger and greater things by my personal performance. While I am trying to play my own game I want my achievements to benefit the whole team: maybe I will keep one end tight and not give many runs away in a crucial session of the match; or bowl a maiden over in a limited-overs game, or break an opposition batting partnership which was overwhelming our side. I want to live every moment, enjoy as much as I possibly can so that I am respected as an individual as well as a cricketer.

Communication is so important to all players. Self-projection by talking to team-mates and captains, giving advice and listening to it, can help win matches. I like to communicate with my wicketkeeper because he is in one of the best positions to give me advice on a batsman's technique, the line and length I am bowling, whether the ball is travelling down the pitch with the seam straight up or is it tumbling all ways out of my bowling hand? The wicketkeeper will see if my bowling arm is high or have I tired and dropped it? Remember too that the wicketkeeper can assist the captain with the angles of field-placings. He stands behind the batsman, in line with the play, and he has a good view of the scoring possibilities.

A captain and a bowler need to talk to each other because there is little point in setting an off-side field when the bowler attacks the leg stump. The captain will probably ask, 'What line are you going to bowl?' and then the field can be set accordingly on the plan agreed. Teamwork in cricket is vital to success. A group playing purely as individuals is unlikely to beat an organised team.

Listen to what others have to say. Have feelings *with* them not *for* them. Your success as a bowler makes you a winner as well as your captain and the rest of your team. Your individual performance can turn the whole team into winners.

Prepare your mind, your body, and look after your action by checking it and asking others to check it for rhythm and body positions. If you are to be a serious cricketer then I must ask you to consider my personal check-list.

Check list for preparing your mind and body

MENTALLY
- Have a desire and purpose.
- Be motivated by setting yourself goals.
- Ensure discipline by total preparation and sticking to a plan.
- Be determined by having a will to win and succeed.
- Give a little bit more than expected by going that extra mile.

TECHNICALLY AND PHYSICALLY
- Have control of line and length.
- Keep sideways as long as possible.
- Keep your head still and think where the ball is to be pitched.
- Vary your pace and the flight of the ball.
- Use the crease for angle variation.
- Follow through after delivery.
- Always run off the pitch, not on it or down it.
- Know your field placements.
- Consult your captain if field changes are necessary.

- Keep cool when bowling. Do not become frustrated or over-react if decisions go against you, or if the batsman is taking the initiative.
- Have good footwear – boots with a heel, leather sole, long and clean spikes and a boot with high ankle support.
- It pays to wear two pairs of socks for cushioning and comfort and to prevent blisters.
- Singlet or undershirt helps to prevent back chills.
- Always put on a sweater after a spell of bowling.

Balls, pitches and control of length

A new ball should be kept well up to the batsman so that he is brought forward. If the ball swings, it can find the outside edge of the bat. By prompting the batsman to a positive attacking stroke there is more chance of his making an error.

An old ball should be pitched slightly short of a length. There will be little movement in the air and the old ball is not likely to seam off the pitch as much as the new one.

On a fast bouncy pitch the ball should be kept well up to the batsman with the idea of bringing him forward – the extra bounce can cause the batsman problems.

On a slow pitch, however, the ball should be pitched short of a length. This serves to contain the batsman. His frustration at being tied down and not allowed to score runs may lead to a risky shot and dismissal.

There are eight different lengths a bowler can bowl but, depending on what sort of bowler you are, you will want to bowl only some of them:

1. *A long-hop* is a ball that pitches halfway down the pitch. The batsman will consider it a gift and easy to score off because he has time to hit the ball almost anywhere. He will probably pull it to the boundary on the on side. The long-hop should not be bowled.

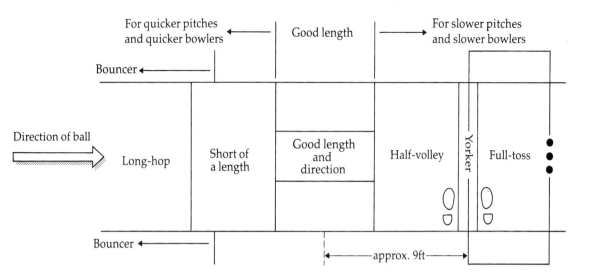

For quicker pitches and quicker bowlers ← Good length → For slower pitches and slower bowlers

Bouncer ←——————

Direction of ball ⇒

| Long-hop | Short of a length | Good length and direction | Half-volley | Yorker | Full-toss |

Bouncer ←——————

|←———approx. 9ft———→|

Bowling lengths

2. *Short of a length* describes a ball which pitches nearer the batsman than the long-hop. Although it is short of a correct good length it can be used effectively to contain the batsman and, on a difficult pitch, it can be a wicket-taker.

3. *Good length* – this ball is directed just about nine feet in front of the popping crease, leaving the batsman in two minds – whether to play forward or back. The actual spot on the pitch will vary according to the firmness of the surface but it is fair to say that 'a good length' creates doubt and respect in the batsman's mind.

4. *Half-volley* – a ball which pitches closer to the batsman than a good-length delivery and one for which every batsman is waiting. The half-volley is easy to drive – the front foot moves eagerly forward to the pitch of the ball and the bat swings through to hit the ball a split second after it has bounced. In fact the batsman aims to hit the ball as it pitches.

But the half-volley can also be a wicket-taking ball when the ball is swinging. The batsman may not quite get the front foot to the ball and he may edge the ball to slip or mistime his drive in the air to a fielder.

5. *The yorker* pitches at the batsman's feet. It is a very good wicket-taker because its full length surprises the batsman and he plays over the top of it, ending up either being bowled or lbw. Try to bowl the yorker with extra speed even though it is a difficult ball to bowl. This is because the length difference between it and a full toss is so small. The yorker is best bowled when a batsman is looking to make some big hits, and you can see it work effectively at the end of a limited-overs innings.

6. *A full-toss*, like a long-hop, is a ball which batsmen relish. The ball does not pitch at all and the batsman can easily hit it to almost any part of the field depending on the height of the delivery. (In limited-overs cricket, however, it is often better to bowl a low full-toss towards the end of an innings, when the batsmen are hitting out, than a good-length ball.)

7. *The bouncer* pitches very short, just about where the long-hop pitches, but it is bowled at extremely fast pace and lifts awkwardly towards the batsman's head or throat or chest, forcing him to play a rushed shot or

to take evasive action such as ducking or swaying. The bouncer is an intimidatory ball, dangerous of itself but also preparation for the follow-up which is often a yorker or a good-length ball just outside off-stump. The bouncer should be used sparingly because it is more effective when there is the element of surprise.

8. *The beamer* is a head-high full-toss. It should *never* be bowled under any circumstances. It can be a very dangerous delivery, in fact it can kill. The batsman can easily fail to pick up the line of flight because it travels much quicker towards him on a direct head-high line. The ball which bounces gives the batsman time to organise his reflexes: the beamer comes like a shot from the dark.

Preparation for bowling

Before the start of a match, bowl to a partner, preferably a wicketkeeper. It helps both the bowler and the wicketkeeper. It pays to put down a marker on a good length or wherever you want to pitch the ball. My good-length mark is usually nine feet in front of the popping crease. After aiming at that for a while I move the marker further up to practise the yorker and then bring it back for the ball rising high from a short length. Obviously you should try to hit the marker as consistently as possible.

At the start of the run-up the eyes should be firmly focused on where the ball is to pitch. Do not look at the front foot for no-balls. A smooth and gradual run-up, increasing in pace, should conclude with the high delivery and follow-through, all coordinated into one continuous action.

Another of my practices is done with a bowling partner. We put down the good-length marker in front of a single stump and have a competition. If you can hit the marker and the one stump it should be easier to settle on a straight line and a good length once the game has started and three stumps are your target.

Some bowlers watch themselves in the mirror as batsmen often do. This works for seeing the correctness of body positioning – head level and still, eyes looking over the front shoulder, front arm up high, and bowling arm coming over the top and finishing down the

opposite side of the body. Technique is most important.

I used to bowl with a golf ball against a brick wall. The ball would rebound off the wall and, on my follow-through, I would try to catch it. This ensured that I completed the follow-through and it helped my reflexes, agility and catching.

When bowling at a batsman in the nets you should try to assess his weaknesses and bowl to them. Practise your rhythm, timing and coordination by doing the basics simply. Practise all sorts of delivery in net practice. This is the place to work on your cutters, for they demand a lot of confidence to bowl in an important match to good batsmen.

In the nets award yourself points, say over twelve balls. Give yourself three points for a ball that pitches on off-stump and is played defensively or beats the batsman; two points if the ball pitches outside off-stump and the batsman has let it go or played defensively; and one point if the ball has pitched well outside the off stump. There are no points for any ball which goes down the leg side. Out of 36 poss-

Richard Hadlee bowling in the Christchurch Test v. England, February 1984

ible points 24 is very good, 18–24 satisfactory, and anything less than 18 means that you still have a lot of work to do.

Bowling is hard work but there is also pleasure in bringing about the downfall of a batsman. What I managed to do in my career was to perfect my skills and repeat them ball after ball. I bowled, I believe, 66,431 balls in my career – a lot of repetition in that! – and by the end I was clinically efficient.

When your bowling spell is going badly, do not give up. Keep running in – that is the only way you can increase your life's wicket tally. Winners make it happen; losers let it happen.

Reading the batsman

When I prepare for a match I open my memory box and inspect the batsmen I have bowled to before. I have always noted their strengths and weaknesses; now I must find out as soon as possible how the pitch will play, so that I can work out my plans to prompt their errors.

33

So let me emphasise two points: know your batsman; and get familiar as soon as possible with your pitch.

For example, I could never afford to bowl too straight to Vivian Richards. He was a master at stroking anything directed at the stumps to the leg side. I used to bowl at his off stump and fractionally outside.

Understanding batting is a large part of the art of bowling. You must be able to 'read' the techniques of the batsmen, and not only at Test level. In club cricket, as an opponent's innings progresses, you recognise clues which tell you what sort of a player he is. Let us imagine that you have not bowled to a batsman before and we are looking for those clues:

- A *tall* batsman will have a long reach and, more often than not, will be a front-foot player. He will be looking to drive, and to push forward to prevent lbw decisions. It is important, therefore, to bowl short of a length, to keep him on the back foot and on the defensive.
- A *short* batsman. The ball should be pitched further up to bring him forward. Because of his shorter reach he may not quite get to the pitch of the ball. He is likely to be a back-foot or crease player.
- A batsman with a *crouched stance and a low grip* on the bat handle is looking to get under the ball to hook or over the ball to cut. He will be a bottom-hand player, meaning that he will often be controlling the strength of his shot with his bottom hand. This may make him hit the ball quite often in the air. The ball should be kept up to him to cramp his movements so that he does not hook or cut. Make sure he is brought forward to the drive because there is a great possibility of him mistiming the ball and scooping it into the covers and/or gully.
- A batsman with his *hands apart in the grip* will look to scoop the ball around on the leg side or cut it on the off. He will also push at

the ball; if his bottom hand dominates (as it will on most occasions) the ball will go in the air if his timing is a little bit out. This type of player will struggle on a wet or slow pitch because the ball will not come quickly on to the bat. The bowler should pitch his deliveries on a good length or short of a length.
- A batsman with *an open stance* is looking to hit the ball on the leg side. His bat is lifting in the direction of gully; when it comes down, the face is angled towards the on side. It is important to bowl outside the off stump to eliminate this batsman's strength, for then his body-positioning and head will be out of alignment with the ball, and he will tend to play away from his body. He might easily snick the ball into the slips.
- A batsman with a *high stance* and *high grip* on the bat is always looking to drive the ball. It is therefore important to bowl short of a length to prevent him pushing forward. Perhaps an early yorker could deceive him.
- A batsman with an *angled bat in the stance* (i.e. the face of the bat is too open and is facing the gully position) is a player who deflects the ball through the gully area. It pays to add an extra slip or gully because the ball could go in the air through the arc, especially the new ball which is hard and likely to carry further. Always attack the off stump of this batsman because, even if it is his strength, it could prove to be his weakness too.
- A batsman *batting outside his crease* is trying to eliminate an lbw decision and to get more easily to the pitch of the ball. He will be a front-foot player, so bowl short of a length. If possible, get the wicketkeeper to stand up to the stumps. If this forces the batsman to stand back in his crease you can settle again into your normal length.
- A batsman *taking a middle stump guard* wants the bowler to bowl straight at him so that he can hit the ball straight between mid-on and

mid-off, into the area we call the 'V'. He will also look to 'work' the ball on the leg side if the line is slightly wayward. He will be a good judge of 'leaving' the ball outside the off stump, so it is vital to bowl directly at the off stump to commit him to playing a shot. Bowl on a good length or just short of a length.

- A batsman *taking a leg stump guard* is more of an off-side player. Anything going down the leg side will be whipped away for easy runs, so bowl at off-stump and do not give him room to play freely outside the off. Early on in his innings it could pay to bowl a little wider because he may chase the ball, not get to the pitch of it, and edge it into the slips. As his innings progresses, a tighter line and length is needed. From a bowler's point of view it should be a great sight to see all three wickets because the batsman has exposed the target you are trying to hit.

Types of batsman

As the batsman's innings progresses the type of player he is becomes more evident. You should be noting his every habit even when you are not in the attack. For example:

- A *low backlift* means that he is a pusher and deflector. Bowl very close to his body, crowding him, and aim just short of a length. Anything very short will be guided away off the back foot.
- A *high backlift* means that he is intent on striking the ball hard through or even over the top of the field. Again you, the medium-fast bowler, should aim just short of a good length. More importantly, changes of pace are necessary, especially if he is driving a lot. If he is driving freely you must assume that you are over-pitching and pull back your length a little shorter.

    If the batsman is hooking and cutting a lot, assume that your length is too short.

- If a batsman *does not play forward or backward* but walks across in front of his wickets, it is important to bowl well up to him. We call him a 'shuffler'; bowlers should enjoy bowling to these batsmen because they expose themselves to being bowled and to lbw decisions. Bowl absolutely straight, at the middle stump.

- A batsman who *backs away from the ball* towards square-leg is a fast bowler's dream. He is obviously frightened of the ball, so the bowler has a good chance of getting him out cheaply. It is important to bowl at leg-stump to cramp his style. In backing away he is giving himself room to swing at the ball, often hitting it in the air. If you bowl wide of off-stump he has a free arc to swing the ball in any direction. The bat-swinger can pick up quick runs but he also tends to get caught. Tuck him up, home in on that leg stump.

- Some batsmen *commit themselves before a ball has been bowled* by pushing the front foot forward. In this case the bowler must bowl short of a length, to prevent him from driving, and bowl wide of the off stump. The batsman then has to make a secondary movement to get into the correct position. If he is not in the right position he could edge the ball to slip or the wicketkeeper.

- Bowling to *an in-form batsman* can be very soul-destroying for the bowler, but you just have to keep at it. Instead of trying to get him out you must be prepared to sit back and wait until he makes a mistake and gets himself out. Bowl very defensively to a well-set field and try to restrict his scoring shots.

    Your captain may be prepared to set a deep field to give him one run so that he loses the strike much of the time. Then you can attack the weaker batsman by bringing in the field and preventing him from escaping the bowling.

    An out-of-form batsman must be pressurised as soon as he comes to the crease; tight attacking bowling to an attacking field.

MASTERCLASS

David Gower always hit strongly on the leg side

Greg Chappell liked to assert his authority as soon
as he came in

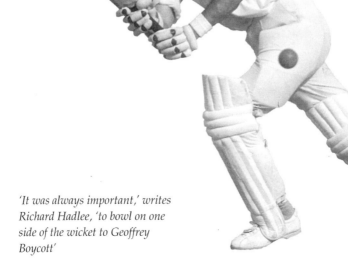

'It was always important,' writes
Richard Hadlee, 'to bowl on one
side of the wicket to Geoffrey
Boycott'

From my own scrapbook of summing up batsmen:

David Gower. The talented England left-hand batsman may have been a little casual or free in his batting style, but he was very strong off his legs and he pulled everything short very well. His weakness was to good-length balls outside off-stump but this was also his prolific scoring area. In Test matches three slips and two gullies would be in position in case it was the bowler's day. In one-day cricket, of course, there may not be any slips, so he is likely to score through that area but he would still be more restricted on off-stump than he would on the leg because he always hit strongly on the on side.

Geoff Boycott was a deflector of the ball. He angled his bat and played the ball fine through the gully or off his hips to fine-leg. He would rarely hit the ball in the air. So he accumulated his runs. He would not hit many boundaries so the field-placing could be always aggressive or restrictive. It was important to bowl on one side of the wicket to Geoff, let him score on the off side to a six-on-the-off and three-on-the-leg field setting. This approach could also encourage him to look for openings on the leg side and maybe persuade him to play across the line of flight.

Greg Chappell could hit the ball anywhere. He was not afraid to loft the ball and he liked to assert his authority when he came to the crease. He was a good driver, square-cutter and hit freely to the leg side. He was certainly a very difficult batsman to bowl to in one-day cricket. It all came back to one thing – to try to contain him by bowling short of a length, frustrate him, and then perhaps he would try a chancy shot and miscue it in the air. Frustrating the batsman brings many victims.

From which end do I bowl?

If possible, use any breeze there is to assist your delivery. If you are an outswing bowler, and fast, you will want the breeze at your back, preferably coming over your right shoulder. Those medium-fast bowlers who bowl out-swing and do not rely on sheer speed often prefer to have the ball held up in the air by a breeze in their face coming from fine-leg or mid-wicket. An inswing bowler will prefer the breeze from over his left shoulder or from cover-point or third-man. It will help him to drift the ball into the right-handed batsman.

Other factors to consider are the slope of the pitch and the texture of the grass.

If there is a slope you must decide what effect it will have on your bowling. If the slope is across the square from right to left it will help the movement of your leg-cutter away from the right-handed batsman. It will also help the leg-spinner. A slope from left to right will help the seamer get movement in from outside off-stump, and also assist the off-spinner to get more turn in from the off.

Note carefully the grass texture over the whole playing surface, the grassy areas and the dry or bare ones too. As an opening bowler I was always looking to bowl into the grassier end in order to get more movement off the seam. No doubt the spinner will want to bowl at the worn dusty patches.

Use the crease

All bowlers should use the crease, i.e. they should bowl from close to the wicket and then from wider. This alters the angle of delivery and may catch a batsman out of line with the flight if he has not noticed your positional change.

I did it this way. I bowled mainly from close to the wickets which I recommend most strongly. Then occasionally I would pull out wider. The best way of disguising the change of angle is to start your run-up from a slightly wider angle but still run in a straight line to the crease. The batsman may find this alteration hard to detect.

A bowler is always looking for variety. You can hold the ball differently, slow down the arm action at delivery or quicken it. You may decide to begin your run-up a yard further back and so complete the action a fraction further away from the batsman than usual.

Where do I place my field?

Field-placing depends on the movement of the ball, the skills and form of the batsman and the accuracy of the bowler, but always you need to have a clear plan in mind. The medium-fast bowler looks to bowl on a good length at off-stump or just outside. Often the best bowlers adopt a split field, five on one side and four on the other. With a new ball which should swing away six fielders on the off and three on the leg may be employed.

There should be no set plan for placing your field. It is a skilful game within a game, rather like chess, and you simply have to work out where you think your wickets will come from and how you stop a batsman getting on top.

I would go further. The more intelligent a bowler the better he understands the possibilities of placing fields to his own bowling. A captain only makes suggestions to the best bowlers and makes an occasional adjustment to the field. Be a thinking bowler and work the chess game out for yourself.

Left-arm seam bowling

The left-arm seamer usually bowls over the wicket, directing his line of attack at the middle-and-off stumps. It is essential that he is able to swing the ball from the right-hander's off to the leg. This gives the batsman crucial problems – does he expect the ball to slant across him towards the slips or will it duck into line with the stumps? Batsmen facing the left-arm over-the-wicket swing bowler often do not know when to play at a ball and when to leave it alone.

The field-setting is important. As long as the ball is swinging late and sharply inward from the off stump, then one or two short-leg fielders should be kept close for the possible catch. Fine-leg, mid-wicket and wide mid-on are also essential – a split field, perhaps with five on the leg side. At least two slips and a gully should be positioned for the outside edge and a straight cover-point.

If a right-handed batsman is plunging forward regardless of length and the ball is swinging in, then the best fielder to add extra pressure is a silly-point, who may well pick up a catch off bat and pad.

The left-arm medium-fast bowler's problems begin when the ball is not swinging so much or at all. Maybe it only swings when it is directed down the leg-stump line, meaning that most balls are going across to the off. In that case, the off-side field has to be reinforced – probably five or six on the off side. At least one slip, however, is always recommended.

Bowlers' problems and corrective measures

Bowling too full a length usually means that you are releasing the ball too soon. You need to let the ball go later but you will have to spend many hours in the nets practising this.

Bowling too short means that the ball is being dragged down the pitch nearer to you than you want because you have let go of it far too late, or perhaps because you have gripped the ball too tightly. Gripping the ball more loosely will help solve the problem. Hold the ball further forward in your fingers with the pressure of the ball felt on the first joints of the first two fingers.

Bowling to left-handed batsmen. Many right-arm outswing bowlers have difficulty here because they appear quite naturally to be drifting the

Richard Hadlee was a fast bowler who cut down his speed to gain more swing, cut, and control

ball down the leg side, the exact line which would be near-perfect if a right-hand batsman were facing. This is accentuated when you bowl from close to the stumps. The left-hander will be collecting easy runs, so the initiative falls on you.

Try bowling from wide of the crease and slanting the ball across the left-hander towards the slips. The ball is less likely to swing and the change of angle could cause a misjudgement of line and bring about a mistake. Many left-handed batsmen misjudge the off-side line and offer catches to the wicketkeeper, slip and gully.

Control. If you are having trouble controlling the ball because it is swinging excessively in the air, it is a good idea to grip the ball across the seam to prevent the ball swinging at all. Once a good line and length have been restored grip the ball again with the seam upright.

Rhythm. I have often found that, if my rhythm is missing, it has been fruitless to persevere with that spell. Runs have been given away and perhaps the new ball has been wasted and would be better off in the hands of another bowler. If that situation arises I have gone quickly to the captain and said 'Let me have a rest for a few minutes and then let me come back soon'. My second attempt has then proved to be much more effective and controllable. It is difficult to explain why, but this works.

If I have totally lost my rhythm and it refuses to come back, I reckon that I am unfit and lack the sharpness needed to bowl effectively. I do 30–50 sprints after the day's play or after the game and make sure that I get my body fitness back up to the necessary level.

Wides and no-balls are frustrating to everyone. We bowlers do not bowl them deliberately. It happens through a lapse in concentration or being too keen to strive for extra speed in order to unsettle a batsman. Wides and no-balls come

directly from loss of rhythm. What a loss of runs for the team and what a waste of effort for us!

Wides will happen, but try concentrating a little harder on where you want the ball to pitch. Perhaps a technical problem has developed at the point of delivery, so do a check on the five positions of the action recommended by Dennis Lillee. Maybe the front leg has buckled instead of being the firm straight pillar of the delivery, or the front arm has dropped and the balance of the body been affected. Only the bowler and his coach can sort that out.

No-balls are the bowler's nightmare. Once a bowler has to worry where his feet are landing, then his concentration on where to land the ball is badly affected. This will cause inaccurate bowling. When the bowler starts his approach to the crease his eyes should be firmly focused on where the ball is going to land, not on a straight line ahead.

If you are foot-faulting you must take corrective measures quickly. First, measure your run-up to see if it is as usual. If the number of paces is the same then you will have to add or subtract a few inches: add to give yourself more room, subtract to allow yourself to take the run-in easily without stretching.

Never continue with your run if something has disturbed your concentration. Maybe you have hesitated, or you were thinking about something other than what ball you wished to send down and where you wanted to pitch it, or the ball slipped in your finger grip, or there is disturbance in the crowd. Stop. And start again.

Loss of rhythm. This can come about for so many reasons. You must think quickly to find out what is going wrong. Ask a trusted team-mate who is standing at mid-off or mid-on to watch you during an over. Ask the wicketkeeper too. It is very complex. These were my thoughts when it happened to me:

1. My run may not be consistent and my acceleration to the crease uncoordinated. My take-off or the jump into my action at delivery may not be high enough, therefore my body positioning at the point of delivery is astray.

2. I may have lacked concentration: my eyes should be looking down the pitch to where I want to land the ball.

3. My back foot may not be parallel to the bowling crease, therefore my hips and shoulders do not turn sideways and I deliver the ball too front-on or become an 'arm' bowler instead of a body bowler.

4. If there is insufficient lean-back at delivery the lack of rocking motion will reduce speed and control.

5. Perhaps the front arm is not getting as high as it should, therefore the balance of my body is falling away too soon from the action of delivery.

6. Perhaps my head is moving too much, taking my body with it. I must remember to keep the head straight and as still as possible with the eyes level. There should be no head movement.

7. If my front foot lands too wide of the pitch, openly splayed out, there will be a tendency for the front leg to buckle, so I lose height and the trajectory of the ball is lower. Tiredness is often the cause, but occasionally a bowler can get lazy.

8. I have known the position of the umpire to be disconcerting. If an umpire's stance prevents you from bowling from close to the wickets ask him to stand back a yard or two. Place him where you want him.

9. I always checked my follow-through when I was bowling inaccurately. If the momentum of the body-action stops, the rhythm is lost. The pull-out of the follow-through should be gradual.

10. If you have an injury, however slight, then psychologically it is difficult to perform well because pain is a dominant thought. Remember too that playing with an injury can do further damage. While you concentrate on protecting the injury you may well place too much strain somewhere else. My advice is to stop, get fit and come back when you are ready.

Conclusion

Although every ball can, in theory, take a wicket it really does not happen that way.

When bowling an over, treat it like having six shells in a pistol. Those shots need to be used effectively, otherwise they are wasted. Sometimes you need to set a batsman up for 'the kill', e.g. if the batsman is coming forward all the time, the first two deliveries may be pitched up to bring him forward again but then you follow them with the bouncer to create uncertainty. The fourth ball can be shortish so that he defends again, the fifth can be on a good length but widish so that he chases it, and the sixth ball can be a yorker at extreme pace. There are plenty of options and variation in that one over – playing to his strength, making him think something different, followed by a possible 'out' shot on the fifth and sixth ball.

Remember that a bowler has to *plot* the dismissal of a good batsman because only rarely does it just happen.

OFF-SPIN BOWLING

RAY ILLINGWORTH

I took up off-spinning because I had an alert schoolmaster who knew his cricket. I was bowling medium-fast in a school match and I tried a couple of off-spinners. 'You certainly make the ball turn,' he said. 'You ought to give up bowling seamers.'

Schoolmasters are vital contributors to cricket. They are the ones who can spot a talent and nurture it. Schoolmasters can also discourage and restrict the progress of a young cricketer, sometimes without knowing that they are doing it. My advice to the master is to look for positive attacking skills in a young person's play. Encourage them to hit the ball hard and, when they are bowling, to spin it a lot. Do not fence off the batsmen from the bowlers from the fielders. Total involvement in

all of cricket's skills will make all-rounders and the ultimate model should be someone like Sir Garfield Sobers. He was Test class in batting, in fast bowling and slow, in close fielding as well as an outfielder.

I was spotted again as an off-spinner of potential by a wicketkeeper in my Bradford League side Farsley, Jackie Firth, who went on to play for Yorkshire and Leicestershire. Jackie had seen me bowling in the nets when, one day, I tried a few off-spinners. Not long afterwards we were away at Saltaire and we got a wet pitch. He told me to try a few off-spinners. I got five for 5, and then, whenever it was a bit wet, I bowled spinners rather than seamers.

This shows how wicketkeepers can be good judges of which sort of bowling is the most

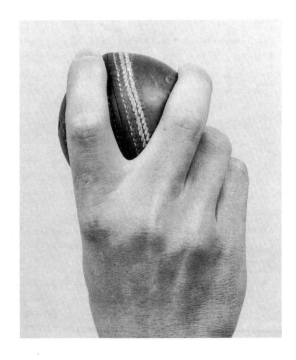

Grip for off-spin, and alternative grip (MCC)

likely to take wickets. They sense that wickets are coming before they fall.

Grip

The grip for the off-break can vary a great deal according to the size of the hand. I have short fingers but a broad hand, so I can get a reasonably firm grip. Whereas the seamer places his fingers on each side of the seam, the off-spinner grips the ball between the first and second fingers with the seam virtually at right angles to them. The ball should be held tightly between the top joints of those two fingers. So the first or index finger is the main spinning finger and is helped by the middle finger: the other two fingers are curled under the ball to hold it in a position which locks it into the fingers but never into the palm of the hand. The ball should not be bedded down in the palm: spin comes from the tops of the fingers. The thumb plays no part.

Keeping the first and middle fingers wide apart can increase the leverage and determine the amount of spin imparted.

If the ball was fairly new and small I could hold it with the index and middle fingers across the seam. If the ball was older and bigger, then I used to push the index finger in alongside the seam. With both grips the idea is to spin the ball hard with the index finger, rotating the hand and the ball in a clockwise direction.

My advice is to experiment with the grip, however long you have bowled off-spin. I found that some surfaces responded if I held the ball a certain way, the ball turning on landing, but that at other times nothing happened – the ball went straight on after pitching. In that case I would shift the grip and experiment.

So whenever you come on to bowl, go for your usual grip, try to spin the ball hard and strike a regular line and length. Once you have built up some confidence, and you see that the ball is not turning off the pitch, try a few changes of finger position. If, however, everything is going well and the pitch is responding, stay with the original grip.

The hand action is rather like turning a high knob on a door. The wrist goes clockwise and, after the fingers spin out the ball, the palm of the hand finishes facing upwards.

Action

I must have been tremendously lucky because nobody really coached me with my action. I grew up during the second world war when there was very little cricket but even so, after the war, when I was sixteen-years-old and attending the Yorkshire nets at Headingley, the coaches used to make others watch me bowling just to take note of my run-up and body action.

Sideways

I will never be dogmatic about bowling actions because people are built differently and move differently. But it was Sir Len Hutton whose advice I never forgot when he told me that cricket is a sideways game. I still believe it is a sideways game.

To run to the wicket, what you need is enough momentum from the run to get to the crease balanced and with enough speed to propel the ball at the speed which comes naturally to you. I do not believe in running thirty yards or so like a fast bowler. I want poise, momentum and balance at the crease. That is all it needs.

The delivery action should then be sideways. Imagine you are a cartwheel. Your front arm is high and the head looks outside it at the batsman. If the wheel turns forward, and you are sideways to the batsman, it is impossible not to bowl a straight ball.

If you keep it in mind that bowling is a cartwheeling game, it means leading down the pitch with your left shoulder. Then, for right-arm bowlers bowling to a right-handed batsman, your right foot will land parallel to be straight so that it makes a rotating pillar around which your body pivots through. The arm comes over, the wrist is cocked with the palm facing upwards and, as the ball is released, the index finger pushes hard against the ball and the wrist turns in a clockwise direction. The bowling arm follows through across the body and finishes pointing towards cover-point. The head is kept level.

Stock ball

How are you going to get your wickets? You must always ask yourself that.

The most productive line for an off-spinner to bowl – assuming he is bowling over the wicket to a right-handed batsman on a good pitch – is at the off stump and just outside. Many bowlers in the modern game do not agree with this, but they have achieved nothing to persuade me that I am wrong and they are right. If you bowl at off-stump and just outside it means that you can get the ball to turn through the gap which often appears between the batsman's bat and his pad. We call that 'the gate'. A good batsman, when he plays forward, has the front foot near the pitch of the ball as the bat comes through the line of flight. If the ball turns after pitching it hits his front pad – in other words he has kept the gate closed as Geoffrey Boycott demonstrates in the forward defensive stroke on page 110.

But the bowler, if he attacks along this line, has another chance. If the ball does not turn but goes straight through it might touch the edge of the bat and be caught either by the wicketkeeper or first slip. Similarly if the stroke is played off the back foot. This is the line I would bowl on most pitches – off-stump or just outside.

My field-placing for this orthodox situation is to have a slip, a short third-man, cover and mid-off – four men on the off side. If it is a very good pitch, unhelpful to a spinner, I would probably put another fielder in the covers to

'Imagine you are a cartwheel,' says Ray Illingworth. 'Your front arm is high and the head looks outside it at the batsman. If the wheel turns forward, and you are sideways to the batsman, it is impossible not to bowl a straight ball.'

the bowling crease, and the left foot in the delivery stride should be taken slightly across the line of delivery towards the on side. I like that delivery stride to be fairly short so that I keep my full height and am poised to release the body pivot and launch the arm towards the batsman.

Reach high at the crease. The front leg should

make four who are trying to stop the single on the off side.

If I am bowling my line accurately then I do not need a man at deep square-leg. He can be at ordinary square-leg saving the single. My five fielders on the leg side will be along the lines of fine-leg, square-leg, mid-wicket, wide mid-on and mid-on, standing close in, or deep, according to how much the ball is turning, how fast the surface is, how well the batsman is playing, how talented he is and, of course, how accurately I am bowling. I would hope to have at least one short-leg.

When the ball is turning a lot I would not change my line from over the wicket. The batsman still has to play at the ball if you are always on the line which allows the ball to squeeze between bat and pad.

Do not be put off by an excellent batsman playing well. Remember that, if you prevent a batsman from scoring, you are frustrating him and pushing him towards a risky stroke. In fact in professional cricket the conditions rarely favour the finger-spinner who has to achieve deception when the ball is in the air. You often hear about a bowler who has a tricky flight. It means that he can draw a batsman forward to meet the ball on the half-volley but that, when the batsman has made his move, the ball appears to dip short of his forward stroke.

Flight or loop

The loop in flight is essential for all good spinners. When flighting the ball I always found that the ball came out over the top of my index finger. The fingers cut less across the ball and more through it, down the pitch towards the batsman. There is as much top-spin on the ball as side-spin. It needs a lot of practice because the arm has got to go through quickly and the ball appear to come out slowly. That is the difficult part of it. The batsman has picked up his own tempo from the speed of the arm and is surprised when he discovers that the ball has

come down slower and a fraction higher than he anticipated.

The turning ball – going around the wicket

There are two reasons for bowling around the wicket. First, it helps your action when you are tired. If I had bowled a lot of overs I would tire, perhaps at the end of a hard day and certainly towards the close of a tough season, and I would find that I was not making the ball turn even when the pitch was helpful. This was the clue that I was losing the spin in my action. My body action, the sideways cartwheel, the pivot and the follow-through, were perhaps lethargic. Going round the wicket makes you put your back into it again because, from that angle, you have to get your front shoulder across and that puts you into the sideways position which makes you pivot and gets your body into the delivery.

So, sometimes I went round the wicket just for a few overs in order to recover my best action.

However, the main attacking reason for

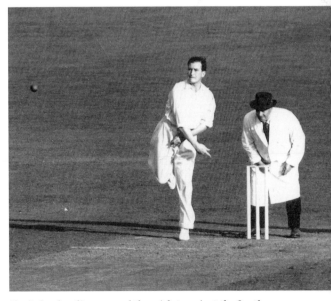

Jim Laker bowling around the wicket against the South Africans at The Oval in 1951 (Hulton-Deutsch)

bowling around the wicket is because the ball is turning, maybe on a wet or broken surface, and when a right-hander is batting you have a much better chance of getting an lbw decision when the ball hits the pads. The line of attack I recommend in these circumstances is off-stump or off-and-middle. I would expect a ball pitching there to be hitting leg-stump if the batsman is not in the way.

The 'arm' ball

The 'arm' ball is another delivery which is meant to deceive the batsman in the action and in the flight. He expects it to be an off-break because he sees the elements of a spinner's action, but last-second deception with the fingers makes the ball drift away to slip.

In this instance, you are a seam bowler with an off-spinner's action. This is how I did it – instead of placing my index finger across the seam I placed it alongside. Many fine bowlers of the arm ball release the ball with the index finger placed down the length of the seam. You can still keep up the pretence of off-spin by

keeping the index and middle fingers well apart. The off-spin grip, that is what the batsman could see from his end. The only difference is this – when you let the ball go you let it straight out, without cocking the wrist or spinning the ball; but it is essential that you finish the action with the arm cutting across the body as though you have made an effort to spin it.

The ball swings away towards the off, but if you do not follow through across the body the ball will not swing and, in any case, the deception is not complete. Spin comes as much from the body action as from the fingers; the arm ball is produced by the off-spinner's perfect body action.

So, when you bowl the arm ball to swing away, you place the shiny side of the ball facing leg, flow into your normal sideways action and follow through across the body. Let the ball out without the hard spin of the fingers. The ball does not revolve in the air like the spinner, and with practice you can develop this ball so that it looks about to spin off the turf but in fact

Illingworth in action

drifts or swings away from the right-handed batsman in the air. The nearer to the batsman it swings the more difficult it is to play, but if you fail in your follow-through the ball may well not swing and instead go expensively down the leg side.

In one season with Yorkshire I took 135 wickets and 41 of those were with the arm ball. My first slip, Phil Sharpe, was one of the finest the game has seen.

What should be the line for the arm ball? If the ball is swinging a lot I would look to start it along the line of leg-stump and maybe outside. You do not want to bowl your normal length. Good batsmen will sweep the good-length ball easily to leg even when it is swinging. Pitch it a little further up, a fuller length, so that when the batsman goes for the sweep shot the ball tends to go underneath the bat. This is not a full-toss but almost pitching on the front crease. If you can do that the batsman will miss the sweep shot into which you have tempted him and you have a great chance of a lbw decision. But a word of warning. You must be sure that the ball is swinging in order to aim for the line outside leg-stump.

The arm ball worked perfectly for me when I pitched it well up around middle-stump. Again the batsman, stretching forward, would expect the off-break to turn in but the ball would move away and touch the outside edge of the bat.

There are two key supporters when you are bowling the arm ball. First it is the variation, not the regular delivery, so your wicketkeeper must be able to tell when it is coming because it usually comes through much more quickly. My Yorkshire wicketkeeper, Jimmy Binks, could tell even as I walked back to my mark if I was going to bowl it and he would wave a glove at Phil Sharpe to warn him to stand back a yard. It was also Jimmy Binks who would tell me where he thought the batsman's weaknesses were. He would say, 'Plug away on off-stump. I can feel a wicket coming.' Always remember that your wicketkeeper and first slip are virtually in line with the play. They really can 'feel' wickets coming in a certain way. Listen to them.

Variations

The 'undercutter' is a quicker ball. It is a faster version of the off-break. It skids when it pitches because when you bowl it, instead of having your hand on top of the ball, you keep your arm and your wrist a bit lower and the hand cuts underneath the ball. The fast undercut usually makes the ball land not on the seam but on the polished portion of the ball and it skids on quickly after pitching.

Be careful with this variation. Often you start undercutting the ball because you are tired and the bowling arm drops from the high vertical, but it is still an important ball because batsmen, looking to pull the ball, are often beaten by the speed of it and are out lbw.

For even more variation you can let the ball go from different positions on the crease. Bowl one from wide of the crease and then another from close to the stumps and you can tell how good a batsman is. Does he truly know the direction from which the ball is coming at him? If not, he will mistake the line of flight and you will be finding the edge of his bat.

Do not concentrate, however, on variety. Remain accurate. Keep control of flight and length and line. Above all, you must achieve these very qualities while you are spinning the ball hard. Spin first, then work at the rest.

Over the wicket to left-handed batsman

When you bowl over the wicket to left-handers it is very important to bowl a good line; there is absolutely no margin for error. So aim for leg-stump or leg-and-middle. Left-handers are usually excellent sweepers, so if you stray you will give away runs. They are also good cutters because they are used to the ball being angled across them.

On an unresponsive pitch, bowl from close to the stumps because the ball in effect is trav-

elling straight between wicket and wicket and you have a good chance of getting lbw's. The arm ball, the one that drifts into the left-hander from off, if well disguised, can be a real wicket-taking ball. Place five fielders on the leg side and four on the off.

There were rare occasions when I tried to pitch the ball four or five inches outside the leg stump but rarely when the ball was turning a lot.

I usually started bowling to a left-hander from around the wicket, pitching the ball on or around off-stump. You have more margin of error from this angle. Place five fielders on the off-side and four on the leg.

If the pitch is turning a lot then you can shift your line in to middle-stump. A slower ball is often a wicket-taker here if you can bring the batsman forward to try a drive through the on side with a straight bat. Try to bowl from close to the stumps. It is impossible to get very close, but I found it easier if the umpire was standing back and I could run in front of him.

In one-day cricket I preferred bowling to right-handers if the pitch was good. You can pitch on middle-and-leg and, if the field is large, you can get a good leg-side defensive field.

Left-handers chasing runs tend to hit the ball to both sides and make you toy with split fields. They can put you under pressure in a run-chase.

The best left-handers I ever bowled to? Gary Sobers played wonderfully, waiting on the back foot. Neil Harvey was always skipping down the pitch, a superb striker of the ball. That's not bad for a couple of names, is it?

Defensive bowling

The skills of defensive bowling are important when international-class players are well set in a Test match. In one-day cricket they are even more essential: you do not want the batsman to score boundaries, so you must set your field to a pattern and force the batsman to strike the ball into the defensive arrangement of fielders. I recommend bowling on the line of the middle-and-leg stump. I would not bowl outside leg-stump, nor would I give the batsman too much room outside off-stump. I would try to tuck up his bat near his pads and force him to play to an on-side field.

So, bowling at the right-hander's middle-and-leg stump I would place six fielders on the leg side, and just three on the off – a short third-man, extra-cover and mid-off. You can vary the depth of mid-off according to the strengths of the batsman and similarly with the third-man. He too can drop back to the boundary. Mostly you are trying to make the batsman play to the leg-side field of three men in the inner ring saving the single and three on the boundary saving the fours. Three on the off side, six on the leg.

To sum up. In a Test match, where taking wickets is the essence of the game, I would persist with my line on off-stump and outside. A limited-overs match is all about the runs you concede. It is a quite different mentality. Pitch the ball on middle-and-leg and prompt the strokes which direct the ball at the most populated part of your field.

The art of bowling is the study of batting

Field-placing is an art. You have to adapt to so many different styles of batsman. My main advice is – watch a batsman in his stance and look for clues which betray the way he plays. For example, Mike Gatting, the former England captain, has the face of his bat open in his stance, so a lot of the time he is going to be hitting the ball square on the off side. Peter May, on the other hand, the best batsman to whom I ever bowled, kept his bat's blade turned in towards his body (see photograph, page 107). I could only see the edge of it when I bowled at him, and so I guessed that a lot of his shots would go towards mid-wicket and

that he might not be hitting me through the covers all that well.

Look at the position of a batsman's hands on the handle of the bat. If the bottom hand is very low and apart from the top hand it should be difficult for the ball to be struck through cover-point. There are exceptions – Asif Iqbal of Pakistan was one, a very wristy player. Mostly, however, those with a strong bottom hand do not stroke the ball through the covers.

What I am saying is that a large part of the art of bowling is the study of batting. Never be afraid to take a batting lesson from an experienced bowler!

Also, if you are to be a professional bowler, or a regular in good quality amateur cricket, you must remember the strengths and weaknesses of all batsmen who regularly face you. You must know where each batsman likes to collect his runs, where he might hit the ball if he has been bogged down for a while, where he lofts the ball, where he is vulnerable. Whenever I saw a fresh batsman come in to bat against my side I only had to push the memory button and I knew exactly what to expect from him. I was not exceptional in this; most good captains and bowlers were the same. I just want to emphasise that everyone, in all classes of regular competitive cricket, should have a complete understanding of their opponent's batting methods.

When are off-spinners best used? When I was captain I always used to try to get my off-spinner bowling at new batsmen. Many batsmen are better against faster bowling and they expect that sort of attack when they first come in. If you can test them with the off-spinner and they are nervous or hesitant you might just get a ball to turn through the gate or have the batsman pushing the bat into the bounce of the ball and squirting it off bat and pad into a close fielder's hands. I really believe that finger-spin bowlers should be used far more often at new batsmen than they are.

The art of bowling is the study of batting. Illingworth is 'reading' the batsman as he prepares to bowl.

I am constantly asked if I looked at a spot on the ground in front of the batsman, or the wickets or whatever, when I was running up to bowl. My gaze was on the batsman but, as well as taking aim, I was trying to read his mind. Whereas some great bowlers always looked at the spot on the pitch at which to aim the ball I simply looked at the batsman and asked myself – what is he doing? Ah! he is going to move back to leg to look for space on the off side. I'll follow him. And so I would direct the ball at leg-stump or outside. Alter-natively, you might have a sixth sense that he is about to come down the pitch to attack you because you have seen his grip tighten on the bat handle, or noticed a slight lurch of the front shoulder, a twitch of the front foot. I was always looking for those signs as if I had antennae.

I never had any need to worry about my run-up. I practised it so much it was automatic. The quicker the young cricketer can run up without any thought about his stride the better. Try concentrating totally on the batsman and see how you get on, but, remember, in the end the best bowlers are the ones who learn by practice, practice and more practice what works best for them.

LEG-SPIN

RICHIE BENAUD

'Over-the-wrist' spin is a world of fascinating variations. Fast bowling is direct, so is medium-pace. True, they contain variations of swing and movement off the seam, and in the use of the brain, but they contrast with slow bowling which, over the years, has developed a reputation for craftiness.

Over-the-wrist spin seems difficult and complicated. I have spent a lot of my time explaining it to children, trying to keep it as simple as possible, but it still amounts to a very difficult art form where the ball comes out of the hand in the most unorthodox fashion at a moment when your body is in a very unusual position. In a way it is a little like a golf swing – another unnatural body action.

Bowling 'over-the-wrist' spin means that your arm is moving in the batsman's direction as your body is preparing to turn in an anti-clockwise direction. Your hand will then deliver the ball in such a way that it is either spinning anti-clockwise, or going straight down the pitch, or spinning clockwise according to your delivery method.

That may not sound simple, but it is and it is important to study it in diagrams from the start. Before you start bowling over-the-wrist you must understand exactly what it is that happens.

The leg-break is the most important ball of all in the right-arm wrist-spinner's armoury when he is bowling to a right-hand batsman. His job is to perfect the leg-break – he must spin it hard, spin it fiercely, and he must teach himself through long hours of practice to land it just where he wants against all types of batsmen and in all situations in a match. The number one goal for the wrist-spinner is that he has complete control of the hard-spun leg-break.

Bear in mind too that it is ideal to create that leg-break with a combination of side-spin and over-spin (or top-spin). All side-spin would mean that the ball will turn a lot but slowly and without a great deal of bounce; all over-spin or top-spin means that the ball will bounce but not turn from the leg.

When you start out as a wrist-spinner, spinning the ball hard is the most important thing. Some people just roll the ball gently out of the hand and drop it on a good length and that suits them mentally, but unless they bowl on a surface that assists them they will never return winning figures. In the long run it will do them little good.

No, the leg-spinner must have the spin first and he must have the fundamentals right and then, afterwards, he can teach himself or he can be coached to bowl accurately.

It is no easy task. I would say that four years of hard and sensible bowling practice is the apprenticeship for the young leg-spinner. Certainly it took me four years after coming into Test cricket before I was confident about what I was able to do with the leg-break.

Grip

I am not dogmatic about the best way in which to hold the ball because I have seen grips different from mine which have been very successful. My grip for the leg-break is simple and orthodox and I use the same grip for the over-spinner or top-spinner, the googly or bosie, and the flipper. I found it was easier to keep the same grip rather than to fiddle around with

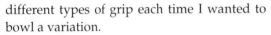

different types of grip each time I wanted to bowl a variation.

The positioning is this: with the seam cross-wise, the first joint or knuckle of the index finger is on the seam; and the first and second knuckles of the third (i.e. middle) finger are also on the seam, on the other side of the ball.

The ball is held quite firmly so that it would be difficult for anyone to pull it out of your hand, though it is *not* held in a vice-like grip. I never let the thumb play any part in the delivery: it can rest very lightly on the ball alongside the index finger or it can be off the ball completely.

The positioning of the hand in delivery controls the way in which the ball will spin. When you bowl the leg-break you start the hand action, with the back of the hand facing the sky as the hand approaches the vertical. Then, as the ball is spun out of your hand, the back of the hand turns towards your face. This means that the ball will be coming out of your hand and spinning anti-clockwise as it goes towards the batsman.

Action

Let me emphasise two important points to remember:

1. Your bowling action should start with the ball at face level so that, in effect, by the time the ball has left your hand it has gone through a circle. Do not, under any circumstances, start your delivery swing with the ball at your right thigh. It is impossible to spin the ball properly from that position and you only go through a half-circle in delivery.
2. Although your wrist needs to be cocked, do not have it cocked so hard and taut that there is no flexibility. You must have a flexible wrist when bowling, and, if your wrist is cocked too much or too tautly, you will put enormous and detrimental strain on your wrist and shoulder.

If you really get the leg-break right it will turn a long way and quite quickly. The amount of turn from the leg depends on how much side-spin you have imparted to the ball: the degree

LEFT
*Grip for the leg-break,
and the grip as seen by
the batsman* (MCC)

*Benaud Masterclass –
demonstrating the grip*

of bounce is governed by the amount of over-spin or top-spin. You must have over-spin to bowl successfully on hard pitches in countries like Australia, otherwise the good batsman will simply give you a great deal of stick.

Applying leg-spin

The leg-break sometimes drifts in the air towards the leg side before it turns away. I used to find that the ideal breeze to help this was the one which blew gently from third-man as I was coming in to bowl to a right-hander. The leg-break delivered with a side-on action and a good pivot would then drift from off-stump to leg-stump and then turn back to the off.

Pivot is absolutely essential. Do not ever allow a coach to gloss over the importance of pivot. Many give it less emphasis than it merits.

The leg-spin bowler, I contend, should be side-on to the batsman in his action; the bowler's eyes should be looking over his front shoulder and inside (i.e. to the left of) the position of the front arm. If you are looking outside, or to the right of your front arm, then you will be bowling front-on to the batsman and pivot will not take place. If you do not pivot on your front foot to turn your body in an anti-clockwise direction then you will invariably be pushing the ball at the batsman rather than spinning it hard.

Be assured that in ninety-nine per cent of cases, when you bowl short, it will be because you have bowled front-on to the batsman. The actual effect of this is that the ball leaves your hand later than it should and is dragged down into the pitch.

Does the leg-spinner get more bounce from the pitch than the orthodox finger-spinner or off-spinner? I am constantly asked that question and my answer is that sometimes he does, but not always. When I first bowled in England, on uncovered pitches, the surface would be like rolled plasticine with no bounce even for the ball delivered with over-spin.

I emphasise again that it is best to have a combination of side-spin and over-spin and to be able to adjust according to the way you judge the pitch to be playing. For example, if

Richie Benaud bowling against Middlesex at Lord's, 1961 (Sport & General)

RIGHT
Shane Warne bowling, 1993

FAR RIGHT
Clarrie Grimmett, Australia's most feared bowler of the early 1930s (Cricket)

you are bowling on a pitch that is very hard and allows bounce, you might wish to use more side-spin in your bowling as you will be getting the bounce anyway.

As for coaching young wrist-spinners, I do not think it ever works if a coach predetermines that a young bowler should become a leg-spinner. He needs to see the lad bowling and, in turn, the youngster needs to be keen on the prospect of becoming an over-the-wrist spinner. There needs to be something there, something a coach can sense or a pupil can tell him about. Keenness and a willingness to work are of prime importance. Unless the pupil has some special aptitude or an unorthodox yet effective style, he will not make it to the top without hard work. That may be unpalatable, but it is also true.

When the going gets tough

On the subject of work, let us consider one very good young leg-spinner in world cricket in 1993, Shane Warne of Australia. Warne's progress in his first two years, one hundred

wickets in twenty-three Tests, was quite remarkable, but he still had to go through a great deal of hard work even when he was being successful. I said to him, when he started out, that he had in front of him four years of solid toil to perfect his hard-spun leg-break which was going to be his stock delivery. That is the ball which must be perfected because, when the going gets tough and the batsmen are attacking, you need to have a standard delivery which you can trust to be on a good length and leaving the bat. It can be war out there, or at least a war-game!

It goes like this. A young leg-spinner making a name for himself threatens to curtail permanently, or temporarily interrupt the careers of opposing batsmen. Batsmen are not fools, nor are they willing to have their careers threatened. The answer they come up with is to try to belt the leg-spinner into submission, so, in turn, the bowler's career is the one that is threatened.

It is here that I underline the reason for working so hard on the stock delivery, the basic

ball in the leg-spinner's armoury, the fiercely spun leg-break which is bowled so accurately that the batsman is unable to score from it. It is your safety net as well as your wicket-taker.

So how do you practise it? First of all, keep it simple. I am a great advocate of bowling in the nets at a mark on the pitch. There is no need these days for a handkerchief, just use a white mark made with one of those scuff-tuff shoe whiteners which will wash off when the groundsman later waters the pitch. Go up to the batting crease with a bat in your hand and work out the spot where you would least like a leg-break to land – probably it is a ball pitching around what many batsmen call the 'blind spot' and then spinning away towards the off side. The spot is where the batsman is unable to score a run, but is forced to play defensively and there is a doubt whether he ought to play forward or back. If you were to play forward you would not quite be able to cover the spin. Put the white mark there on the pitch in line with off-stump, middle or middle-and-leg as seen from the stumps, not from where you

deliver the ball on the bowling crease. Then settle into a routine at net practice of bowling to hit that spot.

My method was to go to the New South Wales practice squad two or three days a week at the Sydney Cricket Ground no. 2, and stay in the one net all afternoon. That way I learned about bowling at all different types of batsmen, openers, middle-order, hard hitting all-rounders, right- and left-handers and tailenders. Tailenders? Yes, some of my most valuable practice was against them because there were times when they were to prove very, very frustrating on the field.

So when I got on to the field in a proper match I still bowled at that spot on the pitch. My eyes were always on it. It was a shrewd little tip I read in an article on spin-bowling written by Clarrie Grimmett, the Australian spin-bowler of the 1920s and 1930s. 'There are a lot of bowlers who use their own method of looking either at the stumps or the batting crease, the batsman's feet, his pads, even his face. This seems an extraordinary approach.

The best question I can ask a young leg-spinner is, "If I were to offer you $10,000 if you are able to throw a ball and hit the top of a single stump, where would you be looking as you throw the ball?"' Logic decrees that the thrower's eyes would be fixed on the spot where he wanted the ball to hit. Why would he look, say, at the base of the stumps if he wanted to hit the top? Why logically would he look at the batsman's big toe if in fact he wanted to land a leg-break on a good spot? I think it is more of a 'cop-out' than anything else, with the bowler saying in effect that he finds it too difficult to watch the spot where he is going to land the ball. Instead he is going to try to land it somewhere vaguely in the region of the ideal spot.

From the moment I turned to run into bowl I always had my eyes fixed on to the spot where I wanted the ball to land, and the spot would vary with different types of delivery for different batsmen. As there is no white mark on the pitch in a match, you will need to choose a little bare patch or slight discoloration in the grass to achieve the same result, but I emphasise again that the spot must be chosen by looking from stumps to stumps rather than from your bowling position, otherwise you risk slanting the ball down the leg side because of the change of eyeline.

Variations

The leg-break is your bread-and-butter ball. Then there is the over-spinner or top-spinner; the googly or bosie; the flipper; the sliding top-spinner; and all the variations of pace, angle of the bowling arm and position on the bowling crease.

Hand position, again, is vital with the variations, and a proper understanding of what happens because of the hand position is very important.

For the leg-break the back of the hand faces the sky and then, in delivery, it is rotated so that the back of the hand is to your own face.

The ball is turning in an anti-clockwise direction, leg to off, as it goes down the pitch towards the batsman.

For the over-spinner, or top-spinner, the back of the hand faces the sky and then, in delivery, faces the batsman. The ball will over-spin all the way down the pitch towards the batsman.

The googly, or *bosie* (or 'wrong 'un'), has the back of the hand facing the sky and then, in delivery, it rotates so that the back of the hand faces the ground. The ball will be turning in a clockwise direction, off to leg, as it goes through the air.

The flipper should *never* be used by young bowlers until their ligaments, tendons and muscles are strong enough. It puts far too great a strain on young bodies. Coaches and parents should not let pupils use it until they are strong enough, and kids themselves should not bother with it until they have perfected the leg-break – which, as I have pointed out, takes a considerable time. The flipper is actually bowled from beneath the wrist and is squeezed out of the fingers so that it is spinning around its own axis all the way down the pitch. The effect is that it will skid straight through or sometimes move off the pitch from off to leg once it hits the surface. But always be careful with the flipper, because it is even more of an unnatural action than the normal leg-break.

Only by hard work will you master these variations. I decided I wanted to bowl well and hard work was the way I got there. In fact, I do not believe I ever truly mastered the flipper. It was shown to me by the late Bruce Dooland in the Nottinghamshire-Australia match at Trent Bridge in 1956. Bruce had completely changed his bowling action to accommodate the flipper and he took me out to the nets on Monday 14 May and showed me the technique of bowling the ball. I worked on it in the nets for the remainder of that tour, returned to Australia and practised it right through the 1956–57 season in Australia but only in the nets. The first time I used it in a match was at Kitwe, in what was then Northern Rhodesia, at the start of the Australian tour of South Africa in October 1957. The result was 9–16 from ten overs. Not only had I never bowled a flipper in a match before but none of the batsmen we were playing against had ever seen one either!

The sliding top-spinner, as its name perhaps suggests, does in fact slide out between the middle finger and the fourth finger. The hand action is *identical* to that of the leg-break, back of the hand to the face, but the ball comes out of the hand with a kind of back-spin rather than leg-spin so that it goes straight on, rather than turns from leg. It is sometimes known as the 'back-spinning top-spinner' and used to be bowled with great effect by the Australian Test player Peter Philpott.

Around the wicket

It was at Old Trafford in 1961 that I used the ploy of bowling around the wicket into the footmarks of other bowlers. More recently Shane Warne, and Mushtaq Ahmed of Pakistan, have done it very well. In 1961 it was an innovation and I sought the advice of Ray Lindwall the evening before I actually put it into practice. He said, 'It could work if the batsmen are attacking, but if you're off line, they'll kill you ...' So it was an attacking ploy that day but it certainly can be used defensively. Remember though, there is no way you can gain a lbw decision against the right-hander if the ball is pitching outside the leg stump.

Nerves

I am often asked if leg-spinning is a craft in which you can easily lose confidence and I have to say, yes. The nature of wrist-spin is such that you can be inaccurate, therefore you will come under punishment from the batsmen. Hence the stricture that you simply *must* perfect your hard-spun leg-break on

which you are able to fall back if you are in trouble.

Nerves can get to you. Over-the-wrist spinners might come on to bowl and not be absolutely certain if they will land the first one on the cut portion. One young Australian playing at the Sydney Cricket Ground had that problem and at the end of his first over, which was considerably longer than usual, Ian Chappell, the captain, asked Brian Taber, the wicketkeeper, if the ball was turning. The answer from 'Tabsie' was that he had no idea if it was turning on the pitch on which the match was being played but, on the adjoining one, the ball was turning 'square'.

Nerves have always posed problems for spin bowlers, and all the more so, I believe, for the over-the-wrist type. There are bowlers who

Benaud bowling around the wicket in the Old Trafford Test, 1961 (Hulton-Deutsch)

have found they are unable to coordinate their run to the crease, even when it was only half a dozen paces, and their careers become threatened. There is no better way of overcoming that type of block than to have complete confidence in that stock delivery, the hard-spun leg-break. Perfect it!

Also, bear in mind that you need a mental approach which allows the batsmen to take a maximum of two and a half runs per over from your bowling. Why would you want to allow more than that if, by having 80 runs taken from twenty overs, you might suddenly find yourself out of the side? If anyone's career is to be put on the back burner, let it be the batsman's, not yours.

Too much variation can be dangerous, however. Although bowling a different ball every ball of the over is eye-catching, it can be expensive against batsmen who are adept at punishing the slightest error in length or direction. Give the batsman nothing. He is dangerous enough anyway so far as you are concerned.

Subtle changes take wickets

During my career I preferred to bowl at attacking batsmen because they offered a real challenge, but there are all types of batsmen, in the same way there are all types of bowlers. I preferred them to come at me with positive strokes and, apart from anything else, that made for better cricket for the spectators. For right-handers I used to bowl with a slip and, most of the time, a leg slip as well. This was particularly valuable for the sliding top-spinner which was the ball Doug Ring showed me how to bowl on a train journey from London to Bristol in 1953. He used an apple as a ball.

It was that ball too, more than any other, which taught me how, on good batting pitches, you did not have to spin the ball a yard. Four inches was enough, so that the batsman was

playing down one line to hit the ball with the middle of the bat, but the ball had deceived him by half the width of the bat. That ball took more wickets for me than the flipper, and the leg-slip fielder was a particularly valuable part of my method.

I rarely bothered to place a silly point or short-leg. I much preferred to have a man at short extra-cover or short mid-on about fifteen to eighteen yards back to pick up the driven ball which was slightly lofted.

Of course mis-drives can be the result of deception in the air but, remember, never try to achieve flight by sacrificing spin. Some bowlers will simply roll the ball out of their fingers, bowl it slower and think that is flight just because the ball goes higher in the air. That is merely a change of trajectory, which is not necessarily a bad thing but is not proper flight.

Do not be obvious. It is the *subtle* change of pace and change of flight that will take the wickets, or at least pose the problems for the batsmen. The leg-break spun just as hard, but bowled a little slower and tossed a little higher in the air, provides perfect variation. The batsman should think it is the same as the ball he has been driving along the ground.

The over-spinner, bowled a little slower, provides a very good change of flight because it will drop slightly into the breeze; but don't sacrifice spin just to flight the ball.

Cricket should be fun

Over-the-wrist spin was enormous fun because there was a challenge every time I came on to bowl to some of the greatest attacking batsmen in the world. It is a highly recommended art, pastime, trade or skill, whatever you like to call it. Over the years there have been some unorthodox bowlers: Jack Iverson and John Gleeson of Australia, Chandrasekhar of India, and now, in different fashion, Mushtaq and Warne are slightly unorthodox in their methods. Iverson was a freakish

Mushtaq Ahmed, Pakistan's leading leg-spinner, 1992

Iverson had not made himself unavailable for the 1953 tour of England, Australia would comfortably have retained the Ashes. John Gleeson, Iverson in reverse, always looked as though he was bowling off-breaks, yet the ball spun from the leg for much of the time. Sonny Ramadhin too was difficult to read, spinning from the off most of the time, although in England he was able to turn the ball in both directions.

One of the regrets of my cricketing life is that I never had the chance to play in limited-overs internationals. The atmosphere in a day-night international is wonderful and I feel that even when sitting outside the arena. These days captains appreciate that spin bowlers play a big part in winning a limited-overs match: Ted Dexter was the first to understand this in the early days of limited-overs cricket. Spinners, and certainly leg-spinners, can play a large part here, providing they bowl well which, after all, is the essential qualification in all types of cricket.

In conclusion

Keep it simple. That is the best piece of advice any young cricketer can have and it is certainly one of the central pieces of advice for any coach. The simplest advice on the matter of over-the-wrist bowling is to perfect that hard-spun leg-break so that you are confident of landing it just where you want, depending on the type of batsman at the other end. Nothing could be more simple, even though it will involve a great deal of hard work.

More important than anything else I have written is the little phrase, 'Enjoy your cricket!'

bowler. He spun the ball off his middle finger by flicking it upwards in delivery. He looked as though he was bowling leg-breaks but the ball spun from the off, though it was not a wrong 'un as we knew it.

I have always been of the opinion that if

LEFT-ARM SPIN BOWLING

BISHAN BEDI

I was about twelve years old when I took up cricket, a little older than is usual in India, but once I started I hardly ever seemed to do anything else. I was always bowling and, in a small town like Amritsar, there was not a lot else to do! There was no television, little other entertainment, so I kept on bowling for about seven or eight hours a day. My coach at the Gandhi ground was Gehan Prakash but he never told me anything special about spin bowling: he was just happy that I was practising, just as I am today when I see a pupil of mine who cannot stop bowling and bowling, *so long as he is spinning the ball.*

Learn to spin the ball hard before you do anything else. I remember Jim Laker, the England off-spinner, telling me that. Try out all manner of grips and arm actions until you know you are spinning the ball and it is turning off the pitch as much as is possible. Sir Donald Bradman used to say that, when he instructed children in the art of batting, he told them to 'hit the ball first' and let the defensive strokes come with experience. And so does Viv Richards. So go out and spin the ball, hard.

Action and grip

Bowl from as close to the stumps as you can, with your head still. Be natural about the grip. Rest the ball in the fingers, not very tightly nor too loosely. Hold the ball firmly enough to be in control. The index finger and the middle finger are stretched apart, the seam is across, and you simply tweak the wrist in a forward, anti-clockwise direction. Pull down and forward with the index finger.

If you simply tug down the index finger across in an anti-clockwise direction you will undercut the ball and it will give you neither the bite nor the bounce at the other end.

When you are practising, as the ball goes through the air, watch the revolutions it makes. The faster they are, the more you are spinning the ball.

I was lucky that I never had to learn an action. I watched a lot of senior cricketers bowl and that is what I recommend you to do, but I was blessed with a natural gift of rhythm. Nevertheless I had to work at it.

Look after your action. Treasure it. Work at it daily to preserve your rhythm because, if you do that, most things will fall into place and develop properly. Think of an action as having a beginning, a middle, and an end: the run-up; a poised delivery sideways-on with head looking over the leading shoulder; and the follow-through. Some bowlers only manage two of the three. Remember, the action is not complete until all three are in place.

There are details to work at within this framework. Make sure that your approach is building up to the actual delivery; save most of your effort for the high rising of the right arm, the bracing of the front leg and the follow-through of the left shoulder and hip.

Be certain about your action. Practise and practise. Never shirk bowling. Then it is possible for you to clear your mind and consider how you might get the batsman out.

Study batsmen and aim to outwit them.

This sequence of Bedi bowling comes from a long study of his action filmed by Patrick Eagar. 'I have always thought', Tony Lewis has written, 'that a great clockmaker would have been proud to have set Bishan Bedi in motion.'

Know their strengths and weaknesses. Research them and if you are meeting them for the first time, observe their habits carefully. I used to hate seeing a fine back-foot player at the other end of the pitch because he would go back and wait, create time for himself and do exactly what I wanted him not to do. I wanted him to be coming forward to meet the ball. Then I would look to deceive him in the flight, to make him play at the ball which is landing shorter than he thinks and, when it turns, passes the outside edge of the bat or snicks it.

That is my vision – the batsman playing a positive forward shot at a ball which is well flighted and turning a lot. It is thrilling to see a batsman drawn forward in this way and become a victim. I feel like a fisherman drifting up my bait waiting for the fish to leap out and make the mistake. But before you run up to bowl, you must have an exact vision of what you want to bowl at, what response you are anticipating from the batsman.

What is a good length? A good length depends on the responses of the batsman. If he is easily brought on to the front foot, then find that length which is just short of a half-volley so that the ball has room to turn and find the edge of the bat or by-pass it. If he is stronger playing back, and likes to wait on the back foot, then you have to pitch the ball further up either to draw him on to the front foot or make his back shot too hurried for safety.

My line was often straight at the stumps, say to the middle-and-off stumps. When a batsman starts his innings he is not sure about line and turn, so I used to place some close fielders around him to make him tense and nervous: get him to push out. Sometimes I would bowl to slip, gully, silly-point, short square-leg and backward square-leg. In my best days for India I was lucky to have brilliant close fielders like Eknath Solkar at short square-leg. If a right-handed batsman feared the ball turning away

to the slips he would often play outside the line and squirt the ball into the leg trap. Even if I was not crowding the batsman my orthodox field would still include a slip and a gully, maybe a short extra-cover too.

To set a close field you have to be exceptionally accurate. This is why you have to learn to bowl by practising hour after hour. If a batsman knows you are going to wander in length and line, then all he has to do is to wait for the loose ball. You cannot expect your close fielders to stay close if you are inaccurate.

If the ball is not turning much, or the batsman is playing well, I suggest you move your line of attack to the off stump or outside the off stump – not to bowl negatively but to present different problems to the batsman and get a little turn even on the best pitches.

If the ball is turning a great deal, I try to bowl a little quicker and straighter so that I make the batsman play every ball. Then I might choose a line on middle-and-leg because, on a turning pitch, you should be aiming to take the edge of the bat or hit the stumps.

If I was asked what sort of pitch I favoured it would be a good one, because then I could probably turn the ball where others could not. This underlines what I mean about learning when very young to spin the ball hard. If you can turn the ball when others cannot you have a terrific advantage.

The best mental approach for a slow left-arm spinner is that of 'the trickster'. You float the ball into the air and invite the batsman to play a positive stroke. I took a lot of wickets against England in 1972–73 and Mike Brearley, who was in India writing for a newspaper, wrote home to say that the England batsmen were not using their feet enough. Fair enough.

But when that series was over I contracted to play for Northamptonshire and I faced Mike Brearley who was playing for Middlesex. Mike had got twenty runs or so when I bowled my first over to him. He jumped out to meet the ball and was about to shake hands with me when he was stumped. Using the feet is not enough. How to use them is the real lesson. The most difficult batsmen to bowl to are those who make not a single movement, not a flicker of the eyelash, until the ball leaves my hand.

I must add some advice about the speed and flight of slow-left-arm bowling. You do not get the desired loop in flight by slowing up the arm action. Maintain your arm speed in regular tempo. Tony Lewis once wrote this about my action:

'When you have seen Bishan Singh Bedi twirl down his left-arm spinners after sixty overs with the same gentle rhythm and control as he first settled into at the start of his spell, you understand why his is a great bowling action. Even more so in his own country, where the test of stamina is more severe in burning heat and on hard-baked grounds which tug on the muscles and jar all the joints.

'I have always thought that a great clockmaker would have been proud to have set Bedi in motion – a mechanism finely balanced, cogs rolling silently and hands sweeping in smooth arcs across the face. Yet it would be wrong to portray him as something less than human – all hardware and no heart – because he bowls with a fiery aggression which belies his genial nature.'

Always try to make your action look the same as the ball before: the changes of speed and flight and line and spin must be as disguised as possible.

To a right-handed batsman, the left-arm spinner bowls from around the wicket. Bowl from close to the stumps and be sure that the thrust of your action is forwards with a strong follow-through. Your left shoulder and left hip should power through towards the target. Do not lurch outwards. If you do not get the proper forward follow-through you will tend to bowl

the ball only with the strength of the arm and without the full body action.

The 'arm' ball is important. This is the ball which swings in towards the batsman in the air. It must be well concealed and controlled or else there will be easy runs to be taken on the leg side as the ball moves in and across the stumps. Do not let the batsman know what is up your sleeve! I used to take a firm grip on the ball at the very last moment. So I would move in to bowl as normal and then, as I approached the wicket and my arms went up, I would place the index finger along the seam rather than across it. Usually I kept the shiny side of the ball, if there was one, on the outside, so that it would swing inwards to the right-handed batsman. Often I would push the ball through quicker to catch the batsman by surprise.

In short, the arm ball works like a seamer. In English conditions I took a lot of wickets with that ball.

The under-cut ball is a useful variation because it is easy to disguise. It is bowled from wide of the crease and looks like a normal spinner but the index finger cuts underneath it in an anti-clockwise direction and the ball, when it bounces, goes straight on. Also, without the usual forward spin the bounce is low and sometimes, if the bowler adds a little more velocity, the batsman, shaping for the turning ball, is left playing hurriedly. I deceived many batsmen who were trying to force the undercut ball off the back foot and trapped them lbw or bowled them.

Over the wicket. I have seen modern-day bowlers, like Phil Tufnell of England, bowl left-arm spin from over the wicket and it is true that a different set of problems is set for the batsman. But I consider that that line of attack should be used only as a variation. The attraction is that the ball may well pitch in the rough ground outside the leg stump created by bowlers at the other end. It is different, of course, when bowling to a left-handed batsman. To bowl from over the wicket to him is only like an off-spinner bowling over the wicket to a right-handed batsman.

One more thought about the rough. Do not base your whole bowling approach on landing the ball in boot marks at the other end.

Conclusion

I would like to address my final remarks particularly to a teenage left-arm spinner who is learning.

I repeat, spin the ball first, before all other considerations. Imagine the batsman is right-handed. If you can spin the ball only a little you have to keep a line outside off-stump. Your little bit of spin might work there and the ball will turn a bit on pitching.

But as you learn to spin it more, move your line in towards off-stump and ultimately, if you can spin the ball a lot, to middle-and-off.

While you are learning your trade as a spinner you must learn also to 'take stick'. There will be a lot of runs scored off your bowling. Get used to being hit. It strengthens your mental attitude because sooner or later a good batsman will hit you. If he hits you for a straight six applaud him. You cannot set a field for sixes. Just congratulate yourself for prompting him to play a positive stroke and, remember, a straight six is only hit off a good ball. Just hope that you get him next time.

Do not be carried away by the negative skills required by one-day cricket, slanting the ball in with a low trajectory towards the leg stump. Always try to get the batsman out.

I always aimed to practise what I preached. I was bowling once to Barry Richards, the South African, one of the most talented batsmen who ever played. I put in a silly-point, slip, and short square-leg. Barry was unhappy with those close fielders and attacked. First ball, he hit me over the covers for four, next ball over

Barry Richards – one of the most talented of batsmen, who had an interesting encounter with Bedi

mid-wicket (there was no mid-wicket fielder) and Jim Watts, the Northamptonshire captain, raced to me. 'Do you still want the same field?' he asked. I said, 'Yes, please. Don't disturb me now.'

Bedi as umpire and coach

Third ball Barry hit me over mid-off for four. Jim, a fidgety, nervous sort of character in these circumstances came and inquired again, 'Shall we move some out?' I said, 'No. Same field.'

Fourth ball and Barry Richards struck it over mid-on for four. No. I did not want mid-on back on the fence.

Fifth ball, he aims to hit me again over mid-off, but this time he wasn't quite there. I flighted the ball a bit higher but with no change of action, and it just drifted inside his stroke as

he came down the pitch, and tickled his stumps. Barry Richards was mine. On a perfect pitch his wicket had cost me 16 runs and the over had produced a wicket.

With great players like Barry Richards, Viv Richards, Greg Chappell, Gary Sobers or Clive Lloyd, you can play on their egos. Sometimes you win, sometimes you lose, but if, as a youngster, you have become hardened by being hit about the field you will have enough steel in your character to try and call their bluff.

65

The field setting at Bedford as Garner bowls for Somerset
in their NatWest match against Bedfordshire, 1982

2

THE FUN
OF
FIELDING

JONTY RHODES

VIVIAN RICHARDS

OUTFIELDING

JONTY RHODES

I was very fortunate that cricket has been part of my life from the earliest times I can remember. My parents were very keen on sport; they have been supportive and encouraging and I simply played ball games as often as possible until I got to the stage when I had to choose to concentrate on one. I managed to play cricket and hockey for a while but eventually cricket dominated.

May I suggest that parents and teachers urge young cricketers not to think of themselves only as batsmen or as bowlers? Skills with the ball in the hand, requiring fast reactions, catching, stopping and throwing at targets can all be part of a small child's growing-up recreation. We had a long passageway at home and my father and I used to throw the ball to each other for hours. We broke a few pictures and windows but that was the sort of household in which I grew up. Out of doors we had a tennis court but we played more cricket on it than tennis. I had the basics drummed into me and I was always running in one direction or another. If you cannot field you are not a cricketer.

I am often complimented on my agility. This too is something I owe to my parents because I have short legs, I am quite stocky, and as a result have a low centre of gravity. I find it more natural than many others to sprint in the covers and make swooping pick-ups. It is easier for me to make a fast pick-up or a diving stop than it is for someone who is six-foot tall.

So learn your fielding skills from the start. In fact, my advice to every young cricketer is to take all three departments of cricket seriously – batting, bowling and fielding – but remember this: scoring a century or taking six wickets in an innings is not such a major contribution to

the team if you also drop an early catch off a batsman who goes on to make a century for the other side.

Whenever fielding and South Africa are talked about the name Colin Bland is mentioned. He was a great hero of South African cricket and he set a fine example to many who took fielding seriously. My own model, however, was Peter Kirsten because, like me, he was short in stature, and pugnacious. He was always flinging himself around, pulling off miraculous catches and playing an inspirational part in the team effort. In all senses he was an attacking fielder eager to get in on the team act.

Watch the best fielders and follow their example. Remember that you are part of a team effort. What you do in the field affects ten other players. Practise fielding, be fit and, in the match, concentrate on every ball.

Run-saving, catching, and throwing

You must not only expect every ball to come to you, you must want it to. Fielding should be fun. Only once did I have doubts and that was when South Africa played in the World Cup of 1992. We were playing against Australia in front of a vast crowd at Melbourne. The atmosphere was awe-inspiring and for a while I was quite distracted. Before the start the South African side went for a trot around the boundary to look into the crowd and we had some catching practice right in front of Australian fans. We slowly relaxed and were in better mental shape by the time the match started.

If you aspire to play first-class cricket you must get accustomed to being watched – cheered or jeered. In your schooldays it could be a parent or a teacher who you know is watching critically. You must be inspired by important spectators and, eventually, by vast crowds. You must want to impress. Spectators should inspire you, not intimidate you.

Stopping the ball and the dive-stop

As the bowler bowls, move forward in order to get your body into a position where you can move quickly in any direction.

My Test cricket began in the 1990s and so I am aware that the main recent changes in the game's skills are in fielding. The one-day competitions in national and international cricket have highlighted the importance of catching, throwing and run-saving. More than ever, the fielder is, as Colin Bland put it, 'part of the attack'. A game of modern cricket includes many instances of fielders diving to save a single run. That was not always so.

It is not much help to your side, however, if you dive badly and miss the ball or fumble it. Then you are on the ground taking more time to scramble into a throwing position than if you had simply stopped the ball with your boot.

As the word 'dive' suggests, the fielder throws himself head first to stop the ball. When the ball is travelling quickly over the ground it is essential that the fielder dives early. In effect you do this once you have decided you cannot reach the ball on your feet. You are diving into the line or as near to it as possible. Your hand may well be outstretched.

Throw yourself forward along the ground and make sure that you stop the ball. It does not matter that you cannot grasp it in the hand so long as you have scooped it away from the boundary. If you did hold it in your hand and you slid over the boundary, then the hit would be adjudged a four. You would have given away the runs you have sprinted to save.

Many fielders dive past the ball or over it. Many get down to ground level too late. So

Colin Bland made a great impression in England with his athletic fielding and superbly accurate throwing. This picture was taken during England v. South Africa at Lord's on 27 July 1965 (Sport & General)

work out the line which the ball is travelling and launch yourself early.

You will also have to work out your own physical possibilities, but concentrate on stopping the ball with one hand and getting to your feet into a throwing position as soon as possible. It is dirty work for the white flannels but only constant practice will give you the perfect timing.

The sliding stop

The sliding stop is rather like a sliding tackle at football. It is excellent for stopping balls close to the boundary, for compared with the more traditional method of stopping the ball with the hand, running past it, turning, collecting it and throwing it in, it saves so much time.

As you approach the line of the ball throw your legs forward and to the right of the ball with the left leg bent underneath the right leg at about ninety degrees. The right leg, the leading leg, is straight.

You will be sliding towards the ball and facing it. You can either knock it back or pick it up. As soon as the handiwork is complete you should push up on the right foot. You are now ready to throw the ball.

If the ball is approaching on your left side then it is the right leg which doubles up under the outstretched left one. Be sure that you are facing the ball and be certain to stop it.

Basic pick-up and throw

Let us imagine that you are fielding away from the wicket. Ideally you have speed over the ground and a powerful and accurate throw.

You are standing exactly where the captain has positioned you. Nothing approximate will do. Mark the spot with your spikes on the out-field if you are uncertain. As the ball is bowled, move in so that, if you have to field the ball, you get a moving start, not a standing start.

How fast should you walk in? Colin Bland always wanted to be stationary as the batsman played his stroke so that he did not commit himself to move in a wrong direction. Also he wanted to push off a firm base which made it easier to turn. Derek Randall, one of the finest England fielders, used to move in at high speed with hops and skips and jumps: the live-wire approach.

Certainly it pays to have both feet on the ground at the moment the ball is played and, ideally, you are moving but not so quickly that you have to pull up and turn with difficulty when the ball goes behind you. I suggest that you move in, keeping your weight moving forward, legs slightly bent and hands forward ready to turn you into a sprinter or a stopper.

If the ball is in front of you, you should run to the ball as quickly as possible, steadying yourself as you prepare to collect it, head as still as possible. Some players have to slow down but the most talented move more quickly to the ball. The better the fielder the faster he can move as he picks up the ball.

This is what we mean by 'attacking' the ball: accelerating into the pick-up wherever possible.

The ball should be approached so that it is slightly to the right side of the right-handed fielder and the reverse for the left-hander. As your head moves downwards towards the ball you lower your hands early, and open the palms, fingers down. The ball should roll or bounce into the hands which are kept together to form a cup. The movement of the hands going forward to pick up the rolling ball can best be described as a scooping action.

Similarly with the one-handed pick-up which, naturally, has its risks at high speed, but in the interests of a run-out, the faster you can perform the pick-up and throw the better.

If you want simply to stop the ball, however, then fall back on what is known as 'The Long Barrier'. As soon as you have established the

'The long barrier'

LEFT *Jonty Rhodes – interception and pick-up*

line of the ball, and before it reaches you, adopt a position with the left knee and lower left leg along the ground at right angles to the ball, with the right foot extending this defensive barrier by being placed next to the left knee. There must be no gap, hence the name 'Long Barrier'. The hands should be together, little fingers touching, in order to gather the ball in front of the barrier with the head slightly forward so that you can watch the ball all the way into your hands. You need to be stationary to perform this purely defensive piece of fielding. From this position you can place the weight on the right foot and step forward with the left into the throwing position.

The Long Barrier can, of course, be constructed to the left or right.

Throwing

For run-outs from my favourite cover-point and point positions I often throw underarm at the stumps. The same is possible to all fielders who are positioned to save the singles. Clearly you have to move to the ball as quickly as possible. I always try to line myself up with the ball slightly to the right-hand side for my right-handed pick-up. When I have the ball in my hand I make sure that I waste as little time as possible in drawing back the arm for the throw. I look for power from a cocked wrist and a fast forward swing of the arm. I aggressively release the ball towards the stumps with a straight arm, with the heel of the hand directed at the target, to keep the ball low, and plenty of follow-through. Young cricketers can begin their practice on this with a stationary ball.

Spend hours practising this and not only with your usual throwing arm. I can pick up and throw the ball with my left hand well enough to surprise a batsman.

As you run in, keep your eye on the ball, head as still as possible, and be sure you have the ball safely in your hand. To make the wicket-taking throw which breaks the stumps

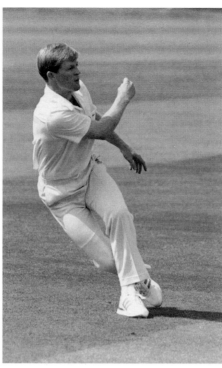

Jonty Rhodes demonstrates, during a Masterclass session at Lord's, the under-the-shoulder throw (above) and the overarm throw (below)

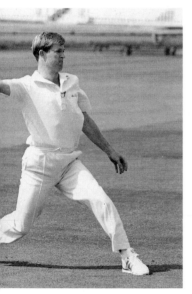

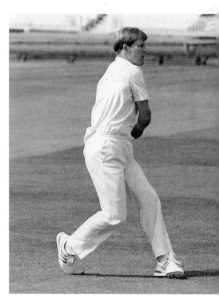

you must take aim. Very often you can see only one stump from sideways-on in the covers or mid-wicket areas and you need to work on a high rate of success with your throwing.

From shorter distances, and for sheer speed, I throw from below the shoulder. I am looking for a run-out. I do not draw back the throwing arm too far but use plenty of strong wrist work. The ball should be gathered when the left leg is leading and the hand is level with the foot: the head must be kept down until the ball is safely in the hand. You must practise this regularly because the fast pick-up and below-the-shoulder throw is the high-speed action which gets wickets but which can also give away runs through misfielding or over-throwing.

For throws over longer distances, when I want to be accurate and to land the ball in the wicketkeeper's gloves without him having to chase around for it, I throw over the shoulder with a vertical arm. The technical points are these:

1. The right foot starts at right-angles to the intended line of throw, with the knee bent and the weight fully on this foot.
2. As the left foot steps towards the target, so the throwing arm, with elbow bent and wrist cocked, should travel on a line straight back from the shoulder. At the same time the front arm and hand stretch out to point at the target.
3. The head must remain level – your eyes looking at the target.
4. As the weight is transferred on to the front leg, so this leg straightens and twists to thrust the body towards the target.
5. The throwing arm should strike as late as possible so that, at the moment of the release of the ball, the chest is facing the target.
6. The actions of the front leg and throwing arm continue, forcing the body into the follow-through: the head now looks at the target over the throwing shoulder, which points at the target.

The advice about the pick-up and throw is obvious but it needs emphasising – make sure, above all else, that you have the ball safely in your hands. No one ever ran out anyone without the ball!

Intercepting the ball and returning

I do not think of the approach to the ball, the pick-up, and the throw as three separate skills. To me they are one, for the more they are one continuous movement, the better.

1. Intercept the line of the ball as quickly as you can.
2. If you have time, turn sideways in the last stride with the right foot landing at right angles to the line.
3. Bend low, knees and hips, to pick up the ball, ideally just in front of the right foot, with the body-weight on that foot and the fingers pointing towards the ground.
4. Get your head in line with the ball: the eyes remain fixed on the ball until it is in the hands.
5. From this position, step forward with the left leg into the throwing position.

Chasing and returning

OVER A SHORT DISTANCE

When you have to turn and chase a ball you must be thinking, from the start of your sprint, of saving runs. In limited-overs cricket especially, every run is crucial. Your effort could win or lose the match.

The important points to remember are:

1. Run as fast as possible.
2. If you throw with the right hand chase the ball so that it is on your right side when you pick it up.
3. As you stoop to gather the ball bend low so that you will not over-balance or have to stand up before the ball is securely in your hand.
4. The pick-up is off the right foot.

5. From this position the body pivots to face the wicket and is immediately in the throwing position.

OVER A LONG DISTANCE

The technique is the same as for the short distance, except that you will be looking to throw the ball further and therefore you will have to get more body-weight into the throw.

1. As you step into the pick-up your last stride should be as long as possible without causing you to over-balance.
2. The pick-up is off the left foot instead of the right.
3. As you pivot, you step towards the target with the left foot: this allows the whole body to come into the throwing position.

Remember that a coaching book gives you just the basic moves which may help you to become a reliable fielder, even an excellent one. If, however, you are a natural athlete and have the gift of exceptional body control, you must not concern yourself overmuch with the theories of fielding. One of the finest outfielders in Test cricket since 1945 was the West Indian Keith Boyce. After a sprint along the boundary he used to pick up the ball one-handed, leap in the air and throw in as part of the same movement, saving seconds of time as the ball flew low, but without bouncing, to the player at the stumps.

Catching

The secret of catching is to get yourself into a good position. Footwork is the key to that and plays a vital part before the hands come into operation:

1. Do not move until you have judged the flight of the ball, its length and line. Remember that it is easier to run in than to run back.
2. Then move quickly into line with it.
3. Keep the head as still as possible and watch the ball all the way into your hands.

A high catch

4. Make sure your hands are relaxed. You spread the fingers comfortably and, if possible, catch the ball at the base of the fingers which should automatically close around the ball.

5. Take the high catch at eye level, letting the hands and arms 'give' naturally with the ball. Try to complete the catch in front of the chest.

The hand position is one of personal preference but for high catches the hands form a cup with the fingers pointing upwards, little fingers touching.

My own preference, however, is to position myself right beneath the ball whenever possible and reverse the hands to make a baseball style catch. The fingers still point upwards but the thumbs are touching.

If the ball is travelling along a flatter tra-

jectory, but still arriving at head height, the baseball style works best:

1. The palms of the hands, slightly cupped, should be facing the line of the ball.

2. Make a wide, but relaxed, target with the fingers pointing upwards and the thumbs touching.

3. The catch should be completed just to one side of the head: your hands and arms will ride naturally with the ball.

Expect a catch off every ball. Move quickly into a good position, in line with the ball and, when possible, underneath it.

Summing up – fielding in the deep

Your purpose is to restrict scoring, take catches and assist or create run-outs. Therefore you need a level of fitness which enables you to sprint to the ball right throughout the day. You also need a powerful and accurate throw.

Taking a high-catch – footwork is the key

Move in as the ball is bowled. Make sure you have an accurate sighting of the ball and move quickly to a good position in line with the ball and under it if it is a high catch. Take aim before throwing and when a team-mate is throwing, be sure to offer cover in case the ball is missed at the stumps and likely to go for overthrows.

Be sure you take up the exact position wanted by your captain. On large fields there is sometimes no need to go right out to the boundary rope. Your distance from the wicket will depend on the estimated 'carry' of a full hit.

For length of return the over-the-shoulder throw is the most powerful and accurate; but keep the trajectory as low as possible: the low throw which arrives at the stumps after one bounce can save vital seconds.

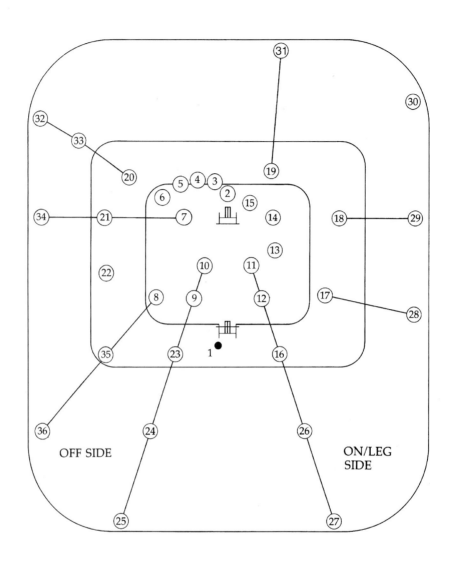

OFF SIDE

ON/LEG
SIDE

FIELDING POSITIONS

1 BOWLER
2 WICKETKEEPER
3 FIRST SLIP
4 SECOND SLIP
5 THIRD SLIP
6 GULLY
7 SILLY POINT
8 SHORT EXTRA
9 SHORT MID-OFF
10 SILLY MID-OFF
11 SILLY MID-ON
12 SHORT MID-ON

13 FORWARD SHORT-LEG
14 BACKWARD SHORT-LEG
15 LEG-SLIP
16 MID-ON
17 MID-WICKET
18 SQUARE-LEG
19 SHORT FINE-LEG
20 SHORT THIRD-MAN
21 POINT
22 COVER POINT
23 MID-OFF
24 DEEP MID-OFF

25 LONG-OFF
26 DEEP MID-ON
27 LONG-ON
28 DEEP MID-WICKET
29 DEEP SQUARE-LEG
30 LONG-LEG
31 DEEP FINE-LEG
32 DEEP THIRD-MAN
33 THIRD-MAN
34 DEEP POINT
35 EXTRA-COVER
36 DEEP EXTRA

Diagram of fielding positions

CLOSE FIELDING

VIVIAN RICHARDS

Catches win matches. I have no reason to change that old saying. Drop a catch and you invite an opponent to score a century. Take a brilliant, unexpected catch and you lift the spirits of the whole of your team.

I have always loved fielding and, when I was young, particularly outfielding. When I first started playing with the West Indies I always wanted to run around the outfield and test my arm. Every boy needed a good arm when I was a boy in Antigua because we used to throw stones into the trees for our mangoes. I usually got a few hits. Then on the beach we used to throw stones on the water to see how many flips we could get. In our cricket games as boys I always wanted to be in the action so I went to cover-point to field while the big boys did most of the batting. Later in my career I was always at slip but I started at cover-point for both the Leeward Islands and West Indies.

I never truly practised close catching until I was in the West Indies side. Then we used to have bowlers like Malcolm Marshall, Colin Croft, Andy Roberts, and Michael Holding throwing the ball on to a slip cradle. It would give us some idea of their relative speeds. As the West Indian daily preparation was more clearly worked out we would conduct the now usual slip-fielding practice – the ball thrown shoulder-high to a batsman, maybe the coach, who steers the ball off the top edge of the bat to three or four waiting slip-catchers. This is an effective simulation of what you experience in a match.

To be a first-rate close catcher you need to have the natural ability of high-speed reactions between eyes and body movements. You must be able to see the ball early and clearly, and

you must be able to move quickly to any corner of your personal space.

If you are coaching and trying to sort out youngsters for close-catching duty, do not believe that size of hands is important. It is the sense of timing which is important. You should persevere with the boy or girl who can make the ball 'melt' into their hands however fast the ball is travelling. To the best close-fielders, the speed of the ball means no extra difficulty. They have the lovely rhythm which allows the hands to 'give' as the ball goes in.

Let me warn you about a common misconception. You often hear it said that someone brilliantly anticipated a catch close to the wicket. I say that anticipation is dangerous when you are standing so close to the bat. You should not move until the ball has left the bat.

For example, no-one can guess how thick or thin an edge will be. If I am at first slip and I anticipate a thick edge my muscles will line up to move right. If the ball flies to my left I first have to go through that split-second of 'freeze' or paralysis as I check and change my direction.

Stance

Be relaxed and natural. I found it natural to bend the knees a little, crouch a little but not too much, with the hands held loosely in front of me.

Be balanced, with the weight on the balls of the feet.

Stand as still as possible. Whatever you do, do not move up or down before you have sighted the ball and judged its flight.

That all sounds easy enough but there are dangers. You see some Test-class close fielders crouch low, but some like Ian Botham, who

Catch at short-leg by David Boon to dismiss Kim Barnett off Merv Hughes, Lord's Test, 1989

was one of the greatest, standing high. Do not copy someone else's stance. If you are too low you may be in a position which cramps you or jams your elbows between your legs: if you are high you may find you cannot get down to the low balls so well.

I emphasise – stand in your own position knowing that you can move like lightning to any part of your personal space, high or low. I also suggest you do not space your legs wider than your shoulders.

What am I thinking?

Think that every single ball that is bowled is going to come to you. Concentrate, but stay relaxed and say, 'Right. Here it comes,' even if the batsman has been batting without a

mistake for hours. You must be ready and you must be relaxed.

Experience is essential because you know how catches come off the differently paced pitches. A hard pitch with bounce produces fast catches but the ball is slowed up by a wet one. If you are a slip fielder you can move in closer on the slow surfaces, but check with your wicketkeeper. Be cautious in the short-leg area for, if you are too close at short square-leg, you can be seriously hurt.

Hands

Some coaches recommend that your hands

Richards catches Gatting off Holding, Old Trafford, 1980. Low down and to his left

should be together and on the ground as the bowler bowls. Again I say, if that is natural and comfortable it is for you.

Practice will make you confident about your hand positions. Basically you are looking to make a soft cup with both hands together, little fingers touching. If the ball comes between the waist and the ground, your fingers are usually turned down towards the ground and probably pointing a little forward. They are easily reversed for a catch that comes waist-high.

It is essential that a good fielder can catch the ball cleanly and quickly with either hand. Practise with both, especially the one you think is your weaker side.

When you practise, be sure to 'give' with the ball and perfect your hand positions.

Watch the ball all the way into your hands. Cosset the ball, draw it into your body and say, 'That's my baby.'

In the slips

If the wicketkeeper is standing back then first slip should be a couple of yards behind him and maybe a yard and a half wide of him. There is no hard and fast rule about where you stand but you must agree with your wicketkeeper how you both cover the ground to be sure that you do not overlap. It is vital that he is aware of exactly where you are standing because then he will know which catches it is safe to leave

to you. He must not fling himself hopefully at every ball that passes.

How close the slips stand to the bat depends on their abilities. You want safety but the truth is – the closer you are the more chances will come your way.

Do you watch the bat or the bowler? I always watched the bowler run in wherever I was standing, even in the positions square with the wicket like gully or backward short-leg. I

picked up my rhythm from the run-up. I would watch Michael Holding build up his speed and I could feel his tempo. I would say, expect every ball to come to me. I wanted every ball to come to me.

On the other hand, if you are happier keeping your eyes fixed on the bat, so be it. It is such a personal matter. Remember that the squarer positions are difficult because you see a batsman play a stroke and it is easy to move with it. Stand still. Head still. Knees bent. Weight on the balls of your feet. Now you're ready for the first sight of the ball.

Fielding close to the wicket is fun and, if you can be very good at it, you will always have a good chance of being selected for your team because, as I say, most chances come close to the wickets and if you catch the opposition's best batsman early on it can be as profitable as scoring fifty runs or taking a couple of wickets.

Above all, enjoy it.

LEFT *Richards, at second slip, catching baseball style, Edgbaston, 1984*

Slip cordon, seen from above in the Bedfordshire v. Somerset match, 1982

*Keep your reactions sharp. Alan Knott catches Dilip
Sardesai off Derek Underwood in the Oval Test of 1971:
'I rate this my greatest catch standing up . . . the wide
deflection finished in my right glove as I dived'*
(Hulton-Deutsch).

3

THE JOY OF WICKETKEEPING

ALAN KNOTT

WICKETKEEPING

ALAN KNOTT

The best wicketkeepers usually pick up the skills of the job naturally and quickly; but it is possible to teach a good technique to anyone who has an aptitude for catching and is keen on becoming a 'keeper. Enjoy this Masterclass; and always remember that, whatever you learn, the two most important points about wicketkeeping are to catching the ball; and sighting the ball clearly.

The mind is vital. One way of making yourself concentrate, when standing up to the stumps, is to think that the bowler is bowling to you, not to the batsman or at the stumps. Another method is to visualise where the ball will come *through* the batsman's stroke, e.g., under the bat when he is driving at a yorker. Mentally, this is very stimulating. With every delivery, you need your hands in line with the ball and on to the height of the ball. Jack Russell, the Gloucestershire and England wicketkeeper, is always saying to himself: 'ball ... hands; ball ... hands'.

When you are standing back, keep your mind alert by thinking to yourself, 'Diving catch ... outside edge', or, if you have kept goal at soccer, try thinking, 'penalty'.

Preserve this concentration over the whole of a fielding session by switching it off and on. In other words, relax between deliveries, between overs, and between throw-ins – but, when the time comes, lock your mind into your job of catching the ball. A wicketkeeper must, on the one hand, be extremely patient; on the other hand he needs to be continuously alert. For myself I used to maintain this attitude, sometimes through a sort of controlled aggression. And, finally, the 'keeper has to remain unflappable in the sense that, even if he misses a chance early on, he can still concentrate on his job as though nothing had happened. Whenever this happened to me, I thought how I might take the best catch of my life next ball.

Some people say that the wicketkeeper's is a dangerous job. True, there are many who have had cuts and bruises but the danger can be lessened by safe techniques. Do not be put off by your physical shape. Some believe that you have to be short to be a wicketkeeper, but John Waite and Ray Jennings, the South Africans, and Jimmy Binks of Yorkshire and England were all tall men.

It is speed of reaction which splits the best 'keepers from the rest. When you see an action brilliantly performed, whether it be an amazing catch or a breathtaking piece of stumping, it nearly always comes down to speed of reaction. Be quick, think sharp.

To sum up, concentrate, sight the delivery, react quickly, and, above all catch the ball!

Equipment

Always be as comfortable as possible in order to do your best job. The right equipment will bring the most out of your talents.

GLOVES

I always thought of my gloves as if they were the natural extension of my arms. They were part of me and I treated them that way. I often used to take my gloves home with me after play. Leaving them in a cold pavilion could make them hard, and they would lose their flexibility. I always wanted them to be supple; and I was never opposed to taking a few catches in the armchair in the evening!

Alan Knott demonstrating the stance he used for most of his career. His hands are between his legs, and the backs of the hands are resting on the ground. 'I am starting to rock forward a little on to the balls of my feet so that, when standing up to the wicket, I can bring my body back in a rhythm with the delivery.'

When I played I was always kneading one glove with the other, shaping them gently. Make sure that the rubber facing of your gloves is in good condition. If it has become smooth or worn the ball may more easily slide out, especially in damp conditions.

Some wicketkeepers like gloves with loose floppy fingers and hardly any front padding, some like no padding at all, but I prefer a heavy leather backing with supple palms. I wanted the palms evenly padded, and to have a soft feel to them. On the other hand, if you are a club wicketkeeper you might prefer a little more padding on the palms if your hands have not been hardened by daily practice.

If your hands become bruised you may not want the ball to come to you. This is the wrong mental attitude. So protect them.

Most wicketkeepers wear inner gloves. Inners can be made of cotton but I wore two pair of chamois leather inners under my wicketkeeping gloves, firmly in place without being too tight. Some 'keepers cut off the fingers of the top pair, others wear just one pair.

Between the two pairs of inners I often used to place a strip of soft plasticine just below the base of the third and little fingers, where I needed most protection. While soft, it was a good unresponsive padding. These days there are more modern materials which serve the same purpose, such as Dermal Pads, known to cricketers as 'fat pads'.

I used sweat bands around the top of my inners to make sure that, whenever I was tearing off the wicketkeeping glove in a hurry to chase for a run-out, the inners would not unravel and get in the way. Today's inners, with a towelling wrist-band attached, are readily available, and many 'keepers use these.

Should you dampen inners? Yes, but not overmuch. If you drown chamois leather and dry it artificially it will go hard and crack. Also, if the chamois is over-wet and slippery, the inners will slide around inside the glove.

Chamois leather goes stiff when it is not used, so I used to wet my hands before putting my inners on, and also sprinkle water on the outside, to moisten them and keep them supple. You might do this process more than once.

I liked to keep my finger nails long for extra protection. If the ball hit the top of one of the rubber stalls, the nails helped to safeguard me from a damaged bone. If you have a finger that needs protection, tape it but not too tightly. This could put pressure on the joint. You might prefer to wrap the tape around the inner glove.

BOOTS

Good boots are vital. If you get sore feet while you are keeping wicket, the pain will affect your technique and concentration just when you should be most alert and ready for action. I often changed mine after every session in Test matches and first-class cricket. I also made sure that the position of the spikes in one set of my fielding boots was different from the second pair. This was particularly important in Test cricket – you could be fielding for six or seven hours, standing up to the wicket on rock-hard surfaces.

Wicketkeepers today quite often keep in 'rubbers'. If this is your style, look for the multi-studded type which gives the best grip. If you like wearing spikes, choose boots that have a sandwich of rubber or other cushioning material between the sole and the uppers.

PADS

Wicketkeeping pads need to be light and comfortable. There are two styles, one which is cut below the knee and the other which gives protection above the knee. Above-knee protection is vital. A bump there can be agonising. I liked pads which were light and which had high top straps that kept the knee flap close to the leg.

Preparing for the match

Imagine that the first ball of the day is going to fly off the edge of the bat and you have to move like lightning to take a difficult catch. This thought always reminded me to loosen up and stretch thoroughly. I made sure I was as mobile as possible. Then I worked with the ball. I like to take a few throws, both overarm and under-arm, some in two hands, followed by one-handed catching. Ask the thrower to make you move to the right and the left, and especially to make you stretch your shoulders and arms wide to either side. This is not always easy to achieve – you need a good thrower! Take some diving catches, both two and one-handed. Feel the ground.

Other 'keepers like to take a few deliveries from the bowlers, some like to join in fielding practice, some like catches hit at them. If it looks from the state of the game that the slow bowlers might soon come on, you should do some standing-up practice with your spinners.

You are now ready for action, but before the game starts I would want to go and look at the pitch to get an indication of its pace and bounce because that will tell me how far I shall need to stand back. Also I check how much grass there is on the pitch to judge how much lateral movement there might be.

Now think of your opening bowlers. Do they like to start off fresh and well-stretched, loose and ready to bowl their fastest, or are they the sort who dislike pre-match stretching and prefer to build up their speed in the middle? This may well be the case in club or school when the bowler has little time for loosening up beforehand. So you have to bear in mind all these factors to answer the question, how deep should I stand?

Most wicketkeepers in the modern game take the ball between hip and knee height, but probably nearer hip height. Personally, on a good surface with even bounce, I preferred to stand further back. I liked to take the ball lower,

One of the stances I used, mainly when standing back. I found that the hands, when outside my legs, brought comfort to the hip area. Jimmy Binks of Yorkshire used this method whether standing up or back.

as it dropped in its flight towards me, at about knee height. That gave me more time to react, In your own practice, experiment with how high or low you like to take the ball.

On pitches which have uneven bounce, however, a wicketkeeper might have to stand a little closer, but it is important that an inexperienced 'keeper is not placed too close to the stumps for safety, in case the ball 'flies'.

So I recommend that, whenever possible, you catch the ball as it drops in its flight towards you. But how wide do I stand? (In all the situations I describe, I am assuming that a right-handed batsman is at the wicket.)

I want to find a position from where I can look past the outside of the batsman and just comfortably see the bowler's arm. If you go very wide your first movement is likely to be strongly inwards towards the leg side but, remember, your job, especially in the higher grades of cricket, is mostly done on the off side. When you have a strong movement inwards it can be difficult to keep your mind and your body thinking 'outside edge'. Also, if you stand too wide you have to move much further to take a ball going down the leg side. The straighter you are standing the easier it is to move to leg. Many 'keepers move their inside leg a little as they come out of the stance, but they try to keep the balance of the body from hip to head even or slightly out to the off side.

So, I repeat, stand just wide enough to see comfortably past the off side of the batsman to view the bowler's arm. Remember, it is vital to sight the ball from the bowler's hand and on its path towards you.

Bob Taylor's stance, hands between his legs, feet about one shoulder-width apart and with the whole of the foot on the ground. His body looks very comfortable with the eyes level. Full concentration has been switched on, ready for action.

If the bowling is left-arm over the wicket the principle is the same, but many wicketkeepers make the mistake of standing too wide. This is because they like to go down into the squat position early and, when they do so, they lose sight of the bowler in his run-up because the batsman is in the way. So they go wide, often too wide. My advice is to remain standing as long as you can, being sure that, when you go down late into the stance you are just wide enough to get a clear view of the bowler's arm on delivery.

The stance – standing back

The most important aspect of the stance is being in a position to sight the ball. Most stumpers keep their eyes level, both eyes looking at the delivery of the ball. They are balanced and comfortable with their feet about a shoulder-width apart.

Some superb Test wicketkeepers placed their gloves outside their legs as they waited. Others had their hands together just under eye level with their elbows resting on their knees, such as Wally Grout, the Australian. Keith Andrew, of Northants and England, did not squat at all. He stood like a slip fielder. Ray Jennings, who

Jack Russell showing a large, relaxed pair of hands, thumbs not forced back but out of the way of the catching area. The butts of the hands are together, with the little finger and the fourth finger of the right hand on top of those of the left hand. If the ball were pitching, his fingers would be pointing more down. Note the areas in the rubber cut for greater flexibility.

kept regularly for South African sides and was one of the best I saw, did the same. I personally found, when I experimented with this method, that it was the best. Unfortunately I did not find it kind to my back, so I adapted by coming out of the squat position to be in Keith Andrew's position before the ball was bowled.

Most 'keepers today squat, with their hands together resting on the ground between their legs. I used to have my weight on the balls of my feet. This was because I am a little short in the calf muscle area, but I enjoyed rocking forward like Colin Metson does today. If you prefer to keep the whole of your foot on the ground, your stance could be more comfortable, especially over a long period in the field on hard surfaces.

Some present-day wicketkeepers use an open stance, for example Jack Russell and Colin Metson whose basic stances tend towards the off side, with the outside hip and foot open to that side. The inside foot stays generally straight so that any leg-side movement is not hindered. This stance helps them to 'think off-side' and to move to that side.

Try out the various stances. Go for good sighting and for comfort. Being evenly balanced can help you to move in any direction.

Coming out of the stance

I preferred to come out of the stance just before the bowler is about to deliver the ball. The main thing to remember when coming up is to be very, very relaxed. Try not to be sudden, or tense. Come out of the stance in a balanced position. My body often used to move a little backwards as I came out of the stance and sometimes on taking the ball. This I found very helpful if the ball dipped, swung or climbed on its way to me. This is important with the modern-day ball which wobbles in the air more than used to be the case before the 1980s.

Many other 'keepers tend to come out of the stance later, however, when the ball is in mid-air; and some come out later still, when the ball actually pitches. Most wicketkeepers stay reasonably low when coming out of the stance, but there are exceptions to this rule who have done well. You will need to experiment to see what suits you best, but whatever you do be relaxed physically and alert mentally.

TAKING THE BALL

Look to get your hands on the line of the ball, and on its height, and then 'give' slightly along that line. If your hands are on line and height you have a safety margin. If you feel it necessary to *emphasise* the 'give' by taking your hands back further and maybe to the side, only do this after the ball is safely in your gloves.

So try to keep your hands on the line and height of the ball because, even if your timing is wrong, you will still be presenting the ball with a large, relaxed glove target which will still enable you to take the ball properly.

For two-handed catching I would want the ball to land at about the base of the little finger of my major catching hand, my right hand. The gloves together form a cup with the hands comfortably spread and relaxed. Do not force the fingers too wide. If you do, you will create tension in the catching area.

As they come out of the stance to take the ball, many wicketkeepers have their hands out in front. This allows them to 'give' with the ball along the line. In photographs many 'keepers appear to have their fingers pointing at the ball, but this is only as the ball is coming towards them. When they take the ball their fingers will not be pointing at it, but downwards, to the side, or upwards, according to its bounce and direction.

CATCHING THE BALL

I like to have my major hand – the right – slightly overlapping and on top of the left hand. Some 'keepers overlap more and others, including Ian Healy, butt their hands and little

fingers together. For the basic, straight delivery my fingers are pointing down. If the ball is to the side the fingers point to the side, and if the ball bounces high the fingers point up. In these positions the fingers can 'give' with the ball and so are generally safe from injury.

Never allow the fingers to remain pointing at the ball when you are catching because, if the ball hits the end of the fingers, then there is terrific resistance and you are likely to do yourself damage.

How do I take the ball that bounces high towards me?

There are two methods. One I call the English method and the other the Australian method.

No thoughts of a stumping here as Jack Russell gets his hands on the height and line of the ball – always look to catch the ball first. Jack is perfectly balanced and on this occasion his predominant hand, the right, has overlapped the left a great deal.

LEFT *A wonderful leg-side catch. The ball flew to Rodney Marsh's right off the batsman's gloves and sheer power has got him there, his eyes focussed on the ball as he takes it baseball-style* (Adelaide Advertiser).

Say the ball is coming at your head or chest. For the English method, move just inside the line of the ball. If needed, you can move your left foot towards the leg side. Turn your shoulders and hips outwards to take the ball, and try not to throw your right elbow high and wide. This can force your gloves lower than you might like, and the butts of your hands are more likely to split apart. On taking the ball, your fingers will point to the side, or up, depending on how high the ball bounces.

The Australian method is to let the ball come at you and catch it 'baseball style' with the fingers pointing upwards. The ball should land at the base of the right forefinger, which is placed in front of the forefinger of the left hand. Top 'keepers usually catch in this style with their head right behind the line. (Be careful if the ball dips on its way towards you; make sure you bend your knees to allow your hands to come lower to meet the ball.)

THE GRUBBER

Taking the ball that grubs along the ground is tricky, so you need to work out a method to counter it. Personally, I usually stood up and tried to get both of my pads in line with the ball, and then I attempted to take the ball in front of the pads. Make sure you get both knees together. If the ball shoots under the gloves or bounces over them, the ball will hit the pads or body and usually land out in front. My head, then, was in a safe position and, as I was on my feet, I was able to get to the ball quickly in case the batsman wanted to steal a bye.

The second method, the long barrier, is the one recommended for stopping the ball in the field (see page 71). It means going down on one knee so that, if the ball bounces off your body you have to spend time getting to your feet to recover it. The head is also in a more dangerous position.

I hope you will have good luck with the first method, but very few wicketkeepers have mastered it. Experiment with keeping your hands to the side of your pads until the final moment of making the stop, in case the ball deviates.

WIDE DELIVERY – HOW DO I GET THERE?

You can use two methods. You can chassé to the side – that is with your body at right angles to the line of the ball so that you are using a side-stride to get to the ball. So if, for example, it is a particularly wide ball down the leg side, your might fit in two or three strides.

With the other method you just turn the body towards the line of the ball and set off after the ball with a running stride – it might only take one. Very often you see a top-class wicket-keeper mix both methods. To a ball wide down the leg side he may start with a chassé stride and move into a run before he makes the catch. So you have the chassé, or the running stride, or a mixture of both.

DIVING – TWO-HANDED CATCHING

If you are diving away to your right and the ball is coming through reasonably high, you can catch the ball with your normal two-handed method. If the ball is very low, dive to take the ball in the right glove and, just as you take it, bring the left glove over on top of it and enclose the ball in your two hands.

Remember, when you are diving for catches take your head towards the ball. Not only does this action bring your eyes close to the catch but it takes the weight and momentum of your body towards the ball and helps to limit the stretching for the ball. Catch the ball late. Bobby Simpson, the former Australian captain, was a brilliant slip fielder. He recommended catching the ball when it was *behind* the line of your body because that gives you extra time. You can imagine that, if the ball snicks the bat and flies very quickly, you need all the time available to respond, to get your hands into the right position and to make the catch.

For one-handed catches I like the ball to land at the base of my right forefinger or index finger, and I then use the web of the glove as a side wall. If you do not use webbed gloves (it is very rare today not to) you will have to catch the ball more centrally with the ball landing probably at the base of the middle finger.

Rodney Marsh's powerful legs propel him easily to this deflection for a two-handed catch off Jeff Thomson. Marsh is taking the ball late, rolling and about to land on the back of his left shoulder. Bad luck for Knott the batsman!

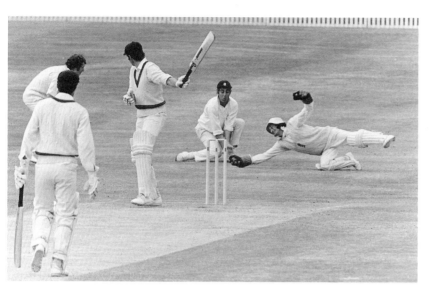

When you have a first slip next to you, think 'low'. Look to catch the edges that will not carry to him. Knott is catching McCosker in the Headingley Test, 1977, against Australia.

In a match, when do you go for a diving catch and when do you leave it to first slip? If the ball is edged high, generally it will reach your slips at good catching height. The balls they will not catch are the ones which do not carry. So you, the wicketkeeper, must think 'low'.

And you must always be ready to dive low. Any edged ball that is below knee height is yours. These edges will almost certainly not carry to first slip. So think low and go!

Standing up to the wicket

The spinners have come on, so now we have to stand up to the stumps,. You need to decide how close you stand. I stood as close as was comfortable in that I always tried to make sure that my pads were not going to touch the stumps, or the peak of my cap dislodge the bails. By being closer you can cut down slightly the angle of the edged ball. If you are a little deeper the ball has travelled further and is moving away from you. Also, if you are standing close, it is quicker for stumping and you can see more easily around a batsman to sight a ball pitching before it goes down the leg side. On the other hand, some 'keepers feel that, if

they are a little deeper, it gives them more time to sight the ball.

HOW WIDE SHOULD I STAND?

I liked to stand with my head as close to off-stump as possible. If a batsman crowded the line of the ball with his bat or body I might have gone a little wider, but I did not like to stand wide of the off stump. I felt that the bowler, generally, is aiming at the off stump or just outside the off stump, so that, if I stood reasonably straight with my head just outside off-stump, I could generally sight down the line of delivery. If I stood too wide, more often than not I had to try and move towards the line of the ball and, if my body was caught on the off side of the delivery, this could be very dangerous. If, for example, a batsman gets an outside edge or a top edge when cutting deliveries that bounce, the ball could fly at the 'keeper's face. Also, standing wide, I have much further to go to take a ball down the leg side. If I am standing straighter and the ball bounces high it is easier to turn my hips and my shoulders outwards so that I can take the ball to the side of my body.

Let my give you a tip about concentration at

this point. When the batsman hits the ball for four or six it is worth analyzing whether your mind was switched on to whether your hands were in a position ready to take the ball, or were you admiring the shot? This will help you to make sure that you are catching every delivery whether the batsman plays it or not.

Another point that helped my concentration when standing up was to say to myself, as the deliveries came towards me, 'Hands on the line of the ball, hands on the height of the ball'.

Whether I was keeping to an off-spinner or to a leg-spinner, I would have my hands waiting for the outside edge. This would mean that, for the off-spinner, my hands were on the line of the delivery, but for the leg-spinner that they were on the *predicted* line: i.e. that that ball would turn and beat the outside edge. Although in both cases the hands are left on the off side, looking for the outside edge, be ready to move them quickly to leg.

STANCE – STANDING UP

For most of my career I used the position I described when standing back. My hands were

resting on the ground between my legs; I believe it helps if 'keepers' feet are about a shoulder's width apart or a little wider. Some wicketkeepers are on the balls of their feet, others have the whole of the foot on the ground.

Being evenly balanced can help you move either way, but the major factor is sighting the ball. It helps if your eyes are level, both eyes looking at the ball all the way from the bowler's hand.

There are other stances for when you are up to the stumps and, if I had my time again, I would try out the one used by Keith Andrew. He used to go into the squat position but, instead of having his hands together, he held them apart although touching the ground between his knees, and he brought the hands together as he caught the ball. So do not worry if your hands are apart, so long as they are together for the take. As the delivery comes towards you, try and bring your hands up with or just under the ball. A great many 'keepers' hands are off the ground before the ball pitches, but try not to get them too high, causing you

Be ready to catch every ball, even if it is an easy full-toss which, to judge from the position of Bert Oldfield's hands, was probably what had been bowled to Wally Hammond.
(Sydney Morning Herald/Fishwick/Fairfax).

to force them down at the ball. This can make taking much harder.

COMING OUT OF THE STANCE

Remember that, when you are coming out of the stance, the balance of your body should be even, not pushed forward. I liked to keep my hands in front of me and coming back with the ball as it came towards me, with my knees starting to straighten comfortably as I took the ball. Do not let your knees restrict your taking of the ball, or the side movement of your hands.

When taking the ball keep the whole of the foot flat on the ground. Although from the hips to the head you might be angled forward, the general balance of the body is even so that, if the ball bounces high at you, it is easy to take the body out of the way and to get the body and head high and safe from injury. If you are pushed forward on your toes, or if you get locked in a low squatting stance, you could be in a dangerous position if the ball bounces high. Be perfectly balanced. Imagine someone being able to rock you slightly back or forward while you are in position for taking the ball.

I feel that it helps if wicketkeepers hardly move their feet at all when standing up to the stumps for basic deliveries just outside the off stump. Simply move from the hips and knees as you take the ball. It is not only your hands which take the ball. Your whole body takes it in a rhythm off the pitch. Keep your knees, and especially your hips, very mobile.

When standing up, the great difficulty in taking comes in the length of the delivery. The hardest lengths to take are the yorker and the half-volley to the batsman. With both of these deliveries there is very little time to read whatever the ball might do, whereas when the ball is short you have plenty of time to adjust and the ball usually comes through at a comfortable height. As you improve with your wicketkeeping I suggest that you practise a great deal taking the full-length deliveries. The method described in the previous three paragraphs will be a great help.

When you are taking the ball which bounces high, you need to turn your hips and shoulders while getting your body inside the line of the ball. Taking the left foot towards the leg side may help if the delivery is straight. When catching the ball now your fingers should be pointing to the side or upwards depending on the degree of bounce. Remember here the position of the outside elbow. (See page 93 'English method'.)

Young wicketkeepers, when standing up, might be worried because they tend to move away from the stumps as they take the ball. Remember, if this is your style, to take only the outside foot back. Try to keep the inside leg reasonably close to the stumps. In fact a movement backwards of the outside foot can help you to get into a good position for the high take which requires the hip and shoulder to be turning outwards. I had periods in my career when I used to move my outside foot back on some of the more lively pitches when I kept to Derek Underwood.

Try not to move both feet back because, if you do, you could be too far away from the stumps to make a stumping.

TAKING A WIDE BALL OUTSIDE OFF-STUMP

Move the outside leg across in line with the bowling crease or even slightly backwards. Try not to move your head to the off side of the delivery. And do not turn your body inwards to face the stumps. If you turn in, it will be extremely difficult to get your hips and shoulders into a position where they can turn outwards again for the high-bouncing ball, and your body, especially your head, will not be in a safe position.

For most deliveries wide of off-stump you will probably need only one stride to reach them. Youngsters may need two strides; if so, move the right leg first, then bring the left leg towards it, then move the right leg again. Try not to go too far wide of the off stump if you are looking for a stumping, but remember that the most important consideration is to catch the ball. So do not stay so far inside the line of the ball that you cannot make a clean catch.

TAKING A LEG-SIDE DELIVERY

First I have to sight the ball. I have seen it from the bowler's hand and I am logging it in my mind to enable me to anticipate its line and where it is likely to land. I try to sight the ball pitching from the off-side, but this is not always possible. For very full deliveries you will need to sight the pitching of the ball from the *leg* side of the batsman. Once you have seen the ball pitch you can make your judgement on where the ball will be coming to you. For example, if the bowler is a left-arm spinner, ask yourself, has the ball turned and bounced, or is it skidding on down the leg side?

If I judged that the delivery could well finish down the leg side, I would move my left foot first, not always a great distance. While I was doing this, I could often be leaning to the off side, looking around the batsman and trying to see where the ball would pitch. Then, when I had decided to take off to the leg side *I led with my gloves*. The hands go first in order to get in line with the ball. The legs follow, chasséing to the left. If the ball beats the hands, then the left leg can become a second line of defence. As with off-side taking, move the feet in line with the bowling crease or a little behind.

Once you are moving down the leg side you must be trying to re-sight the delivery with your head and hands facing the ball. Do not turn the body in to face the stumps. This would probably mean that your head and hands would have to do the same, making both sighting the ball and catching it very difficult.

Sometimes you will find that you cannot get a sighting of the ball as it pitches. This is when you use the knowledge you have logged in

For this legside take Jack Russell's hands have led towards the line of the ball, the legs following fractionally afterwards. If the ball had been missed by the batsman and Jack Russell's hands, the left leg might have just got behind the line to act as a second line of defence.

your mind from the delivery coming towards you, flight, drift, etc. You know the state of the pitch, the speed of the bowler, and therefore the likely height of the bounce or the amount of turn. But still look to sight the ball on the off side of the batsman, then on the leg side. Remember, for leg-side taking, move as late and as quickly as possible. Speed is vital. Move late, but like lightning.

For leg-side taking when keeping wicket to a left-handed batsman, I would try, after moving my hands to the line of delivery, to place my right leg on the line of the ball without moving it on further to the leg side. This would keep my body nearer the stumps, and make easier reaching the bails with a two-handed method. If I tried to transfer the ball to my weaker left hand, it would prove clumsy and time-wasting.

When you are keeping to a left-handed batsman, use your same natural catching method – right hand slightly overlapping the left. Other than this, and the method of leg side taking, everything you have done for the right-handed batsman can be used for the left-hander, if you see it all as the mirror image.

STUMPINGS

For stumping chances you can use your arms and your hands in the action to remove the bails. But most 'keepers, especially for wider deliveries move their whole body, led by their knees and hips. Your hands and arms follow. For really wide deliveries I know that some 'keepers, including Jack Russell, run at and past the stumps as they remove the bails. I suggest, however, that you do not become too preoccupied by stumping. Even when the batsman charges down the pitch, think just about taking the ball. It could be a catch after all. Try thinking 'edge'. See if that helps, but do not get tense. So many young 'keepers say 'Oh! I get so scared about stumping'. So let me suggest a method of practice.

Get a batsman to charge down the pitch, hit some deliveries, play at and miss others, but do not let him tell you which ones he is going to hit and which he will let through. When you take the ball, just throw it back to the bowler. Do not even bother to go for the stumping chance because, as you improve as a wicket-keeper, stumping will come naturally. Even when the batsman plays the ball, do not take your hand towards the stumps in a stumping action. No-one ever made a stumping without the ball in his gloves. When a batsman is out of his ground, Jack Russell says to himself, 'If I catch the ball, he's out'. Some stumpers take their hands back to the stumps after each delivery. If this is your style, and it doesn't affect your game, don't stop.

Give yourself sessions where you practise your stumping method, building up speed, but use the practice I have just mentioned until you are happy with your game.

Conclusion

Work at your wicketkeeping skills, and keep fit and mobile for the job. Your talent will get expressed all the more if you enjoy what you are doing. Keep your game as natural and comfortable as you can.

No matter what happens, think 'lucky'.

Alan Knott stumping Lawrence Rowe at The Oval in 1976, to pass the then world record of Godfrey Evans for Test dismissals (219). 'The hands have led the stumping action but the body, especially the knees and hips, have all worked together.'

4

BATTING

VIVIAN RICHARDS

GEOFFREY BOYCOTT

DAVID GOWER

THE NATURAL APPROACH TO BATTING

VIVIAN RICHARDS

My first cricket was on the beaches of Antigua on the hard, wet sand close to the sea. Often the ball would skim through fast in a spray of water. Our bats were often flat pieces of wood shaped to be like the bats of the heroes we watched playing the occasional game of first-class cricket that we were able to see.

When I was older, the fields we used for matches were rough and uneven. I am still amazed how we used to race in to field the ball, picking it up in one hand although it was bouncing in every direction, and hurling it into the wicketkeeper or at the stumps.

The Antiguan way was the natural way and that is what I ask all readers of this book to consider seriously. I say to coaches, consider the natural instincts and talents of the young player and let him develop his own style.

No-one will ever persuade me that there is one method of batting, common to all, which can be imposed on young cricketers by the book. I do not see it like that.

The reason why I am happy to contribute to *MCC Masterclass* is because there is a balance between suggested methods, orthodox and well-tried, and the priceless experience of the Masters who all know that good cricketers should be helped to find their own strengths. Allow young cricketers to be free and relaxed; do not complicate batting with too much theory before they can hit the ball. I will never confuse a young mind by talking about the bat and the pad being close together so that the ball does not squeeze through. I will say, show me how you can hit the ball to all parts of the ground and bowl accordingly to help him.

This is why the greatest West Indian batsmen have looked to score off every single ball they faced. When they have played a defensive stroke it has been the secondary instinct taking over; they were simply rejecting the ball saying, sorry, can't hit that for runs, I'll just stop it.

It is not a technical matter. It is to do with the approach in the mind to batting. Let the mind of the youngster fly; let him see the best cricketers play and show him a big field with no fielders, no barriers, no batting rules, and let him whack the ball in all directions.

When you develop such enthusiasm for scoring runs the young player will be so heart-broken at getting out that quickly his curiosity will be aroused about some hand-me-down safeguards. When I first went to England I attended the Alf Gover Cricket School where I was told that my left elbow should be pointed upwards and my left shoulder ought to be leading down the pitch and so many other physical adjustments while the ball was coming my way. In fact all I learned – all I required to learn – was that I needed to play a little straighter.

Again I concentrated on the mind not on the body. I began to look to play the ball much straighter down the pitch within the arc of mid-on and mid-off. It meant ignoring some of my favourite areas square with the batting crease, but I was soon playing longer innings and avoiding the disappointment of being out early.

It is the same with the grip and the stance. Do not tell young people that they are standing

Vivian Richards: A characteristic and powerful finish.
West Indian batsmen look to score off every single ball.

too open or too closed unless they appear to be getting out because of an obvious fault. Emphasise the ability to be balanced on their feet and able to see the ball right the way down the pitch from the bowler's hand. Relaxation leads to sharp reactions; tension slows down the mind-to-body messages.

Playing an innings

The night before a match I often dreamed that I would make a century. I never dreamed that I would make a duck. Some things play havoc with your mind before you get out to the middle and have an innings, but fear of failure was something which never hit me, I am delighted to say. I have often been called arrogant and over-confident but I do not believe that any cricketer should ever go for second best. Always expect to play right to the limits of your ability. Go right for the top.

As a young boy I was always playing innings in my mind and I was always scoring centuries by hitting sixes to get from 94 to the three figures. My actual career was in part a realisation of those dreams. I always encourage the youngest batsman to have a vision of success. In the Caribbean we enjoy hitting the ball hard and I must remind all coaches that enjoyment is one of the keys to creating entertainment, and both are the fathers of victory because winning cricket is positive cricket – the only cricket worth playing and watching.

Keep cool when bowlers try to annoy you and wind you up into a temper. Always believe that you can master the best even though they get you out from time to time. Never let a previous dismissal or run of dismissals have you intimidated. I think back to my battles with Dennis Lillee, the Australian fast bowler, and think what a superb clash of personalities it was.

Maybe I had a sort of brashness but I never had doubts about his ability or mine and, even though I knew he was special, I felt that it was not so special that I could not achieve. Nothing Dennis Lillee bowled was going to be unplayable. When Dennis was in harness with Jeff Thomson they were capable of the total destruction of a Test batting line-up but still I backed Viv Richards. Richards was going to do what he could do. I never felt too cocky but I knew that I was pitching my skills against bowlers who were just as arrogant and dominating.

So without worrying what they were up to I got on with my own concentration and stroke-play. Dennis used to come down the pitch and look you straight in the eye, real angry stares, but I always loved the confrontation. That is what I mean to say – look forward to the tough, crunch moments, relish them, and think that that is the fertile earth you need for your own talent to grow and blossom.

Dennis Lillee was going to have his day and Viv Richards his. I just wanted to make sure that I had more than he did. One day he would get me out and point me back to the pavilion, the next I would raise my bat and acknowledge the applause of the crowd, Dennis included. There was mutual respect but neither of us lost the belief in our own roles.

Batting is not war – relax and express yourself. Some of us are belligerent, some are coaxers of the ball, some delight in hearing the ball smash against the hoardings, others love to steer the ball wide of fielders for just a couple of runs. Each approach can be dominant. And come what may, you must always be trying to be on top.

BASIC TECHNIQUE

GEOFFREY BOYCOTT

Not everyone can expect to bat well. Natural abilities are necessary, for example ball sense, the ability to sight the ball and to judge its length quickly. Perfect timing of the stroke, the magical moment when the ball meets the middle of the bat, is almost a secret which cannot be taught, though it can be improved by study and practice.

Some people have ball sense and timing, others do not, and coaches will do well to make an honest judgement of a young cricketer's potential as soon as they are certain. Successful batting is not about physical strength. An experienced coach will know whether your game can be improved; whether you have enough natural talent to develop so that you can enjoy a cricket career that can give you fulfilment and enjoyment.

When I coach young players I try to develop and strengthen the qualities they already possess. I do not think that coaches should lay down rigid rules of technique – this might well inhibit a young player. It is true that each shot may be best created within a framework of orthodox technique but do not be a slave to orthodoxy. Coaches must allow the individuality of the pupil to come out.

A coach must be critical but encouraging. Confidence is one of the key words and that can only come from success and the likelihood of success. Success is more likely to come if you can create for yourself a sound technique, from how you hold the bat, to how you execute

Boycott Masterclass – coaching the positioning of the feet

different strokes, to how you and your partner run between the wickets.

NOTE: *The text and diagrams that follow are written and designed for a right-handed batsman. For a left-hander reverse 'left' and 'right'.*

The grip

Your grip on the bat is important because your hands have to work together. You need flexi-

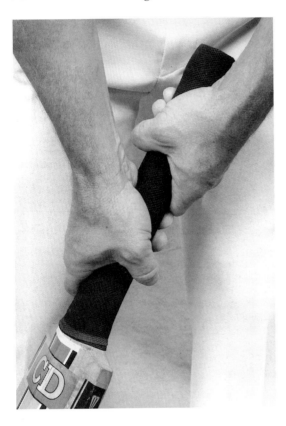

bility of stroke but without change of grip. It is one thing to play hefty drives, but you also need to play strokes which require relaxed hands or manoeuvrable wrists.

The hands are close together towards the top of the bat handle. The 'V' formed by the thumb and forefinger of the top hand is directly above the corresponding 'V' of the bottom hand, and the line of these two 'Vs' is between the outer edge of the bat and the splice.

Personally I like my top hand turned around slightly more than the majority of players towards the back of the handle, the top 'V' points more towards the splice of the bat. This gives me more control with my weaker hand, the top hand.

Taking guard

The most usual guards are leg-stump, middle-and-leg (or 'two legs'), and middle-stump. Which guard should you take? When I am asked this I explain that the reason you take a guard is to know exactly where you are stand-

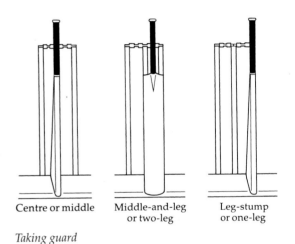

Centre or middle Middle-and-leg or two-leg Leg-stump or one-leg

Taking guard

Batting grip: hands close together. The 'Vs' of the hands are on the same line, between the outside edge and the splice.

ing in relation to the stumps. You must know where your wickets are, particularly the off stump.

Take your normal stance and ask a friend to stand directly behind the wicket at the bowler's end, where the umpire stands. Shuffle around until your friend tells you your eyes are over the off stump, and then ask for the exact position of your bat in relation to the stumps. That will be your correct guard.

Batting stance: Peter May, 1953. Shoulder pointing at the bowler, the head fully turned, the eyes level. Easy and natural (Photograph by J. G. Dunbar)

Stance

An easy stance is important. The feet are parallel to the crease to enable you to stay sideways to the bowler, though many players favour a slight opening of the front foot, say, towards cover-point. It is important that the body is sideways to the bowler with the weight equally distributed between the feet, which are comfortably apart but no more than shoulder width. The toe of the bat rests behind the back

toes and the hands comfortably lean against the thigh. The knees should be slightly flexed. The left shoulder points down the pitch and the eyes are level.

The batsman's weight should be on the balls of the feet. Batsmen have to be like dancers, light on their feet and able to transfer their weight quickly from one foot to the other depending on the length of the ball. The stance does not mean that you have to stand immov-

The back-lift: the basis of a sound technique, the left arm has pushed the bat over the stumps; the face of the bat is open; the eyes look squarely at the ball. No movement yet of the batsman, Graeme Hick's feet.

able, like a statue. You are simply putting your body into a position from which you can move swiftly in all directions.

Back-lift

If your stance is correct, it is a natural movement to pick up your bat in the direction of the slips, as the great batsmen do, such as Sir Donald Bradman in a picture here from his book *The Art of Cricket*. Then, at the top of the back-lift, loop the bat and bring it down over the line of the stumps.

Many tutors teach more traditionally that, if you pick the bat up straight it will come down straight, so they suggest you take the bat back directly over middle-stump. I feel that the best players have never done that. It simply is not a natural movement and it will let you down under pressure.

Some batsmen take a stance with the bat held

Sir Donald Bradman says in his book The Art of Cricket: *'my back-lift was usually in the direction of second slip, as depicted here'. But of course he came down straight.*

Graham Gooch's stance with bat raised looks strained. Geoffrey Boycott does not advise it.

a long way off the ground – Graham Gooch of England is one – but this is a stance for hitting. I do not advise it. Pick the bat up naturally but bring it down straight. It is worth pointing out that Graham Gooch did not start his career with an unorthodox pick-up. He took up his stance with the bat on the ground. No-one began their career with the bat held high in the pick-up. Would Graham Gooch have been an even better player if he had stood more naturally? It is worth asking.

THE STROKES

GEOFFREY BOYCOTT, DAVID GOWER AND VIVIAN RICHARDS

All cricket strokes are played with two fundamental movements, forward on to the front foot, or back on to the back foot. The aim of every batsman should be for equal competence off both feet. Only by practice can a batsman judge length, but it is the judgement which enables a batsman to select the right stroke.

Never make up your mind to go backward or forward before you see the ball leave the hand of the bowler. Guessing is a dangerous pastime.

Correct footwork is the essential part of all strokeplay. Try not to think of back play in defensive terms and forward play as attack. The best players defend and attack equally well off back or front foot. In truth, batting should not be split up into compartments of defence and attack except for ease of analysis and study. Be balanced in your stance and ready to move either way.

'Go right back or right forward,' says Vivian Richards. 'Use as much of the crease area as possible. Let the ball come to you.'

'Once you have settled in,' adds David Gower, 'you can by judicious strokeplay force the opposing captain to move some of his men back.'

Forward defence

The forward defensive stroke is played to a straight, good-length ball, which is too short to drive, but too far up for a back-foot stroke.

Lead with the head and front shoulder, and

Masterclass group on how to play the forward defensive stroke

the front foot will then follow to the pitch of the ball. Place your front foot as close as possible to the pitch of the ball. The top hand is in control while the bottom hand is relaxed, with the bat held loosely between thumb and forefinger.

The ball is played with an angled bat as near as possible to the front pad, so that the ball cannot squeeze through.

The body's weight is on the front foot, the front knee is bent, and the head is over the point of contact. The back leg is fully extended from the crease but raise the heel of the right foot: get the weight on to the inside of the right toe because that will move your head and whole balance that small bit further over the point of contact. Be careful not to drag the back foot out beyond the popping crease as you play.

Backward defence

The back-foot defensive stroke is used to counter a short-pitched ball on the line of the stumps, but the delivery is not short enough for the batsman to play an attacking shot.

Pick up the bat, then step back and across with the back foot so that your head is in line with the oncoming ball. Keep your full height and stay sideways by keeping the back foot parallel with the crease. The front leg draws back naturally to join the back leg.

Stay sideways, because the bat then has room to move through in an uninterrupted swing and also because, if the ball is short and rising towards the head, you present a narrow target to the ball.

Although you are going back, the head must be over the ball. When you play the stroke, therefore, the weight will be slightly forward.

The front elbow and top hand control the stroke, and contact is made in a line under the chin. You will need to raise the elbow high to keep the bat straight. The bottom hand takes a gentle hold between thumb and forefinger.

LEFT AND ABOVE *The forward defensive: as played by Geoffrey Boycott and Glenn Turner – left leg bent to 'shut the gate', right toe behind the batting crease, elbow high, head over the ball at the moment of impact*

A fine example, by Ted Dexter facing Wesley Hall at Kingston, Jamaica, in February 1960, of getting behind the line of a fast rising ball; or, as Dexter himself comments, 'not so much behind as beside and close to the line, keeping the sideways position'.

The off-drive and straight drive

The off-drive is played with a full swing of the bat to an over-pitched delivery or half-volley and, as with the forward defensive shot, the head and front shoulder lead towards the line of the ball, with the front foot following.

The ball is struck just in front of the front foot, and, with an accelerating arc, the bat follows through over the front shoulder in the direction you want the ball to travel. The top hand should remain in control and the head is kept still as contact is made.

Some batsmen prefer to check the follow-through, and they keep the face of the bat open and stop it at about shoulder height. That is fine. Whatever works for them is what matters, but all obey the basic tenets, that the top hand should remain in control and the head is kept still and above the ball as contact is made.

The straight ball you hit past the bowler, but if the delivery is very wide you could be aiming to the right of the cover fielder's left hand.

At the completion of any well-hit drive, the batsman should find himself with his weight firmly balanced on his front foot, with his head still leading, and knowing that the whole face of the bat has moved down the line of the ball at impact.

Off-drives. Different batsmen, different styles: (left) David Gower stroking it square; (above) Ian Botham and Vivian Richards vigorously on the offensive; (right) Steve Waugh, watchful, effective, very correct.

The on-drive

If the ball is over-pitched on leg-stump, play the on-drive.

The on-drive can be a difficult shot to play and many players have trouble with it. The ball comes in on the leg stump and the secret of playing it, and of keeping good balance, is to place the left leg *outside* the line of the ball. At the same time the batsman's head and front shoulder will dip towards the line of the ball. (Many players place the front leg inside the line, but this means that the batsman never has his head over the ball. His body then falls to the off and forces him to play across the line of the ball.)

The front knee bends as the weight leans forward into the shot. The bat moves naturally along a line from slips to mid-on, and the ball is struck just in front of the front toe.

The basic principles for the drive apply, including a full swing of the bat, though some players check the follow-through and stop the bat when it is just below shoulder height. With the on-drive the bottom hand comes into the stroke in a more positive way.

The lofted drive

The lofted drive is a particularly effective attacking stroke, played mainly to slow or medium-slow bowling. It can be played from the crease or by advancing down the pitch.

Although it is important to get close to the pitch of the ball to avoid skying it, the ball should be struck earlier and a little further beyond the front toe than if you were aiming to hit the ball along the ground. The head must stay down and not be lifted too soon. A full but controlled follow-through will help you to clear the inner ring of fielders.

David Gower adds: 'When you want to hit the ball in the air the body may lean back, but keep the head down, watching the ball as long as possible, as you would with any normal shot. Whether you are trying to loft the ball off

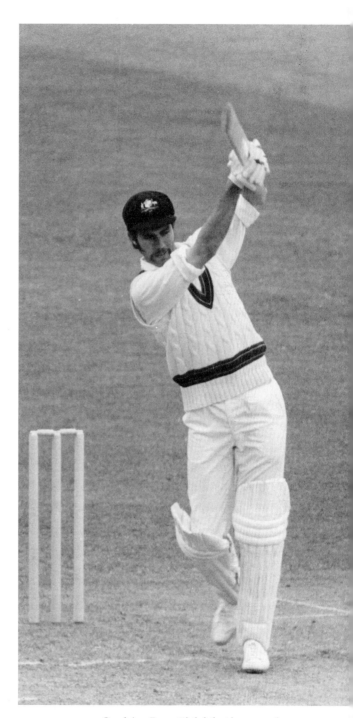

LEFT AND ABOVE *On-drive. Boycott's left foot has opened to lead the body on to the line of the stroke; Greg Chappell's head has led the transference of weight on to the front foot.*

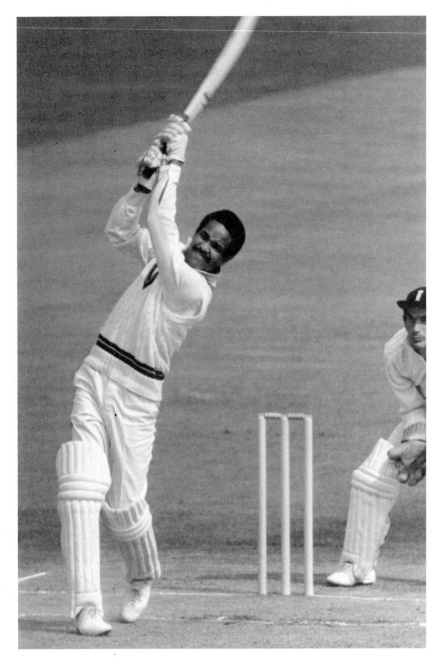

Gary Sobers' lofted straight drive is as elegant as it is powerful. Note too how the front foot points towards the covers.

FAR RIGHT *Gavaskar – the follow-through of a forcing shot off the back foot. The toe of the right foot, which was pointing towards cover at the moment of impact, has swivelled round with the power of the shot and the body is now leaning forward.*

RIGHT *Martin Crowe shows the ideal balance to make a powerful stroke off the back foot* (All-Sport)

the front foot, or the back, just remember this – you are going to hit the ball better if you've got into position to play the ball on the ground first and then, at the last movement, you make the final adjustment to hit the ball over the fielders, not at them.

'Keep your eye on the ball. Watch the ball right on to the bat. It is just like golf when you are trying to hit a long wood. If you are looking up towards the target you are never going to hit it far: if you keep your head down and watch your club actually make contact with the ball, it will take off. It is the same with driving the ball at cricket.'

Hitting a full pitch to leg

Off the front foot. Make sure that your head is in line with the flight of the ball, eyes looking straight down the line. The front foot will land more or less pointing down the pitch towards the bowler.

Swing the bat across keeping the head absolutely still. Your weight is on the front leg which bends as the body moves into the stroke.

Try to strike the ball with your arms at full stretch from the body in front of the left leg. Angle the blade of the bat upwards if you are aiming to hit a six, or, if you are looking for

runs along the ground, bring the bat down on the ball from a high back-lift and roll the wrists.

Forcing shot off the back foot

The forcing shot off the back foot is played to a short-pitched ball. Stay sideways as the back foot is taken towards the stumps to land parallel with the crease – allow room for the bat to swing through the line of the ball. Although the movement is backwards, the weight, as you play the stroke, is slightly forward.

The bat is controlled by the top hand and the high left elbow. The bottom hand adds power just as the ball is struck past a braced back leg. Make the most of your height so that you are on top of the bounce of the ball.

Square-cut and late-cut

David Gower writes: The square-cut is a run-scoring shot played to a short ball wide of off-stump. First step back and across with the back foot, and then, with a pronounced turn of the front shoulder, throw the arms outwards and downwards from a high back-lift to strike the ball at full arms-length. The high back-lift is recommended because the best time to hit the ball is when it has reached the peak of its bounce. The body-weight should be moved on to a bent back leg and, generally, the toe of the back foot points in the direction the ball is intended to travel.

Against slow and medium fast bowlers it is possible to play the cut off the front foot. The front leg is thrust well across to the line of the ball and, as the front knee bends into the stroke, the bat is thrown out to meet the ball just as it gets to the top of its bounce.

Against fast bowlers you get quickly on to the *back* foot and it helps to have the bat high because when the bat is up early, you can get on top of a cut. (If you have got the bat down low and your hands low, down at your waist, you've got a lot of extra movement to make before you are properly in position.)

Although the text books usually advise you to throw the arms at the ball I would mark some caution here. Ideally you should wait for the ball and let it come to you rather than force the stroke. (See page 143.)

The late cut is similar to the square cut but the ball is played later in its flight, and finer, to

The cut. David Gower (left) and Robin Smith (right) cut square. In each case the full weight has gone into the shot and the ball has been kept down.

a straightish third-man or through the slips area. Unlike the square-cut which requires power, the late-cut needs gentle hands. Again watch the ball right on to the bat because it has to be played behind you. The ball is met almost in line with the stumps before contact. Thus you make use of the speed of the ball on to the bat for its velocity off it.

The pull

The pull shot is played to a short-pitched ball with the bat horizontal – a cross-bat which 'pulls the ball to leg'.

Move the back foot back towards the stumps and let the swing of the bat open up the body so that you end up square, or chest-on, to the bowler.

The head must be kept still for as long as possible. Hit down on the ball with a horizontal

Bradman enjoys the delicacy of the late cut, 1948

RIGHT *The finish of the pull stroke, as played by Mike Gatting (All-Sport)*

bat from a high back-lift and try to strike it well in front of your body to avoid being cramped in the stroke. Aim for mid-wicket or square-leg. Your weight should finish up on your front leg.

The hook

This is another stroke which looks pre-meditated when you see an expert play it. The movement back and across the crease, inside the line of the high, bouncing ball, is so fast that it looks as if the batsman knew a bouncer was coming. This is because the best batsmen

West Indian cricketers are brought up to hook. Vivian Richards plays it magisterially square. Clive Lloyd (below) has hit the ball later towards fine-leg. His body has pivoted and cleared the line of the ball which has been hit down.

know they have the shot available and it should come out naturally.

It is important to have a thorough understanding of the nature of the pitch. Hooking fast bowling off a surface which is bouncing unevenly is extremely risky, even daft, because the shot is played with a cross-bat.

You need to have the bat high in the back-lift so that you can move it easily along the plane required to play the hook. Your feet should be balanced in the stance and full of lightness and anticipation.

Get your weight quickly and firmly on to the back foot, which has not only moved back but far enough across to be just on the off-side of the line of flight and it points towards mid-off. This means that the body enjoys a full pivot as a strong stroke to leg opens up the body towards the bowler. Aim to hit the ball down, as square as possible on the leg side.

The leg glance

This is one of the most delicate strokes in the game and is played to a ball narrowly missing the leg stump. No power is required here, just good balance and a sense of timing which will gently help the ball on its way with a turn of the wrists on impact. It can be played off the front or the back foot.

Two things to be wary of are either attempting to glance the ball too fine, or attempting the shot at a ball too far away from the body – the likely result is a nick to the wicketkeeper.

The sweep *(see picture opposite)*

The sweep is an attacking stroke usually played to a slow delivery, well pitched up and just outside the leg stump. The head leads the weight forward towards the line of the ball. The front leg is bent, the head is still, and the ball is swept by a horizontal bat around behind square-leg.

Unless the ball is wide, the front pad should be placed in line with the flight of the ball – not inside the line, as that will expose the leg stump.

LEFT *The leg glance: off the front foot, and off the back foot. In both cases the ball is met just in front of the left leg, and the batsman's head is on the line of the ball.*

RIGHT *Gower, always strong on the leg side, plays the sweep*

Gatting shows how you can play the reverse sweep, but Geoffrey Boycott does not recommend it

The reverse sweep

This is a high-risk shot, writes Geoffrey Boycott, which is attempted, sometimes successfully, by batsmen who have not got enough shots or by good players who need to show bravado or be outrageous. I have seen it work cheekily on occasions but when it fails the batsman looks foolish. Set high standards for yourself, model your batting on the best and remember that the great batsmen never contemplated playing the reverse sweep. You would never have seen Graeme Pollock, Sunil

Gavaskar or Greg Chappell play the reverse sweep.

Using the feet to get to the pitch of the ball

Leave your decision late to move down the pitch when playing a slow bowler, and move so late that he cannot detect your plan. Be on the lookout to leave your crease but do not go until you have spotted the suitable ball. Do not predetermine a move.

Allan Border uses his feet to drive Emburey through the mid-wicket area. Perth, 1986.

Move the front foot well forward and then allow the back foot to glide up alongside; then move the front foot forward again to the pitch of the ball. From this position several yards down the pitch you play exactly the same strokes as you would from the crease – the off-drive, straight-drive or on-drive.

PREPARING TO BAT AND BUILDING AN INNINGS

GEOFFREY BOYCOTT

So many cricketers waste net practice. Even professional players abuse the opportunity of good practice by failing to concentrate, by slogging, or by relaxing too much for their game's own good. This is not only irritating and unhelpful to the bowlers who are also trying to work at their technique but it is dangerous to the batsmen themselves.

In a net you need to simulate match conditions. You cannot expect to practise one way in a net and play an entirely different way in a real match.

So when you are set up to bat in a net, start slowly before looking to play your shots, as you should in a match. Do not have half a dozen bowlers queuing up sending down a barrage of balls. With just three bowlers you can study each action as you do in matches and take time between balls to think about each stroke you have played. The bowlers benefit too because they have time to think what they are trying to bowl.

Prepare your mind for batting in the middle

Preparing the mind for batting was always vital to me. I started thinking about it the night before, but with club or occasional cricketers that might not be so easy. However, on the morning of a match you have to give some thought to it – who you are playing against, and what bowlers you will face. Then, when you get to the ground, it is important to take a look at the pitch.

If it looks to be a very slow pitch you know that the ball may not come on to you quickly. On wet ground it may even sit up and then you know in your own mind that you will have to get right forward, absolutely to the pitch of the ball if you are playing a stroke off the front foot. You deduce, though, that most of your runs will come off the back foot with pulls and cuts. On the other hand, if it is a fast bouncy pitch, you will not envisage pushing forward too often into a steep bounce, and you may suspect the ball is going to turn.

I tap my bat on the pitch, and that tells me whether I am on soft ground or firm, spongy or loose, whether it will be fast or slow. I bounce a ball on the pitch to see if it bounces high or low. If the ball always comes off the pitch at the same height you know it will play true. If it comes off at differing heights I expect the bowling to bounce unevenly.

Spend time weighing up the possibilities because the first few balls you face in the middle are absolutely vital. Get it wrong, and you could be out.

In the dressing-room

When I open my bag I find my kit clean, trousers and shirts pressed, sweaters neatly folded. I like to keep a permanent place in the bag for each item. If my bag is organised then my approach to batting should be too. Whenever I arrived at the crease to take guard my world was in order and I was ready for the most important minutes or hours of the day, the batting.

Try to get a net before the match or at least get a bowler from the team to turn his arm over on the outfield so that you can get your feet moving backwards and forwards according to the length of the ball and find your best timing: feel the ball making sweet contact with the bat. Do not force it. Do not show off and try to thump the ball into the boundary benches. Just be inwardly happy with your footwork and timing.

In the dressing-room I think that batsmen are best left quiet before an innings. Before I opened an innings I did not want to talk to anybody. If my mother had knocked on the dressing-room door I would have told her to go away. I did not even want my partner to chat to me. I really wanted to cocoon myself, surrounded only by concentration. In short, I put the blinkers on.

Playing yourself in

Let's imagine that you are a schoolboy going to the crease to bat. You have inspected the pitch and you anticipate that some shots may be unwise to play – perhaps it is a rain-affected, soft surface and you think it will be impossible to drive. Do not say to yourself, 'I must cut out the drive'. That is too negative. You must also know in your mind which shots should be profitable. Just take your time: be wise enough to say 'That shot will be risky, I am aware of it'. It is just a particle of the whole mass of concentration you need in order to be a very good player – and especially at the start of an innings.

When you go out to bat, get yourself accustomed first of all to the pitch and the bowlers, and let the runs flow naturally. Playing yourself in is vital. I have seen very few batsmen in the world who can take an attack apart right from the word go. Sir Gary Sobers and Vivian Richards were probably the only exceptions, truly great players, who could do that in my playing days.

Runs will come, as I said, but how and where? Look carefully at the placing of the field. See the possible gaps for a ball played along the ground. Keep the ball on the ground. It is fine for Viv Richards to butcher the bowling because he has the talent. The majority of batsmen have to restrict the chances given to the opposition by shunning the lofted shots at the start.

Put yourself occasionally into the mind of the bowler. It is frustrating for him if every good ball he bowls keeps hitting the middle of the bat even when no runs are scored, and then, when he strays in length or line, the ball keeps disappearing through the gaps for runs. It can be demoralising for him and you are on your way to getting on top. It is essential to dominate but many players have a false idea of what domination with the bat amounts to. It can be resistance to a fine spell of bowling, it can be impudent singles pushed to mid-on and run quickly. You can conquer and infuriate by stinging like a bee as well as by devouring like a lion.

I prided myself on a good technique, and an orthodoxy which has stood the test of time.

The stance is crucial, but the emphasis of my teaching has always been on balance. When a batsman stands at the crease to face a fast bowler his foot movement has to start somewhere. Just before the bowler releases the ball, as his arm is on the way over, some decide to play back to fast bowlers, back and across the stumps. It does not matter which way they go as long as they are not committed to the ultimate stroke, backward or forward. This is the important thing. Look at Sachin Tendulkar, his front foot moves a little bit forward and across, say two inches, and the back one moves in line with it, but they are small movements and always on the balls of the feet. These movements are to get ready, to prepare, not to take up the final position for the stroke. If the ball is well up he can get quickly forward, but he can also move quickly back from the poised position. Do not move around on flat feet. It is heavy movement which destroys the essential, nimble approach.

I used to move a little back and across that fraction of a second before the ball was in the air. Greg Chappell did the same, but on the

Sachin Tendulkar – on his toes, and hooking

balls of the feet with the weight just that little bit forward. This meant we were poised, ready and waiting to see the ball's length and then make the big, positive move forward or backward.

So let me tell you how I got my innings started. If you have a good technique it should be bread-and-butter to play off your legs to the on side. The ball is coming on to you, your wickets are not exposed, you are sideways-on and you simply help the ball on its way. You say to the bowler 'thank you very much' and run to the other end.

Thus I recommend the state of mind which concerns itself only with singles. This playing-yourself-in process cements the detailed knowledge you have built up of where every individual fielder is standing. Ask yourself – is there a single to cover or mid-off or wherever? How deep are they standing? How square is gully? Which fielders are close behind me on the leg side? Most importantly, which hand does each fielder use to throw the ball?

You will not collect these early singles if you have too tight a grip on the bat handle. Let the ball come to you: do not push out at it all of the time, but, just as the ball is about to hit the bat, relax the hands a little and the ball should drop down within a few yards. If your partner is anticipating short singles he will be backing-up at the non-striker's end and there is nothing fielders at cover-point or mid-wicket can do to stop you stealing the single.

I am a great believer in the short single because it rotates the strike. Suddenly the bowler is having to bowl at your partner who has different strengths and style. Perhaps, for that matter, your partner is left-handed and you are right-handed. That means the bowler

has to change the line of his attack and the captain needs to readjust his field and so that simple single, completely unspectacular, has presented your opponents with a problem or two.

Again, put yourself in the bowler's mind – you have just bowled a good ball and a run has been taken. Your own confidence goes up because your score and the team's total ticks over, while the bowler cannot get a full over to work on your weaknesses. To sum up, the quick single is good for you and your team, and a blow psychologically for the bowler.

Dealing with the new ball and bouncers

An opening batsman's job is to see off the new ball which is hard and may bounce high, it is shiny and so might swing. The seam is firm and pronounced and you must expect the best bowlers to land the ball on the seam and get late and fast movement off the pitch. The bouncers will come flying at your head. Your reflexes must be sharp.

Bouncers are a test of a batsman's character and courage. They threaten physical danger and prompt many batsmen to play inept strokes which are born of the physical and mental reactions to fear. Techniques fall apart often because apprehensive batsmen are more intent on avoiding being hit than with keeping their eyes on the ball and their method in place.

You can be a good-looking batsman and have a sound technique but still be useless against fast bowling. I urge everyone to think positively and understand that it is part of the beauty of batting to be able to play fast and short-pitched bowling.

First of all you must learn to watch the ball, and I mean really *watch* it, and not freeze. It requires courage to stand and watch the ball until it has passed by or you have hit it with

Dealing with a bouncer: Robin Smith drops his hands and, keeping his eye on the ball, sways out of the line

the bat. The bad player watches the ball until it is nearly going to hit him and then he is stuck like a rabbit in the glare of a car's headlights. All he can do is turn his head away. He has no chance of playing the ball well and, of course, as soon as the fast bowler sees the fear he will keep flinging down the bouncer challenge.

Watch the ball and then, if you are not playing a shot, sway out of the way or duck. Watching the ball is the key to finding your courage. It may fly past you three or four inches from your nose or over your head, but that distance, in batting, is a million miles away.

Look at the ball . . . all of the way . . . and then everything will fall into place.

I am not a great believer in helmets. I used to wear one towards the end of my career but by that time almost everyone was wearing one and, if I had chosen not to, it would have been like waving the proverbial red flag at the bull. It was like saying to a bowler, 'Look at me I'm so good I do not need a helmet', and he would try twice as hard. That is foolhardy, silly.

My advice to youngsters is: play without a helmet for as long as you can, possibly forever, but not because of bravado. Viv Richards never wore a helmet but his talent was exceptional. Be sensible and consider the advantage of batting without a helmet – helmetless, you truly have to watch the ball. You cannot be lulled into a sense of physical safety which is dangerous because it is tempting to say 'well, if I get hit I will take it on the helmet and I will be all right' or 'I am not a good hooker but I will have a go because I cannot get hurt'. A helmet often gives false confidence and then the golden rule can be broken – batsmen do not watch the ball right the way through the shot.

Work out what is right for you and always feel comfortable at the crease.

If you are uncertain, practise at playing the bouncer. Get a friend to bowl or throw a tennis ball at you on a hard surface so that it rises

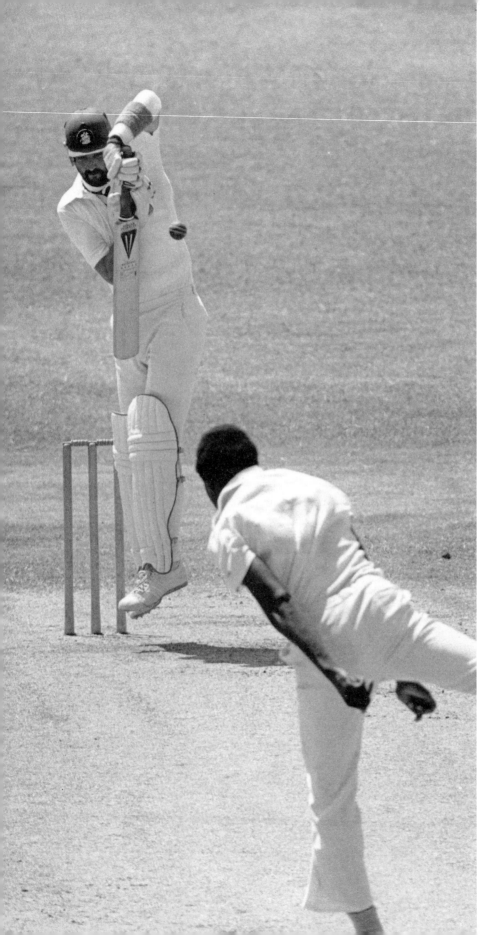

Graham Gooch counters a very fast delivery from Andy Roberts which rises more steeply than he expects. In order to stay on top of the bounce and not give a catch, he uses a fine back defensive shot, but has to be airborne at the moment of contact.

RIGHT *Boycott cannot evade Lillee's outswinger this time, but luckily for him he is missed in the slips*

to head height, and practise ducking and weaving, keeping your eye on the ball at *all* times. You will soon learn to cope with bouncers without having to worry about injury at this early stage. Graham Gooch, when he was opening for England, used to go to the nets padded up and helmeted ready to face team-mates who stood halfway down the pitch and threw bouncers at him. They hurled the ball hard into the ground and sent it whizzing at his head. This is when you need to be the dancer, light on your feet, quick in reactions and elusive.

Do not fool around with this form of practice. It is dangerous. Choose a thrower in whom you have confidence.

Let me emphasise here the constant message:

If you have been ruffled by a bouncer, clear your mind before the next ball. It could be a fast 'yorker' or a slower ball which catches you on the back foot. You have to be prepared for anything.

Dealing with swing

When the ball is swinging say to yourself, 'What does the bowler want me to do? How does he want me to play? What strokes is he hoping to see?'

For example, Dennis Lillee would bowl out-swingers and pitch the ball well up: he would have plenty of slips and gullies behind me for the nick and there were huge gaps in front of the wicket on the off side. Maybe he would have only one fielder in front on the off-side

and you would say to yourself 'H'm, that's very inviting. But why?'

Obviously Dennis wanted me to drive at the ball, aim for the open spaces and he did not mind my making a good stroke for four off the front foot because he wanted me to feel comfortable there. Next drive, snick, caught. Dennis is saying to himself, 'Thank you very much, Geoffrey, England 12 for 1. Four more like that and England will be 50 odd for 5.'

Always be aware of where the fast bowlers have set their fields. Understand where they want you to play the ball but never do what they want you to do. You yourself must decide which are the safe areas.

This it not to say, for instance, that you cannot drive at Dennis Lillee with the new ball, or at Kapil Dev whose body action is ideal for bowling outswingers, but before you do so make him pitch the ball right up to you. Wait. Have patience. Let him see you refusing to drive so that he is tempted to land the ball an extra foot closer to you. Then bang. Get on to the front foot and drive the ball away.

So what I am saying is that the batsman, from the start of the day and right through the early overs of his innings, must have antennae to make him aware, not only of the ball and the field-placings, but of the whole environment so that he can understand the complete plot.

Do not thrust out at the swinging ball: let it come to you. Play it as late as possible.

Dealing with spin

Let us think now about the middle-order batsmen. When they go to the crease they are faced with different problems: having to start an innings with the ball turning and the fielders crouching close around. Very often too, at Test level, there are many thousands of spectators screaming for your downfall. In club cricket there may be league points hanging on your wicket and you find as many as six fielders around you who can almost stretch out and

Kapil Dev, with his left shoulder right round in his body action, pointing at fine-leg, is in the ideal position for the bowling of outswingers

touch you. It has happened so often to English batsmen in India who have looked intimidated and hopelessly short of technique against spin.

First of all you must have enough confidence in yourself to play the ball with the spin *towards* the fielders. It is easier and safer to play with the spin. Play into the fielders and if possible through them. I see a lot of batsmen who, when they come in and see the fielders close on the leg side, try to play the ball away from them to the off side. Or sometimes the pressure is too much and a batsman will try to hit the ball over the fielders into the outfield even though he is not settled and has not gained the feel of the pitch, nor understands what the bowler is doing.

Play *into* the fielders. You can indicate that you are in control of a spinner without hitting him for four or six. Play him with the middle of the bat towards the fielders. I cannot repeat often enough – it is easier and safer to play with the spin.

Do not plunge or grope forwards. In a perfect world you will see the ball early and play it late. You will be amazed how long you can wait to move the bat at the ball if you are balanced and if you have 'gentle' hands. You see it, and wait and wait and wait. It takes confidence but that is the way to enter a cage of fielders with the ball turning.

I do not recommend plunging forward, nor do I recommend playing the turning ball by pushing forward into the spin with the bat hiding behind the front pad. Batsmen only get away with that because umpires do not give enough batsmen out for padding the ball away without trying to play a stroke. The law says you are out if the ball striking the pad would have hit the stumps and you are not attempting a stroke. I have talked to many of the great players about this and Gary Sobers always advises cricketers to play at the ball *with the bat*. Your pad or, more accurately, the front foot and pad, go forward just inside the line of the approaching ball and act as a secondary defence.

Which brings me to my usual emphasis in forward play – balance by keeping the weight on the ball of the front foot. Many players put their front foot heavily down on the ground with a bump. It is a flat foot. I like to see my pupils balanced on the ball of the foot like ballet dancers. This means you can manoeuvre your knee to go with the spin whichever way that

is. Never put your foot down with a bump: the front leg goes rigid; you cannot move anything; your body becomes wooden.

Let the ball come to you. Do not push out in hope. There is an old adage – if in doubt push out. Rubbish. Don't be in doubt. Make up your mind. Be positive.

Only play forward when you know you can smother the spin. Never pre-judge. Never make up your mind beforehand and, after every ball, clean the slate. Forget what has gone before. Play the ball late. A lot of the fine play against spin is on the back foot. You have more time to follow the deviation off the pitch and back play helps you to obey the eternal discipline: let the ball come to you. Play it late.

It is important to learn what spin is coming your way and it is an advantage if you can 'read' the googly from the top-spinner, from the flipper, and so on. But it is not essential. I would go as far as to suggest that it is not imperative to know which way the ball is going to turn if you are defending but it certainly is if you are going to score.

Some players say that they can tell which way the ball is spinning as it comes through the air. I never could. Just remember that some of the best batsmen the game has seen did not know which way the ball would turn. They did, however, judge the length and the line perfectly and then they played the ball off the pitch.

Vivian Richards puts his own gloss on this. When he was asked, 'Do you watch the wrist of the spinners?', he replied, 'I never did'. 'Just think about it this way,' he went on. 'Very often the spinners themselves do not know which way the ball is going to turn, so why should you? A leg-spinner who runs up to bowl a googly sometimes will overspin the ball and it will respond like a top-spinner. Maybe it will keep low. You have to watch the ball all the way down its flight but especially you should never bank on the ball turning one way or the other just because you have seen signs from the bowler's hand. Turn is not dependable: don't rely on it . . . until it happens.

'It is much simpler to say to yourself – if I get to the pitch of the ball, it does not matter which way it is going to turn, I have a half-volley before me and I can drive it hard. When I could not get to the pitch of the ball I simply concentrated on getting my head over the ball.'

Building an innings

So let us imagine that your innings is under way. You have played yourself in. You are beginning to find the gaps.

Moving down the pitch to meet the spinner is an excellent way of making good-length balls into half-volleys and you create problems for the bowler by disturbing his line and length; but practise this in the nets first.

You have to move late. Be ready to move in your mind, even store the idea in the front of your mind, but do not move before the bowler bowls. When the bowling is very slow you can leave the decision until the ball is in the air and you know you can go down the pitch to meet a half-volley or full-toss. The best professional spinners, however, have quite speedy arm actions which produce a high but fast-dipping loop in their flight. You can set off down the pitch at the split-second they release the ball so that they cannot alter the ball's flight.

The warning is this – if they sense you coming they will be able to flatten their flight, widen their line and perhaps leave you stranded halfway down the pitch.

In the nets persuade one of your spin-bowlers to bowl at you and, if he senses that you are about to use your feet down the pitch, he must not let the ball go. You will be amazed how late you have to leave the move down the pitch. Go too early and the best bowlers will get you out.

Another point is this. If you are down the pitch and think you cannot arrive at the pitch of the ball, do not forget that defensive play is called for. Because you go down the pitch you do not have to hit the ball for runs. And when they do hit the ball, too many club batsmen get caught. This is because they have not put the front foot absolutely to the pitch of the ball, and are not bending the front knee or leaning the body into the shot. The key to it is to get your weight forward over the front knee.

If it is not in your nature to hit out and score quickly then don't do it; however, after playing yourself in you should begin to look for chances to score instead of just waiting for the really bad ball. Just like when you are driving a car, you think about moving into a higher gear. So be more positive. Forward defensive shots to the ball pitched well up can become more powerful drives if you take bigger strides forward to the pitch of the ball and use more follow-through of the bat.

If you feel you are getting bogged down against a medium-fast bowler, try to break the stranglehold by moving eighteen inches or two feet out of the crease to take your stance. You are now nearer the pitch of the ball if the bowler persists with the same length. He will have to adjust. Make him think and change. Runs should come.

Never forget that, as the team searches for runs, the non-striker too has a role to play. As the bowler releases the ball he should be walking forward, ready to run. Then, if the striking batsman calls, he is already on the move and can get to the other end more quickly.

But be prepared for the straight-drive back to your stumps. Regain your ground quickly in case the bowler touches the ball on to your stumps. You can be run out that way. Even

Bread and butter shot. Boycott, taking advantage of the bowler straying down the leg side, plays the ball easily off his legs through the on-side field.

though you are not facing the bowling – concentrate. You cannot turn concentration on and off like a tap. Only relax at intervals or at the end of the play or when you are not out.

The best bowlers will often change the line of their attack. Great fast bowlers such as Dennis Lillee and Michael Holding will deliver the ball from a different position on the crease. You need to spot the change and always concentrate on the exact line of the ball's flight. Some bowlers – Bob Willis, Michael Procter and Malcolm Marshall are instances – could bowl long spells from around the wicket. The ball then comes to the batsman at an unusual angle.

I would always try to counter this by narrowing the angle. I would take guard on middle-and-off and turn to face the bowler chest-on, in a very open stance. I was then playing on the bowler's line, not across it.

Calling for runs

The general rules for quick, clear calling are these:

a) The striker calls for the run if the ball is played in front of the wicket;

b) The non-striker calls when the ball goes behind the wicket because he can see better and he is the one who is running to the danger end – the wicket nearer the fielder;

c) Call quickly and clearly – 'Yes', 'No', or 'Wait'. The batsman taking strike should run down the side of the pitch from where the bowler is bowling and the non-striker down the other side.

d) For a second run or more the call is best made by the batsman who is running to the danger end.

A problem arises when right-arm bowlers bowl around the wicket or left-arm bowlers bowl over the wicket – the non-striker cannot run on his usual side. Both batsmen are on the same side. The solution is for the non-striker to run well wide of the striker. (There is no

Malcolm Marshall switches to bowling round the wicket

limit to how far out he may stand so long as he is behind the batting crease.)

Do not risk getting run out. Lots of calling by both batsmen is preferable to no calling at all. Remember, in a batting partnership, silence is not golden. And as you complete your run, ground the bat early and slide it into the crease to prevent being run out.

Conclusion

To succeed as a specialist batsman you must work hard and be single-minded about improving your skills, but always try to play the innings which your team most requires.

ATTACKING PLAY

DAVID GOWER

Perfection for a batsman is to dominate the bowler. You do not suddenly decide, however, to launch an attack – runs should come more naturally out of your play than that – but it often helps if the match situation requires you to attack. It can be in Test or county or club cricket, but you know that the timing and the pace of your attack will be the keys to winning the match.

An attacking innings

To play an attacking innings, first clear the mind of anything that is going to prove negative. For example, in Test matches you know that you will be coming up against very fast bowling, and bouncers, so clear the mind about any possible dangers. Think about that at night if you must, but remove it when you are at the crease. Concentrate instead on getting relaxed, comfortable, and in a position to see clearly and to react quickly.

You want to feel that you are in the right place, that you know where your stumps are, and exactly from which direction the bowler is coming.

As you look around the field-placings, you must visualise the possibilities for scoring.

If Michael Holding is the bowler, or another of the great fast men, you need to understand the possibilities, that he can bowl extremely quickly, that he can bounce one at your head, cut one off the pitch, or whistle in a yorker. Understand his ammunition, not because you are going to be afraid and may take cover, but because you want to prime your body to perform the right reflexes. You want to be still and perfectly balanced. If you cannot move easily backwards and forwards your innings

will be over very quickly. You would feel stupid if you gloved a ball into the hands of gully for nought and went back and said to the team, 'Sorry, I didn't expect him to bowl a bouncer'.

Batting is essentially about picking the bat up and moving instinctively into the right positions.

Watch the ball, and wait for it, but never commit yourself beforehand. In an attacking effort the main danger is that you commit yourself to the scoring shot but find that you have not watched the ball for the last two or three yards on to the bat. Then you make errors of timing and miscue.

In Test matches, with large crowds excited and a bowler at the end of his run, I always used the trick of watching the ball only. Nothing else, not even the bowler. Watch the ball when it is still in the bowler's hand: watch it all the way down towards you. After all, it is the ball, not the bowler, that you should be aiming to hit!

Getting the scoreboard to tick over does not necessarily require violence. However aggressive your intentions you must remember the priorities of batting – to concentrate and to watch the ball *all of the time*. If you do not watch the ball on to the bat, consider what a waste of time and energy it has been. Furthermore you could well be out if you have taken a terrific swipe just hoping that the passage of the ball will be interrupted by the middle of the bat.

I hit the ball better when I do not try to hit it too hard. This does not mean I cannot play shots which might be described as aggressive or glorious or punishing; it means that I have played them just as if I was defending, as if I

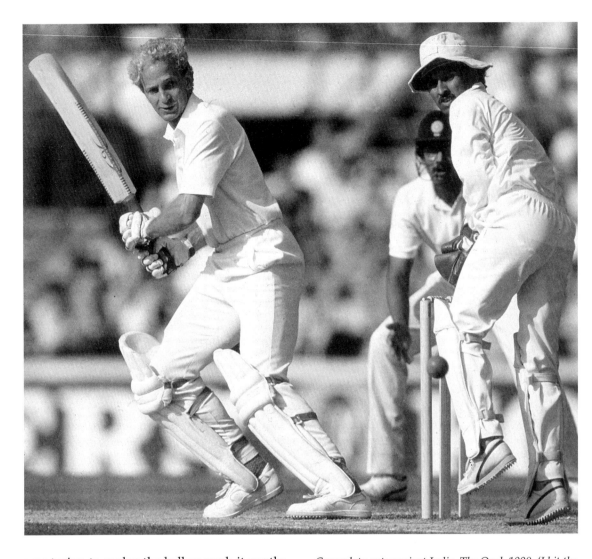

Gower late-cuts against India, The Oval, 1990. 'I hit the ball better when I do not try to hit it too hard.'

was trying to nudge the ball or push it gently through the covers. I keep concentration, balance, and bodily control over the shot, and follow through when I feel I am making sound contact.

To play an attacking innings you must know where every gap is in the field. I recall one one-day international at Edgbaston when Mark Waugh and Allan Border scored five or six runs an over comfortably without a single violent movement. Allow yourself to place the ball. Attacking batting is a delicate balance between maintaining control over the ball and the bowler as best you can without losing your head and therefore your wicket.

Equipment

Your choice of bat is important. Go for comfort. Personally I am not built to carry big weights, therefore I do not use a huge bat. Mine are, say, 2lb 9oz which would include the weight of a couple of rubber grips on the handle. I like a thicker handle. With that I feel I can manoeuvre the bat through straight batting shots as well as the cross-batted ones. Basically, though, pick up your bat and feel comfortable.

The right cricket shoes are important too. To feel light-footed you look for light footwear, but you also need protection in case the ball lands fast on your foot. For that matter you need a secure grip on a variety of surfaces. Just think of poor Mike Atherton getting run out at Lord's on 99 against Australia in 1993. He slipped as he tried to turn and ended up crawling back to his crease, but not in time to escape being dismissed.

So you should look to wear spikes on any surface that looks grassier and therefore more slippery than usual. All-rubber soles are most comfortable, especially in dry conditions, but my own choice in those circumstances is to have at least half of the sole with low spikes. These are the choices, of course, of the professional who has many pairs of footwear.

For the schoolboy or club player who, maybe, has just one pair I recommend that plenty of time is taken in choosing a comfortable design. You want shoes that allow your feet to breathe and be healthy. Aching feet make good fielding impossible. For the amateur I recommend spikes both at the front of the shoe and on the heel.

On being left-handed

Basically the game is the same whichever way you stand – you try to position your feet, manipulate your hands and get the blade of the bat square on to the ball, playing as straight as possible and with a firmer hold with the top hand.

Whenever you are batting, however, left-handed or right, always be aware of the direction from which the ball is coming at you.

Just think what the difference is for the left-handed batsman. The standard right-arm over-the-wicket bowler is slanting the ball across the left-hander and the temptation for the batsman is to try to play the ball out on the off side which means usually playing across the line. Similarly playing back down the line involves playing the ball slightly to the on side of the wickets.

But let me emphasise one further point – 'the leave', letting the ball pass without a shot. This is an essential weapon when facing the ball which slants across you. As well as being safe it can frustrate a bowler who then might pull his line in more towards your body where it is safer for stroke-making.

It is the same for a right-handed batsman when he faces a bowler who bowls left-arm over-the-wicket. The line of the ball, unless it is swinging, is across the stumps.

When I face a right-arm over-the-wicket bowler I take leg-stump, or one-leg, guard. For a left-arm over-the-wicket bowler I move across towards the off stump and take 'two legs' or even perhaps middle-stump on a day when the ball is moving a lot in the air or off the pitch.

Try not to make a huge academic business of being left-handed. Be relaxed and natural, but ask yourself all the time if you are lined up physically and mentally with the direction of the bowler's hand.

There is, though, one perpetual penalty for batting left-handed, at least in first-class cricket. Left-handers are often faced with rough ground outside their off stump, the result of right-arm bowlers following through. My advice is: Don't panic. Even though there are fielders crouching close around you, concentrate on playing right back or right forward. Relax your grip. Don't waft at the ball, which will probably respond to the rough ground by turning a lot and bouncing unevenly. Watch the ball. Play it late.

Line and length

Assessing the line is important because you need not play a stroke unless the ball is coming towards the stumps; but we are discussing attacking batting here and the best batsmen, the ones you love to watch like a Viv Richards or a Gary Sobers, prey on any ball which is not of a line and length to force a defensive shot. A short ball, however wide, goes for runs; an overpitched ball, however straight, goes for more runs. Such batsmen are always ready to pounce, and this is why I repeat and stress: *Start with your bat reasonably high, the face of the bat opened outwards as you break the wrists, so that your hands are ready to play an attacking shot in the first place.*

This gives you room to swing the bat and if you spot any minor errors of line or length by the bowler, a simple swing of the bat will give power to the stroke.

Increasing the tempo

A lot of people come to me and say – 'Look, David, I'm a club cricketer, I'm in a weekend match and it is time to do something, the team needs me to increase the scoring rate. How do I play it?' It is a good question. It is at times necessary to change the tempo when batting.

I know that the sudden rush for runs has to happen from time to time, but how much better a player you will be, and how much more prolific a run-scorer, if your instinct is always to score off the bad balls right from the start. Perhaps, at first, you simply push them away for singles, but you can always pick the bat up high and follow through. In other words, in your pick-up and footwork you are making attacking strokes possible from the first ball, even though you are there initially to survive and defend.

If you go from a defending game to sudden attack you telegraph your intentions to the fielding captain. Also you tend to perform rather like a car which has first gear and top gear but nothing in between. Your innings may get stuck in the middle!

But let us say we have decided to accelerate the run-scoring. The first point I make is this – it is amazing how much time you've got. The great mistake we all commit at times is being too eager to dominate: it persuades us to move too early. Very often you can give signals to the bowler who can, in the last split second of his action, change the length, line or speed of his delivery.

If a slow bowler is on, then you may want to advance down the pitch to destroy his control of length. Yes, fine, but always make sure that you leave your first move until that last split second, the second when the ball actually leaves his hand.

Practice

If you are successful in the middle that is your basic confidence booster, but to be continually successful you have to groove many of your actions both in defence and attack – your arms may not be working along the right plane, your footwork may be imprecise, the back-lift is wrong. All sorts of tinkering may be needed for the mechanism of the batsman, running repairs, you might say.

You must practise constructively, always with a plan. If you want to practise a particular shot you ask your bowler, or whoever is throwing the ball to you from halfway down the net, to provide what you want.

If there is nothing specific you wish to practise, ask for bowling on the off stump. Half of the art of batting is to know where your body is in relation to your off stump, to help you recognise which balls to play and which to leave alone.

At school you might only have ten minutes in a net. First, you exaggerate your footwork to make sure that you are getting right forward to the balls pitched well up and right back to the shorter ones. You ensure you are always getting in line, and nicely sideways so that your bat is coming straight down the line of the ball. Try to play the ball back in the 'V', that is, into

Playing strokes

The key to playing all strokes is to see quickly the line and the length of the ball and to move early into the appropriate position. Being in the correct position gives you room to play the shot. If you are playing a cut shot, for example, obviously you have to get on the back foot even if your initial movement is forward. A lot of players have initial movements, almost nervous tics, but, as Geoff Boycott says, they do not matter so long as they leave you balanced, on your toes, and ready to move positively in any direction once you recognise what sort of a ball is being delivered.

So let me repeat. See the ball early; make up your mind quickly; move to the right position to play the shot.

In a match I see a ball that is short, coming down the line outside off-stump, and I can see also that I have the room to play a square-cut. I first step back and across with my back foot and then, giving a pronounced turn of my front shoulder, I throw my arms outwards and downwards from a high back-lift to strike the ball, if possible, at full arms-length. (See also above, page 118–19).

Although the textbooks advise you to throw the arms at the ball I suggest a little caution here. Ideally you should wait for the ball and let it come to the bat rather than force the stroke. With all attacking strokeplay you must have the strokes in your mind because your mind is set in the attacking mode, but you only play the shots when they come naturally. In other words you have to be relaxed while you are attacking. This may seem a contradiction but it will lead you to the perfect form of attack which is natural rather than premeditated and forced. Force your shots and you pay the penalty – you may be too close to the ball or too far away, under the bounce or over it, and you will edge the ball rather than meet it with the middle of the bat in the fullness of the swing of the arms.

Gower cutting. Being in the correct position gives you room to play.

the narrow arc between mid-on and mid-off, to ensure that you are meeting the straighter balls with the full face of the bat.

Then, as you expand your range of practice strokes over the second five minutes, consider how you are getting out in matches and try to repair the flaw in your technique which is causing any repeated failure. You can always ask bowlers to provide you with the right tests. Net practice provides the opportunity to simulate what happens in an actual game so that you are training your instinct to do the right thing when you see it in play.

So the attacking batsman always stands at the crease with an open mind. Just consider your range of scoring strokes as 'available'.

Batting in different countries

Not everyone has the chance to test their skills around the world, but if the opportunity comes to go abroad on tour, then it is as well to be aware of the varied conditions that you will encounter and how to come to terms with those conditions as a batsman.

England in itself can provide a large variety of playing surfaces, which all require minor adjustments of technique and timing. The county professional, who sees much of the country on his travels, will find that the preponderance of pitches tends, however, to be slow or merely average in terms of pace and bounce.

English conditions and coaching tend to encourage front-foot players, who will think of cover drives as their stock method of scoring runs. Such methods will often hold good in countries such as Pakistan, India and Sri Lanka, where pitches can be absolutely true, devoid of grass and therefore pace and bounce, and beautiful to bat on.

However, conditions can also be vastly different, and it is not unknown, to say the least, to find real turning wickets in the subcontinent, ideally suited, in the case of India for instance, to the great tradition of spin bowling that produced the likes of Bishan Bedi, Chandrasekhar, and Prasanna. The front foot might still be the better bet overall, but a new technique has to be learnt alongside one's old knowledge.

And whereas the front foot dominates technique on these slower pitches, the true test of the best players comes when they are confronted with the sort of conditions traditionally found in Australia and the Caribbean, where local climate and turf characteristics quite often mean hard, quick and bouncy pitches. At least

that used to be the case, for even in these countries you will now find that many of their pitches have become more placid with the passage of time.

For instance, in Australia only the WACA ground at Perth still retains the sort of pace and bounce that make bowlers add five yards to their approach, and batsmen an extra layer of padding to the body; and in the Caribbean even the legendary Kensington Oval at Bridgetown, Barbados, always true in the old days, but fiery sometimes in the early stages of a game, seems to have lost some of its verve.

With quick bowling the key in modern cricket, when these conditions are encountered batsmen need to have learned all about backfoot play. It is no mere coincidence that Australians and West Indians all seem to have learned about the cut and the pull at an early age, simply because these are the shots needed to score runs. The West Indian fast bowler, Michael Holding, summed it up perfectly when describing how to bat there: 'You want to drive, you go hire a car'.

Batting is always about adapting to the conditions of the day, something that can be done more easily if the basics of one's technique are already sound. Experience of different conditions adds to a batsman's overall knowledge, and comes with time spent at the crease. But it always pays to be prepared and to be aware of all the problems one is likely to face.

A career

Is cricket a viable career? It would be pleasant if it was a $64m. question, but the sums involved are not usually that great! True, there are players who can now make a properly profitable career out of the game – nothing, of course, to compare with the world-domain sports such as golf or tennis, or the multi-million-dollar American sports – but nevertheless a more than useful income by many people's standards.

The truth is that we all start playing the game because we want to enjoy it as a sport and relaxation, perhaps as a challenge as well. Because we enjoy it, and then a certain few discover that their talent is such that an opportunity arises to think of turning a game into a profession, a decision has to be made.

One accepts that not everyone with a talent for cricket is necessarily as talented in other fields to the extent that there will be a plethora of career options available. However, sensible advice normally dictates that those with the option should take degrees or acquire suitable business qualifications before risking a sporting career with its imponderables and pitfalls – not least the whims of selectors or the danger of injuries.

Ways of testing the water include the youth sides run by the counties and local cricket associations, from which a player can proceed on to the lower rungs of the ladder which can lead to county second-eleven cricket, up to first-class and – who knows? – even beyond. Many fine players, Ian Botham for one, have begun with an apprenticeship on the MCC groundstaff at Lord's where, over the years, the first disciplines have been instilled into some quite raw material!

A degree of self-appreciation, in the true sense, and honesty, comes in handy in the early stages: whatever one's dreams of scoring the winning runs against Australia at Lord's – and there are many gifted players who will never achieve that – it is best to acknowledge early one's limitations. Only the chosen few make it to professional levels, and many fall by the wayside in the process.

For those who make the grade, the game is rewarding in many senses, with personal achievement always inextricably intermingled with that of the team, with true satisfaction coming from being able to contribute fully to your team's success. There are friendships to acquire, the pundits to endure, the public to pat you on the back or hurl brickbats if things don't go too well, and a lifestyle unique to the sport.

I have had precious few regrets in my career but, there again, much of my time in the game has been filled with success, so for me to carp would be churlish in the extreme. I have seen others despair and sink without trace, but almost all of them have known that they tried and gave the game their best shot. Nobody can ask more than that, and nobody who tries will spend the rest of their lives thinking: 'I wonder what would have happened if . . .'

For those who make it to the top, the rewards are significantly better now than ever before. Success on the field in itself is rewarded, but for the best players there are extras to be won from endorsements, sponsorship, and various other spin-offs. What is important to remember is that cricket is what feeds the rest of it, and that one's performance on the field should be the only motivation required. Once you have that point sorted out, the rest will almost take care of itself, and everyone will love you!

In short, if the opportunity is there to use cricket as a professional tool, then take it. People will always be jealous that you appear to be making a living out of something that started simply for pleasure, so whatever you do, don't forget to enjoy it all along the line.

5
CAPTAINCY

Mike Brearley setting the field for John Emburey, a bowler as meticulous over his field placings as his captain. Old Trafford Test, 1981.

CAPTAINCY

A DISCUSSION BETWEEN
MIKE BREARLEY AND TONY LEWIS

TONY LEWIS: *Why is captaincy so important?*
MIKE BREARLEY: In cricket of all games captaincy is of crucial importance. One reason for this is that cricket matches last so long that there is less chance of adrenalin carrying one right through; cricket is the only game that can go on for a week, and at the end neither side be nearer winning or losing than at the beginning. There's more time, and need, for thought. Also there's such a range of skills involved and the captain has to have an idea of what they amount to and how to use all of them effectively. Moreover, conditions change; on the first day they can favour the fast bowlers more than the batsmen and spinners, and later on vice versa. Even in a relatively short match there's time for tactics and strategy, and a need for someone to hold the process together. Also cricket is a game of individual contests within a team context, and that balance – between self-interest and team-interest – has to be attended to and sometimes modified by the captain.

If you're looking for a captain, what qualities would you value most?

Well, I'm glad you said qualities (in the plural) because there's a whole range. Broadly they may be divided into two sets. The first is a matter of tactical inventiveness and knowledge of the game; the second is the ability to get the best out of the players.

So there's a technical side to captaincy, which embraces what?

It embraces the whole game. At one end there are longer-term, strategic considerations, such

as building up a strong side over a season (or seasons). There are questions about the balance of the side, whether in general or for a particular match. Then for each match the captain needs to form some flexible, overall policy on such matters as how the pitch will play, who his main attacking and defensive bowlers are likely to be, what the main strengths and weaknesses of the opposition are, and so on. Finally there is the nitty-gritty, tactical detail of such matters as changing the field and the bowling, and of making declarations.

And the second part of it is the human side and the understanding of people?

Yes, and being able to get through to people, to excite them, and make them feel they're better players than they are, or at least as good as they are.

So if we're picking the captain of our club this week, amateurs now, would we go for the longer serving?

No, not necessarily, though it depends on what sort of a club it is. Naturally if it's a club in which the longest-serving player has always been captain, and the aim is to play socially, without being concerned overmuch about winning or playing purposefully, then why not? But if, within a friendly atmosphere, you want to play cricket properly and as well as you can, if there is some wish to try to win (even though it may not matter too much), you won't necessarily want the longest-serving player as captain. Many clubs will value as captain someone who combines tactical skill and a sense of purpose with a recognition that opportunities should be shared; for instance a weekend cricketer can expect to be given a chance with ball or bat, and someone who has scored 50 to 100 may be expected to give his wicket away and/or bat lower in the order next time, even if such moves may tell against winning.

One of the more famous statements about captaincy is that the sovereign virtue in a captain is unselfishness. Would you agree with that?

Unselfishness is important. If you have a captain who plays for himself, then all the players start to think they're entitled to play for themselves. As I've said, in cricket there is this fascinating balance between self-interest and team-interest. You've got to score runs and take wickets and catch catches, you've got to do well for yourself in order to be doing well for the team; but, on the other hand, some self-interest needs to be sacrificed, at times, in the interest of the team as a whole. I believe a captain should be an example of one who is willing to be unselfish but who has also got a shrewd idea how well he can do himself, and makes the most of his own abilities. So both come into it.

Let's turn to your own career. There's always a

difficulty, isn't there, in separating one's own performance from the welfare of the team – your other job, so to speak. Did you find that difficult?

Yes. At times I found it difficult captaining England when I clearly wouldn't have been worth a place as a batsman alone. This wasn't always the case, but there were occasions when I wondered if I had a right to be playing. Then I started to wish that I did not have to be active and energetic, or be seen in public; sometimes I just wanted to crawl away, as in one Test in Melbourne.

But your question has a wider scope, hasn't it? It raises the issue of how good a player a captain needs to be. In an ideal world the best captain would be an automatic selection as a player alone. It doesn't matter whether he's one of the best players in the team, but it makes matters easier if he's worth his place in the team for his batting or bowling alone. But it may well be that the best captain is not one of these eleven, and then selection may be a nice question. What I am sure of is that a good captain is like the conductor of an orchestra. He can transform a team and get the players to perform better than anyone imagined they could.

There is a huge challenge, isn't there?, in captaincy to separate one's own performance from the job of skippering the whole team – the Graham Gooches of the world who have to field and scheme then, ten minutes later, need to turn round, as you used to, and put the pads on. Suddenly you're no longer the captain so much as the opening batsman.

Captaincy can certainly become a burden and, as a captain you can feel het-up, over-involved and anxious. If the captain is an opening batsman, and has got into such a state in the field, it's hard then to be single-minded enough to go in and bat. I think there is a similar problem for the captain who is a fast bowler, who has to work himself up to bowl with maximum hostility and yet at the same time be calm enough and detached enough to captain the team on the field. On the other hand, the job is also very stimulating. It makes the whole game ten times more interesting. In county cricket I think I batted better for being captain than when I wasn't captain, because it kept my interest alive all the time.

Thinking about captaincy in the field while fielding at first slip, as you often did, must have been a considerable help?

First slip is a good place from which to captain a side in the field. From there you can see exactly what the bowler is doing; you are right next to the wicketkeeper who has the evidence of how the ball comes into his gloves as well as his privileged view of what the ball is doing. You are within conversational reach of several other fielders, and it is easy to contact the bowler at the end of the over. The only problem is in concentrating fully on the slip-catching while simultaneously being totally committed as captain. This difficulty explains why so few wicketkeepers have been successful captains.

Pursuing the technical side of the job, how much did you need to understand the abilities of your players?

The more you understand them the better. Technically you need to know who bowls best in different conditions. Also, some bowlers need longer spells than others. For example Bob Willis, who was a great trier and optimist, tended to ask for an over or two beyond his limit, while John Lever found his best rhythm in much longer spells. You certainly have to know who will keep going on a hot day when you're up against it, and who will exploit, say, a patch of loose earth just outside the off stump. You also need to be able to widen people's

horizons, give them ideas of what else they can try out, learn to do, or develop into. So the question brings in both sides of captaincy.

Yes, I wanted to ask you about the personal relationships because, famously, you produced the best from the players who played for England. Ian Botham comes to mind immediately, of course – someone whose career suffered a bit of a blow when he was captain and then you came back and took over. That sort of sequence.

Of course, there was an awful lot of luck involved in the events of 1981. But I did help Ian, I think I was good for him. We were very different kinds of person and we respected each other. I'd been his captain when he first came into the England side, which made things easier for us both when I took over after he resigned. I often gave him his head, I admired him so much for his attacking flair that I often told him to run up and bowl the way he felt like bowling, or to go in and let the bat go. I rarely had to calm him down, but I could do that too. He also had a lively mind as far as cricket was concerned especially for attacking ideas, so he was helpful to me; we had good interchanges. Sometimes he didn't like being told but, having given it a bit of a thought, he would usually come round.

And Bob Willis' was another successful career which you had much to do with.

Yes, though it took me a long time to realise with Bob that if he wasn't feeling good about himself, he wasn't quite as robust as I thought when it came to teasing or joking. With Ian Botham, you see, you could get more out of him by knocking him, saying 'You're bowling slower than my Aunt Edith'; he would bristle and come in much faster. But when we did this with Bob we realised at a certain point that it would get him down, that he was actually less confident and needed to be helped rather than teased. So, yes, I think it went well with Bob on the whole but there was that area where I didn't get it right.

Still trying to line up the captaincy with the club situation as well as the county one, I'm thinking now of the team talks. Would you recommend for teams a sit-down before a match, with analysis and open discussion? Or are you one for more instinctive performance on the field?

I've tried both ways. There's a great danger of becoming either a sergeant-major or a colonel when you give team talks. If you get the mood wrong and the flavour wrong, they can be banal. And for a club captain to start talking as if it was a Test match would be ridiculous. On the other hand, if there's been an interval and you have discussed certain things with the right people and you've thought about it and you get the players together and say, 'Look, I think we should try this and this is what we want to do, don't worry too much if we don't get anyone out, it's a good wicket', or whatever is appropriate, that can be for the good of the team, if you do it with humour.

Discipline is a difficult word and difficult to impose on the players. That must be, I've always thought, more difficult for the amateur captain who may be a bank manager all week and then suddenly has to come to give the grocer a rocket on Saturday. Is discipline simple? Is it essential?

Well, even in the most relaxed teams there are some things you wouldn't want players to do. You wouldn't want certain attitudes to develop, so there must be means of getting people to organise themselves or be more self-controlled or behave in a certain sort of way. Usually there is no need to be heavy. The best teams are those in which self-discipline predominates, and people do things because they

feel them to be right, and they have roughly the same sort of values. But even in a club side there must be occasions where discipline is needed – for example, if someone's always late or doesn't turn up when picked without letting anyone know.

What about criticism, criticism of individual players, technical more than otherwise? Is it best performed by a coach, a senior player, or does the captain have to take this on all the time?

I never had a manager in the way that many current England and county team players now have a manager, so I'm talking mainly about situations in which the key figures would be the captain and the coach. In my experience it's mostly down to the captain as far as first-team players are concerned. He's the person on the field with the players day by day and hour by hour, and there are times when he has to tell people that they are not doing as well as they could do, or if they carry on like this they'll only get so far in the game.

We have asked other captains what they make of the job of captaincy and who they think might make a good captain. So, Mike Brearley, Captain of England and Middlesex, I want you to talk me through a day in the shop here at Lord's, arriving in the morning, skippering Middlesex. Talk us through the day.

We have probably got twelve, thirteen or fourteen players from whom to pick on the basis of fitness, pitch, and weather conditions. The first thing I'd do, having arrived an hour and a bit before the match, would be to have a look at the pitch, because the whole match hinges on the pitch and I'd try to assess it. At Lord's I'd know the pitch pretty well but often I'd ask the groundsman how is it going to play; whether, say, it's damp all through. I might want to put my knife into the pitch or scratch the surface, to see how hard it is and to see if it's at all damp underneath, because sometimes it can look brown and yet be quite damp underneath; and if so we might want to field first since the ball would move around on the first day. What the pitch was like would affect selection, which I was keen to do as early as I could so that everyone knew where they were. There's nothing worse than hoping to play or being anxious about playing and not being told till about fifteen minutes before the start.

Sometimes a player would have to have a fitness test, or he and I would have to talk to the physiotherapist about whether playing could do damage. Obviously, I'd want to find out how the player thought about it himself, though I'd have to evaluate responses differently. Some players are always aware of niggles and make the worst of them, others ignore them and want to play even when unfit, so one has to know the players in this respect as well as in other ways.

Then I'd want to talk to various people – the chairman of selectors might be on the ground, or there might be just senior players and the coach there. We might discuss the strengths of the opposition, or debate how far we wanted to go all out for attack, playing five bowlers, a specialist wicketkeeper, and just five batsmen, or whether we'd be better off being a bit more careful by packing the batting. Or is it, we might ask, a bowlers' pitch on which four bowlers ought to be enough to get the wickets and so we need to play the extra batsman? In the championship it was nearly always worth going all out for a win, since, because of the points system, a draw often wasn't much more use to you than a defeat.

Once the team was settled I'd try to get a bit of practice before the match. Some players like to have a net every day, some don't. I did think that on most days it was good for people to do a few exercises together and a little fielding practice, partly to get their eyes sharpened up

and partly for everyone to feel that we were in it together, even if it was only for ten or fifteen minutes. And then there would be the toss, by which time you'd have to have decided what you were going to do if you won it. The two captains would find each other half an hour or twenty-five minutes before the start. That left time for the players to get ready, physically and mentally, for whatever the task was, batting or fielding. So there's quite a lot to cover. I might also have met the coach, or spoken to him by phone, about what the second team had done in their last match as, apart from immediate questions of selection, I needed to keep tabs on how the whole staff were getting on. There might be one or two players who'd want to talk to me, too. Or maybe somebody was losing confidence and I would want to talk to him about that; or somebody had become a bit over-confident, and needed to quieten down a little, get himself in before he started trying to hit the ball all over the ground. Whatever it might be.

Let me take you on to the field for some specific incidents in cricket and hear your recommendations to the many people learning the game and playing the game. First of all, appealing and mass appealing.

We didn't always behave quite according to the standards that I advocate. For instance, we would sometimes get annoyed, feeling that the umpires were against us, or that the other side was cheating, and we'd retaliate. But discounting that, I always thought we should appeal only if we thought the batsman might be out, that it's wrong to appeal when you know it's not out, especially to appeal with conviction as if you are sure it is out when you know perfectly well that it isn't. So there are standards to be kept. It's a matter of integrity, really. There's no harm in appealing loudly and concertedly if you all think it's out; you're not intimidating the umpire, you're not trying to pull a fast one on him.

What about 'walking', a debate in every clubhouse throughout the world? I've snicked the ball – shall I walk or shall I stay and wait for the umpire's decision?

It does make a difference which era you play in and what the general atmosphere is. Non-walking – the Australian and the Yorkshire League method – has always had a certain attraction to me. The umpire is there to do a job, and players have to take the rough with the smooth. Everyone is sometimes given out when he's not out, and not out when he's out. The main thing, if you are given out, is to accept the decision and get off the field briskly. Even if the umpire is wrong, don't embarrass him by making a scene. Don't show dissent whether as batsman or fielder. So I repeat, on the whole I'm in favour of not walking, it's straight-forward and honest provided the players respect the umpire. I also believe strongly that you should never claim a catch when you know it's not out, never ever in any circumstances. Occasionally we pick up the ball so close to the ground that we're not quite sure ourselves whether it was a clean catch, in which case we should admit that we're uncertain and the decision should then almost always be 'not out'.

Do you therefore regret the necessity for referees at international matches these days to impose the code of conduct?

To be honest, I've never been quite sure what these referees do! I suppose they do come in when there is a row, when someone behaves badly. In Tests, players are under stress, it's a tense situation with a lot of involvement and excitement, and a lot of competition. So maybe it's not a bad thing to have someone on hand to back up the umpires and sort out bad cases. But I regret it if it's necessary. Nine times out of ten, I'd say it's a free lunch for the referee!

I make the point because it does seem to be an abdication of the true role of captaincy . . .

Yes, and of umpiring.

Declarations. So many questions are asked, aren't they? How do you judge them? How will you change your batting order to chase the runs?

It's hard to argue generally. On the whole I would have thought the main purpose of a declaration is to give yourself time to bowl the other side out. So you don't really want to declare if you've no chance of getting them out. If the only side that can win is the other side, when, for instance, there is very little time left, it seems a mockery to declare. Having said that, there are two ways of thinking about declarations. One is that you make the game so safe for yourself that you can keep attacking fields and force the other side to play defensively, because all they've got to play for is a draw. Some captains and some bowlers like that. The other way is to give yourself an extra chance of winning by inviting the batting team to take risks in going for the runs, and in my experience that is more often the reason for declaring, especially in club cricket. In these cases the good declaration is when the carrot is kept dangling in front of the nose of the batting side just enough to keep them interested and long enough for them to lose wicket after wicket in the chase until you eventually get down to the tail. It's often a matter of balancing the match delicately. One of the pleasures of captaincy is the art and skill of declaring and following it through in the field.

As for changing the batting order, probably sides change their batting order too rarely. The trouble is, it's amazing how conservative batsmen are, how much they dislike having their position changed, especially at short notice. They feel insecure and often superstitious. One reason for conservatism among players is that they do not, on the whole, like the batting order to be fluid. Part of the resistance derives from whim or superstition that they have had their successes in one position and, even more positively, have had no success when moved up or down. Another part stems from the fact that most of us like to know 'where we are'. Batsmen get used to a certain routine and when this is changed they feel, as Ranji put it, 'like fish out of water'.

I believe there should be agreement within the whole team that the batting order can be changed in order to make tactical sense. At Middlesex, we agreed that as professionals we should be sufficiently successful to be able to play according to the needs of the side.

However, I think that I should have done more to make batsmen more open to the possibility of such changes, as they often make good tactical sense.

You've captained England internationally and different countries must have presented different problems. Any special observations?

There are different problems in different coun-

tries. I never captained in West Indies, but I was told that a problem for visiting sides there had been inadequate practice facilities. Above all, though, it is the quality and quantity of West Indian fast bowling. So maintaining an attitude of courageousness against this sort of battering must be an essential part of captaincy, as well as helping to figure out how best to play against the fast bowlers. On one hand, if you stay in long enough against fast bowlers who are really good on pitches that give them some assistance, they'll get you out sooner or later, so you have to play some shots and take some risks. On the other hand, you can become 'stroke-happy' against fast bowling, and people can play so many shots that you need one or two batsmen who are willing to stand firm and take the blows, players like Brian Close or Geoffrey Boycott or Ian Redpath. I think that's the biggest difficulty in the West Indies.

In Australia one of the difficulties can be the crowds. For example, in one series, whenever I went out on the field at Sydney and Melbourne, at least 50,000 people booed! Keeping one's sense of balance within that sort of atmos-

Another of the jobs of captaincy – taking the press conference. (Old Trafford, 1977)

phere was not easy. Also, as in the West Indies, it's pretty hard, the game is played hard, the pitches are hard, the fast bowlers are hard. The hardness of it is quite difficult.

And when you think of India and Pakistan you get different problems again, the spinners – especially in India – men round the bat, tremendous artistry of spin bowling and close fielding, a lot of appealing, a lot of bat-pad decisions, very excitable crowds. And sometimes the excitability would get through to the players and umpires, and decisions made too quickly. I personally found playing in India a pleasure. The Test matches there were mostly played in good spirit. Indian cricketers have a different attitude from others. They appreciate friendliness and show a more obvious respect in contrast to the Australians who respect out-and-out toughness. So creating and keeping a good atmosphere in India is a different matter from doing so in Australia or West Indies. Pakistan cricket is a mixture of both, with a tradition of excellent wrist-spinners supplemented, in recent years, by formidably fast swing-bowlers. In both India and Pakistan some English players find the culture alien, and one task of captaincy and management is to maintain enthusiasm without allowing paranoia to develop.

Captains obviously bring their own qualities to the job and they'd be different qualities to their predecessors', and the fellow that comes afterwards; but just re-establish for everyone, the basic qualities which are essential.

One basic quality is to do things your own way. You can't copy somebody else, you can learn from other people but you can't copy them. The good captains that I think of, people like Ray Illingworth, Greg Chappell, Ian Chappell, Keith Fletcher, the good captains were totally different in personality. Having said that, I'd add that all captains have to combine the willingness to tell with the willingness to consult. Sometimes you must tell people what to do, expect them to do what you tell them to do, and tell them off if they don't do it. In other words you have to be willing to be autocratic, you can't have full-scale democracy in the middle of the field near the end of a tight match, there just isn't time. Then the message should be: 'Do it because I say so, we can discuss it later'. You have to be able to get that across clearly and firmly. As captain, you have to take full responsibility, to take the rap. Equally, though, you need to be capable of being democratic, consulting players in your team, both to get ideas and to make players feel that you value their opinion. Consultation also helps the captain to get to know where there's opposition to his point of view. Some captains fail to seek out opinions from people if they expect them to be hostile to or in contradiction with their own, but this results in an atmosphere of fear and concealment. You lose the dynamic support from the team as well as tactical liveliness.

So a cricket captain is quite a special individual?

I don't know about that. No doubt the best captains are rare and in a sense special, but everyone has some capacity for it and everyone can improve by listening and learning. Not that captaincy is a matter of thinking everything out in a dispassionate and logical way, as I've been trying to do here. It's more a matter of going ahead and doing it, communicating your enthusiasm to others. But of course intuitions and enthusiasm aren't enough on their own, they also need to be developed and sharpened. Cricket captaincy is not only an opportunity for doing precisely that, but is a wonderful way of being totally involved in every aspect of the game from beginning to end. Yes, it can be a headache, but I found it – all in all – great fun and rewarding.

Postscript

TONY LEWIS WRITES: The subject of captaincy is always a difficult one for books of cricket instruction – it is easy to generalise, hard to be constructive – so, for our Masterclass, I chose to interview Mike Brearley, the author of *The Art of Captaincy* and probably the most respected England captain of recent years. However, amongst our other Masters there are five other distinguished captains – Ray Illingworth of Yorkshire, Leicestershire and England; Geoffrey Boycott of Yorkshire and England; David Gower of Leicestershire and England; Richie Benaud of New South Wales and Australia; and Vivian Richards of West Indies. By way of a postscript to our discussion I decided to ask each of them the question, 'What makes a good captain?' The degree of unanimity in their replies is interesting:

What makes a good captain?

RAY ILLINGWORTH: I think there are many things: it's not exactly one question, let alone one answer, but I think first and foremost you must be a good tactician. You must understand the game. I cannot believe that, if you are making mistakes about whom to bowl and when, your players will want to follow you.

Next I would go for man-management. Try to be honest with players. It is not easy, but any player should be able to come up to you and ask you a question and have an honest answer even though he might go away disappointed or even angry.

Sometimes you have to be a little tactful if you are hurting a player, but I would be happy to answer the question with those two statements – understand the game and be honest.

GEOFFREY BOYCOTT: I have always felt that there are two requirements of captaincy, the one is reading the game, knowing the intricacies of field-placings, knowing the batsmen's weaknesses, getting it right on the field, and the other is reading people.

One way for a young cricketer to learn about captaincy is to pretend to be captain on the field. You might be standing at third man and you are just doing your job but you can play a little game in your mind. I used to do it when I was young with Yorkshire. I would decide for myself about bowling changes and which end I would bowl the bowlers, where I would place the fielders and so on. Then, during an interval, I would hear Brian Close, the captain, discussing the tactics and I would say to myself, 'Yes, I thought that one through well. I think I got it right.'

Reading people is far more difficult. This is where some captains have no experience at all. No-one teaches the ability to read the players. There are no lessons on it. You need to run the side which means coping with the strong-minded individual as well as the soft fellow who needs coaxing. This is where a lot of captains fall down.

I truly believe that captains from an early age need help from schoolteachers both on the basic cricket problems of changing the bowling and setting the fields and also in the study of individuals, watching the different characters around the school. I do not think we do enough of that.

DAVID GOWER: The ability to communicate is a leading quality for a captain. I have ignored the obvious answer, however, of knowing the game thoroughly. That is imperative but I am concerned about the wider ability to find common ground in discussion with your players. The game is full of so many different characters and you do not survive as a captain if you have one approach for all of them.

You must understand the way every player works so that you can add little bits of motivation or restriction. You have to spend a lot of time with players as well as time with your own thoughts, responding to the way the team is playing.

So in my book, the basics of the game and the communicative process are the two pillars of captaincy. If you fail to get the messages over then they will be running around the field like headless chickens wondering what is going on and you are going to get nothing done at all.

RICHIE BENAUD: The first requirement is luck. I have seen a lot of very good captains walking the street, metaphorically, with the soles out of their shoes, because luck went the wrong way at the wrong time.

The captain should keep it simple. Do not be flamboyant and effervescent and start waving your arms about setting your fields like a sergeant-major or a policeman on point duty.

Above all, keep two overs ahead of the game and then you will find that you make your own luck. The unsuccessful captains are those who are only up with the game or even just behind play, but this, I guess, applies to life as well.

VIVIAN RICHARDS: You can never succeed as a captain without having reasonably good players around you. The quality of your team is crucial and, in my case, the rich talents of the West Indian players made my job all the easier. On the easier days all I had to do was to point the boys to various positions and they would do the job.

You have to know people. I took over the captaincy when I was twenty-five, so I didn't really have much time for learning. Looking back, I realise I needed to have more patience with players: I set my own standards high and I was perhaps a little intolerant when they failed. I was trying to fit into a big man's shoes, Clive Lloyd, and because of his remarkable record I felt I needed results and needed them quickly.

But a young captain must get a rapport with his team and not rush. They see him in a position of authority and trust, so he should concentrate on learning the game from A to Z and relaxing. Gradually, as I became more experienced, I never left my team out of any decision-making I thought was important. Know your game: know your players: know yourself. I guess that's it.

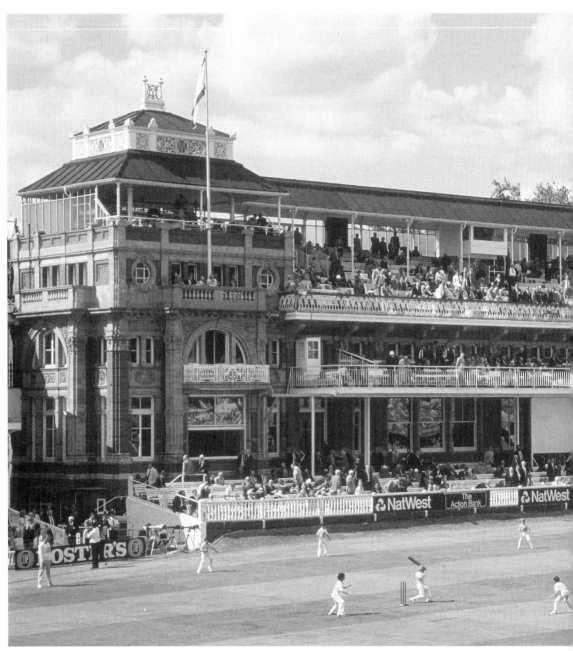

*Kwik cricket being played in front of the pavilion at
Lord's during one of the intervals in the NatWest final,
1989.*

6

COACHING YOUNG CRICKETERS

COACHING YOUNG CRICKETERS
HUBERT DOGGART

The role of the cricket coach is extremely demanding. It takes time, study, instruction and practice to master the techniques of cricket – which is in many ways not a natural game – and then to communicate those techniques with clarity and conviction. It is also a role that can be exhilarating and rewarding.

The coach will, of course, be explaining the skills of batting, bowling, fielding, wicket-keeping – and, later, the important art of captaincy. But in addition, he should convey to his charges something of cricket's history, tradition and literature, and the spirit of adventure, fair play and enjoyment in which the game should be played.

The coach will be able to point to top-class players, past and present, so that young players begin to feel themselves part of the fraternity of cricket; and he will shrewdly be able to put the immediate practice into a wider context, so that the coaching session is not an end in itself but a pointer to future match play, at whatever level.

The expert cricket coach needs a wide range of qualities: the patience of Job, the wisdom of Solomon, and the knowledge, sympathy, sense of humour, and enthusiasm that go hand in hand with good teaching which should always be instructive and enjoyable. At the same time, the coach can inculcate lessons of discipline and involvement that have an educational relevance far beyond the particular net practice, match practice, or match, which the coach is overseeing.

Each of these three – NET PRACTICES, MATCH PRACTICES and MATCHES – is important to the coach evoking the interest, skill and satisfaction of the players he is coaching. Finally – but as important a point as any – the coach must at all times nurture, not repress, individuality. The ability to foster the flair which a young cricketer already possesses is a hallmark of a good coach.

Net practices

Net pitches should be in as good condition as pitches in the 'middle' – something not easy to achieve at a time when there are fewer groundsmen and less understanding of their crucial importance. Artificial pitches, however, are an ideal substitute, in the middle as well as in nets, and advice on their installation is available at Lord's, and from advertisements in the cricketing press. Proper measurements of pitch and crease are important, and all kit should be kept behind the net, not in front where it too often interferes with the bowler's run-up.

All those attending nets should be active for as much of the time as possible. This is especially important when coaches have more players to look after than is ideal for one net. The best number for a net is probably six – with one batting, and one getting ready to bat, but also watching, listening and learning after he or she is ready – and four bowling. Enough cricket balls and the proper kit are necessary.

Each batsman should have sufficient time at the wicket. I was taught by Harry Altham – most inspiring of coaches as well as the co-author of the original *MCC Cricket Coaching Book* – to divide the time available for the batsman into three. So, assuming that there is time for a quarter of an hour for each batsman, you would spend the first five minutes assessing him, noticing such things as:

1. a comfortable stance and grip of the bat – with a firm top hand and a 'softer' bottom hand;
2. the ability to keep the head still and eyes as level as possible;
3. the ability to judge the line and length of each delivery, so enabling him to move the feet quickly into good positions for his strokes;
4. the ability to play straight;
5. the crucial importance of the left shoulder, arm and wrist in the playing of each shot.

In the second five minutes you would concentrate on one shot that needs special attention – one, for example, that may be getting the batsman out regularly.

For the final five minutes, let the batsman play an imaginary Test-match innings, in which he is set a target of twenty runs to make in two overs, say, with three wickets in hand, and is awarded runs for good strokes, especially the one on which the coach has been concentrating.

It is notoriously easier to coach batting than bowling, and it is probably better to get some of the bowlers bowling to the wicketkeeper in a different net, where they can receive advice about such problems as the following:

- The length and smoothness of their run-up;
- The bowling action, with good balance and a sideways position, and a follow-through that must always be seen as an essential part of the delivery;
- Those two familiar aims: the line and the length of each delivery;
- The way to swing, seam and spin a ball;
- The plotting of a batsman's downfall over a period rather than trying to get him out every ball;
- The concentration of a bowler for a stated number of balls, bowling to a batsman's weakness.

Wicketkeepers need specialist advice – see Alan Knott's chapter on page 86 – but practice for wicketkeepers is as important as for the batsman and the bowler, with balls bowled and thrown at them from every angle.

Match practices

One of the themes of this book is the need for all practice to be geared towards some kind of match-play, and match practice is a sensible middle way, between nets and a full-blown match, of achieving this. It assumes a pitch in the middle of, or on part of, a cricket ground, with the correct measurements, the creases properly marked out and stumps available at both ends. The numbers of such a match may not be known in advance, but the coach should have in his mind the framework of the practice.

There are different conventions to suit the ability of the players and the time available, but basically some sort of competition adds edge and enjoyment to the practice. The coach will be the umpire at each bowler's end – unless there is the luxury of two coaches. If not, one of the batting side will stand at square-leg to adjudicate – impartially – on any stumping or run-out decisions.

Eight-a-side cricket works well, for which the following are the conventions:

- Each team consists of eight players;
- Each innings shall be of sixteen overs, time permitting;
- The batting side shall bat in pairs, each pair batting for four overs. Thus, there will be a change at the end of the 4th, 8th and 12th overs;
- Batsmen shall have unlimited 'lives' but each 'life' results in eight runs being deducted from the side's total;
- Batsmen change ends at the fall of a wicket, except on the last ball of an over;
- Each fielder, except for the wicketkeeper, will bowl and no bowler may bowl more than three overs. Catches and run-outs earn eight extra runs for the fielding side;

- Each team starts with 200 runs, and the winning side, self-evidently, is the side scoring most after additions and deductions have been made. Watch that every fielder in front of the wicket stands the requisite 11 yards away from the stumps.

Emphasis will be placed by the coach on such matters as:

- The calling – 'yes', 'no', 'wait' – made loudly enough to be heard by one's partner;
- The kind of backing-up, which can turn one run into two, two into three, and so on;
- The batsman changing his bat into the hand that enables him to watch the fielder in action, as he turns for the next run;
- The art of reaching out for the crease to save distance and time – but beware of not crossing the line of the popping crease!;
- Bowlers' over-long run-ups;
- The falling-away of the pivotal front arm in the bowling action; and
- Failure to follow through.

Coaching – of the batsmen, the bowlers, the wicketkeepers and the fielders – can go on during the match, but too much interruption of the flow of play is unwise. Encouragement should always be the prevailing mood, particularly if the level of achievement seems not to have noticeably improved since the last practice. The coach will have a discussion after the practice about what went well and what went wrong. He should never concentrate solely on what went wrong!

Matches

The aim of a coach is that match-play should follow on from nets and match practice, although this may not always be easy to arrange. Matches of, say, eight-a-side are excellent value at first, since there is more action for more players – plenty of gaps in the field, and consequently more runs, more fielding, more

throwing in, more backing up. Eleven-a-side will naturally be the final aim.

For each side there should be a captain who sets his field – not without advice! – and each player should be encouraged to captain in his own mind, working out what field he would set to each bowler, and noticing the strengths and weaknesses of each batsman. For example, one who holds his bat high up the handle will usually be a driver, another who holds it low down the handle will usually be a nudger, cutter or puller.

Coaches will take notice of the batsman's thought processes – playing himself in but looking for the singles, remembering that he plays only one ball at a time, etc. – and the bowler's need to understand the concept of line and length. Length may well vary slightly, for a particular bowler, to a particular batsman, on a particular pitch. There is no better definition of good length than 'the pitching of the ball so that the batsman is not sure whether to play forward or back, thus inducing indecision and doubt'.

All our Masters have emphasised the need to attack in order to gain psychological and tactical advantage. Their attacking instinct, however, is always tempered by good sense and a good method of defence. Judgement about when to hang on – shortly before an interval, for instance, when the loss of one wicket may often lead to a second – and when to go on to the offensive, is something that a coach will talk about – or, better still, ask the young cricketer for his view, with the hope that later the correct assessment comes to him instinctively.

Any match needs to be well run and involve as many players as possible. Thus, retirement for batsmen at a set score will enable more players to have an innings; and a set ration of overs for a bowler will have the same effect. At close of play the young cricketer will wish to return to base exhilarated by involvement and

The wall or sight-screen catching game. A useful and enjoyable practice, being played here inside Lord's ground. (MCC)

success, or disappointed by failure but determined to put the record straight on the next occasion.

Fielding practice

It is a truism that 'catches win matches' and that nothing gives more satisfaction to the non-bowler batsman who has made nought than the contribution to victory, or even to staving off defeat, of a blinding catch. Conversely being an 'immortal butterfingers' (as Waymark was called in James Love's poem of a Kent v. England cricket match in 1744) is sometimes hard to come to terms with. 'Practice, practice and more practice' is the best advice.

There are three enjoyable ways of training your close-to-the-wicket fielders, other than slip-cradles which do help to sharpen reactions:

1. Take a bat, have balls thrown at you full-toss from about six yards, and angle them towards your slip and gully cordon. Switch catchers after a time since the middle of the cordon is the easiest part to reach;
2. Stand five metres away from your slip cordon and constantly fire catches to them with your hand. They return the ball to you and you can indulge in some enjoyable

sleight of hand – dummy-throw, flipping the ball from behind the back, looking one way and throwing the other. Enjoy it. Make it competitive. Both methods help to sharpen reactions and to increase confidence. The need to stay down, so that a player's eyes are on the line of the ball for as long as possible, should be stressed;

3. Wall or sight-screen catching. Split fielders into two equal teams – catchers and throwers – and place them in two parallel lines facing the wall. The catchers stand approximately three metres away from the wall and the throwers at six metres. The throwers throw tennis balls on to the wall, and the catchers try to catch the rebounding ball, and flip the ball back over the shoulder to the thrower. Each successful catch could score five points. The catchers and the throwers change over after a timed session.

Here are three ways of practising your away-from-the-wicket fielding:

1. Stand by your wicketkeeper and send balls on the ground or in the air, calling out a name or number. The fielder, moving quickly in – as he would do in a match as the bowler bowls – either fields or catches

Underhand attacking interception. Or trying to run the batsman out. (MCC)

the ball and returns it over the stumps to the wicketkeeper. Stress the need to catch high, so that the eyes are on the ball for as long as possible, and to keep the head still and let the hands 'give' with the ball at the moment of catching.

2. Rebound catching (not unlike the practice in paragraph 3 above). Teams of any numbers, but equal in strength, line up in single file facing a wall or sight-screen, fifteen metres away. On the word 'go', the first player in each team throws a tennis ball at the wall and then sprints to the rear of his team. The second player in each team catches the rebounding ball, throws at the wall, sprints to the rear, and so on until the first player is back at the front of his team.

3. Underhand attacking interception. Trying to run batsmen out. Have two teams of equal numbers, one team with bats and the other without. The object is for the fielders to run forward, pick up a stationary ball and run out the batsman before he reaches the popping crease at the wicketkeeper's end. Five points can be given for each successful strike.

The coach can work out his own variations for keeping as many people as possible active and improving their fielding skills. These two schemes have also proved effective:

1. Divide your players into two teams. Each first member runs to a stump some twenty-two yards away throwing, as he does so, the ball in the air, alternating a short throw and a high throw and catching it as he runs. At the stump he rolls the ball back to his second team member, and so on...

2. The coach stands at one wicket, a wicketkeeper at the other. The coach throws the ball into the off side and fielders in turn race from behind him, pick the ball up and throw in to the wicketkeeper, trying to beat two batsmen practising their running between the wickets. Overthrows are, of course, retrieved by the thrower responsible!

Coaches cannot over-emphasise the satisfaction that good fielding and good catching can bring to an individual, nor the contribution they make to the success of the team.

Learning by watching

A coach can also teach by taking his team to a match, and commenting before, during and afterwards. Sitting behind the bowler's arm, just to the off side, enables a young batsman to imagine himself at the crease, watching intently the trajectory of the ball and whether the batsman moves early or late; and it enables a young bowler to watch the crucial qualities of line and length, and when the batsman is able to take advantage of any lapse. I once took my yearlings side from King's School, Bruton, to Taunton, and saw Somerset's Ian Botham play with awesome power against a Hampshire side which included Malcolm Marshall. There was little the coach found to say, that day, in the presence of such a great innings!

In most matches it will be possible to note:

- the care with which a captain places his field and looks after his bowlers;
- the particular field-placing for a particular bowler, and bearing in mind the batsman's special strengths and weaknesses;
- the position of the slips in relation to the wicketkeeper and to each other;
- the stillness of the batsman's head, and the way the back-lift is an important part of the shot, as in a pendulum, whether attacking or defensive;
- the art of good running between the wickets; and the importance of fielders backing up to prevent overthrows.
- Watch from square-leg to note the movement of the batsman's feet – does he go right forward and right back? Study also from the side the rhythm of the bowler as he runs in.

A coach can teach effectively from videos especially since he can stop the video to emphasise a particular point. Young players can take only a certain amount of indoor chat and video-watching, however; real practice should follow immediately at outdoor or indoor nets.

A coach can also teach by collecting his team around a net when a top player is batting or bowling, and draw attention to the secrets of his success – or, for that matter, the occasional error which may creep in. He will emphasise that, while all great players have their own style, they all follow the same basic principles.

Watch is a useful watchword for all coaches. Watch the way top-class players do it. Watch carefully the techniques explained by the Masters. Batsmen watch the ball all the way on to the bat. Bowlers select their target as they run in and watch it as they deliver the ball.

When fielding in the slips some players watch the ball from the bowler's hand on to the bat. Otherwise, for everywhere else in the field, expect the ball to come to you: watch the bat and never take your eyes off the ball until it arrives in your hands. With high catches, watch and wait to judge the ball's trajectory and keep on watching even as you move.

In addition, watch your captain at all times so that he can move you without fuss – when, for instance, he is trying to prevent a top batsman from stealing the strike. Yes, watch is a useful word for coaches, and for players.

Group coaching

Group coaching is an important way of starting the young on their cricketing career. It must never be confined merely to playing the forward defensive stroke (as some critics have claimed) but ought to encourage the playing of attacking strokes as well. The point about defence, however, is that a batsman will not stay in long enough in a match to play his attacking strokes if he has not learned to keep out the good balls bowled to him, and this he will do by means of a proper defensive stroke, whether off the front foot or, equally important, off the back foot.

There must be a sufficient amount of kit available to make a session of Group Coaching worthwhile. This comprises:

1. Enough bats of the right size and weight, with a decent 'pick-up' or balance, and not too heavy for young batsmen to use;
2. Enough 'team balls' or 'wind balls' for each 'bowler' to throw at each 'batter', whether straight for the defensive shot, or the cut or the pull, or dropped from above and hit on the second bounce, for the drive. Fielders can practise their skills by fielding the attacking shots.
3. Permanent marks in the shape of wickets, creases and length-targets to encourage bowlers to bowl a 'length'.

A way needs to be found of providing activity as continuous, varied and satisfying as possible for every young cricketer. Here is a suggested programme, depending, of course, on the number of coaches and boys present:

FIRST HALF-HOUR

10 minutes: Warm up with fielding game after a brief talk on fielding skills, illustrated in this book by Jonty Rhodes of South Africa.

20 minutes: Main activity. Stroke demonstration and practice in groups of five. Then bring them back for the coach to make a fresh point and further practice.

SECOND HALF-HOUR

Basic bowling demonstration and practice in five groups. Again, bring them back regularly for a fresh point and further practice.

THIRD, FINAL HALF-HOUR

A game either of eight-a-side cricket or mini-cricket so that the players finish on a high note, using skills they have learned during the earlier lesson.

Eight-a-side cricket has been described earlier under 'Match Practices'. Mini, or Continuous, cricket is played by twelve players as follows:

● The batting team is divided into three pairs.
● Each member of the fielding side takes up his position on one of six fielding discs. (See diagram.) The fielder on disc 1 is the first

bowler, and the fielder on disc 4 is the wicketkeeper. Outfielders must be in contact with their discs until the bowler starts his run-up.

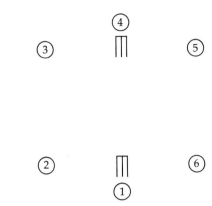

Fielding positions for Mini cricket

● The batting side starts with 100 runs.
● The first pair bats for two overs, whether they are out or not.
● The batsmen must run every time the ball is hit, and they may also run for byes and leg-byes.
● Every time a wicket falls the batsmen change ends, except after a run-out.
● All bowling must be overarm.
● At the end of each over the fielders move round one place in a clockwise direction, and the batsmen change ends.
● At the end of two overs the first pair of batsmen retires and the second takes their place.
● When a batsman is out three runs are deducted from the side's total.
● Coaches will point out how batsmen can steal singles by good placing, and fielders can save runs by being alert.

Kwik Cricket sets and the accompanying rules are an ideal start for the young who, however, will want and need to move on quite quickly to a more advanced game.

The aim is to keep young players interested and involved throughout – without too much repetition. At the finish, they must feel that they have both made progress and enjoyed themselves.

Cricket equipment

The coach will want to be able to help young players with their equipment – what they will own themselves and what to borrow from a common pool. Here is a framework of advice:

BAT

A young player needs a bat that is easy in the pick-up, not too heavy, with a good 'drive', and one with which he feels comfortable. Advice should be sought from a coach rather than a parent buying a bat in a shop that does not specialise in bats. The coach will also advise about the oiling of the bat – never on the splice and not excessively.

BOX

A young cricketer should, on the advice of a coach, wear a box or protector, since it helps to give him confidence and prevents painful injury. Most players now slip the box into a jockstrap.

GLOVES: BATTING AND WICKETKEEPING

Gloves should be comfortable, and also give protection when, say, the lifting ball hits a batsman or a wicketkeeper on the hand.

PADS

Pads must both give protection and enable freedom of movement. If they have straps, these should be cut short and worn on the inside of the leg to avoid batsmen being given 'out' caught off the pad.

HELMET

The young player should get advice from his coach on the right moment for him to wear a helmet, depending on the speed of the opposition bowlers and the quality of the pitch. A helmet that gives protection but still enables the batsmen to hear calls and feel comfortable is important.

FOOTWEAR

Footwear – boots rather than shoes – should above all be comfortable, give support and strength to the feet, and protection too, particularly as deliveries will occasionally hit them. It is important to have spikes if the ground is wet, but normally the boots will be ridged to enable the feet to grip while going for a quick run, or fielding and throwing on the turn to prevent an extra run. Footwear, like other kit, needs to be kept clean all the time.

SHIRTS, FLANNELS AND SWEATERS

The coach will have a policy over these, for they are expensive. Cricket largely remains a white flannels game – and long may that continue! Shirts need to absorb sweat and shirt-sleeves must never flap. The use of a long-sleeved sweater on a cold day is important, especially for fast bowlers between overs. A sleeveless sweater is often useful too.

CRICKET BALLS

The more they are cleaned and looked after the longer they will be of use.

Some useful also-rans for the coach

- The younger cricketer should be encouraged to think of cricketers being well-turned out for practice as well as for a match. A well-turned out side starts with a bonus in terms of confidence and psychological advantage.
- The young cricketer should learn how to umpire and score, with fairness and efficiency. Thus, he ought to learn the Laws of Cricket and any regulations that apply to his age group.
- The young cricketer must be encouraged to learn the values and etiquette of a game in which both are important. 'It isn't cricket' still contains an important core of truth for life as well as for sport.
- The young cricketer should also be encouraged to read about the game.
- The game should always be played and victory achieved within the Laws of Cricket (see especially Law 42 on Unfair Play) and the spirit of the game which they reflect.

'A WONDERFULLY INTRICATE GAME'

BY TONY LEWIS

MCC Masterclass will be, I hope, a cricket tutor and a trusted companion. It is not just a collection of memories from former Test players, nor a book of advice for those with outstanding talents. It is everyone's book, lessons from famous players who want you to get the most out of cricket and have a lifetime of fun and friendship. Once I had completed my interviews with the eleven Masters I appreciated that I had in hand precious words of advice, solid technical know-how all enriched by an understanding of the game which came from performance in successful international careers.

They all impressed me with the depth of thought they had put into their own games. Whatever question I put to them was greeted with clarity of opinion, though all emphasised the importance of an individual approach to the game. Their message is that we are all different in bodily shape and mental approach and we must allow our individuality to grow within the framework of a reliable method of batting, bowling or fielding.

Cricket is such a wonderfully intricate game. The result is a matter of mathematics – who scores more runs, but along the way, what nuances, what twists and possibilities! Just think of it – the weather conditions play their part even before you have tossed the coin for innings. Perhaps the heavy cloud will enable the fast bowler to swing the ball dangerously; maybe a pitch that is cracking will make the spinner a match-winner if you are fielding at the end of the match; then a catch may be dropped or a batsman bowled off his pads; or a no-ball bowled in a crucial last over – so many elements can come into a cricket match. Like a kaleidoscope you can shake it and each time the brilliant pieces fall into a new and exciting pattern.

How many times have you tried to explain the complexities of cricket to a non-cricketer? Where do you start? I always begin with the totally unpredictable possibility that the ball when bowled towards a batsman might land on the upright seam and change direction because of that. Which way does the bowler expect it to go, to the off or to the leg, I am asked? In fact the bowler does not know the answer himself though some are better able to predict than others. The ball landing on the seam might simply go straight on. What a game! How does a batsman meet the ball with the appropriate stroke if the bowler himself does not know which way it is going to deviate.

I have always believed that players can help each other, sometimes more than coaches can help them. For example, if you are a batsman and are not making good contact with the ball, go down the pitch between overs and ask your partner if he has spotted a fault you can quickly put right. I need hardly say that your adviser needs to be someone whose judgement you trust. For example, in 1974 I played in an England Test trial at Worcester and was struggling to get going against the bowling of Derek Underwood. After an over or two of pushing and prodding my partner came down the pitch to talk to me. It was John Edrich, a most experienced Test batsman. 'You are not getting your front foot out to the pitch of the ball,' he said. 'You're only going halfway.'

Next over I got right out to the ball, struck a cover-drive for four and was on my way to scoring a half-century.

So it can be with bowlers. If you are inaccurate and cannot work out why, ask your team-mates to take a look at your run-up and delivery. Someone standing at mid-on or mid-off can spot some unevenness in the run-up and the wicketkeeper especially will be able to tell you if you are falling away at delivery or failing to follow through, or whatever.

The best results are obtained through practice. All of our Masters say that. I played against most of them and can back them up. I remember Dennis Lillee and Richard Hadlee charging in to bowl with fast but untidy actions. Study and practice turned them into classic models of rhythm and control without loss of speed. Good actions last.

Bishan Bedi bowled tirelessly on grassless pitches in Amritsar, made for batting, and by repetition and from necessity learned to turn the ball on surfaces where others could not.

Richie Benaud practised 'the flipper' for nearly eighteen months before he tried it out in a match; and he still says he never really mastered it! When Geoff Boycott went missing on an England tour you could be sure he was taking a net somewhere, often with a group of local bowlers recruited for his personal practice. Nothing has been achieved by any of these Masters without hard work and deep concentration on their craft.

MCC, founded in 1787, has always stood for tough competition and sportsmanship. Throughout cricket's history standards of behaviour have lapsed from time to time and now in the 1990s, towards the second millennium, the game's administrators all over the world have been addressing some undesirable examples of gamesmanship and petulance – umpires are pressurised by a chorus of appeals when most of the fielders cannot be sure of the dismissal; batsmen stand at the crease looking disgusted after being given out. Cricket, as I have written earlier, is a game requiring fair-minded participation.

Nowadays, because so much international cricket is transmitted by television into the homes of young players it is even more important that every Test player in the world sets sporting standards of behaviour, a code to copy which will lead all cricketers to the ultimate enjoyment of playing a full part in a team game.

Remember this. The respect you have for the Laws, for the umpires and for your opponents is really the respect you have for yourself.

NOTE ON 'THE MASTERS'

BISHAN BEDI

Bishan Bedi's first-class career extended from 1961–81 during which time he took 266 Test wickets with his left-arm spin. He was an attacking bowler whose action was a model of rhythm, yet the purity of his style belied an aggressive approach to bowling which all the best bowlers have possessed.

RICHIE BENAUD

Although Richie Benaud played for his state at the early age of eighteen and for Australia in Tests when he was only twenty-one, he was a dedicated student of leg-spin throughout his career from 1948–68. He took 248 Test wickets, mastering control of many variations of flight and spin. When his playing days were over, his abilities as writer and television commentator made him the ideal communicator of the wrist-spin skills and much more.

GEOFFREY BOYCOTT

A most prolific and single-minded batsman for Yorkshire and England who dealt in the minutiae of technicalities. Since his retirement in 1986, with 48, 426 first-class runs which included 151 centuries, he has become one of the foremost teachers of the game, passing on the method which made him one of the biggest run-scorers in cricket's history.

In his Test career which began in 1964, he amassed 8114 runs at an average of 47.72 in 193 innings, and scored 22 centuries.

MIKE BREARLEY

Mike Brearley proved in his 31 Test matches as captain of England, and in his eleven seasons leading Middlesex, that captaincy in cricket is a crucial force. He was the only England captain, after Len Hutton, to win the Ashes and then successfully defend them. He led England to 18 wins in 31 Tests including a record unbeaten 19 home Tests.

He applied a considerable intellect to the game. He grew to know cricket in its every detail and understood the hopes and fears of his players.

HUBERT DOGGART

Hubert Doggart was a stylish middle-order batsman, a useful off-spinner and a fine slip catcher who played first-class cricket between 1948 and 1961. After an outstanding start at Cambridge University, his cricket for Sussex and England was restricted by his commitment to teaching, first at Winchester College and finally as headmaster of King's School, Bruton. His contribution to cricket continues with MCC, where he has been President and Treasurer, and with the English Schools Cricket Association.

DAVID GOWER

Left-handed and elegant in style, David Gower created impressions of insouciance which disguised the determination that brought him 8231 Test runs, at an average of 44.25, more than any other England batsman to date. His career with Leicestershire and Hampshire extended from 1975–93. He captained Leicestershire and England and, especially in his early career, was a superb fielder.

RICHARD HADLEE

Richard Hadlee began his Test career at Basin Reserve, Wellington, in 1973 as a fast and furious bowler off a long run-up and ended it at Edgbaston, Birmingham in 1990 off a much shorter run but with wonderful control of seam and swing and with a model action. Indeed in that last Test he took five wickets in a Test innings for the 36th time, making 431 in his Test career, then a world record.

RAY ILLINGWORTH

It was Ray Illingworth's move from Yorkshire to Leicestershire in 1969 which raised his profile in Test cricket. It was then he became England's captain and masterminded England's recovery of the Ashes in Australia in 1970–71. He led Leicestershire to their first-ever county championship in 1975 and to four one-day titles.

His off-spinning was shrewd and frugal and based on a rare perception of the possible weaknesses of those who batted against him. He took 122 wickets in Tests and 2072 in all first-class cricket. In 1994 he was appointed England's Chairman of Selectors.

ALAN KNOTT

Alan Knott played in 95 Tests for England between 1967 and 1981, surpassing all previous records for an England wicketkeeper, by totalling 269 Test victims.

He was a diligent student of his art with an eye for the smallest detail of preparation. His remarkable reflexes were married to a regime of strict physical fitness. As a batsman he was good enough to score five Test centuries.

DENNIS LILLEE

Dennis Lillee possessed all the fast bowler's virtues – a fine physique, a superb action and an unquenchable fire raging within him. He was a technician too, always seeking improvement. He signalled his ability to take wickets at the highest level with 32 wickets in five Tests in England in 1972. In all he took 328 wickets in a Test career which extended from 1971–84. Since retirement he has coached fast bowling all over the world.

JONTY RHODES

The Test career of Jonty Rhodes began in 1992 soon after South Africa returned to Test cricket following a twenty-two-year absence. His fielding immediately put him in the class of the finest the cricket has produced, and set him alongside his legendary compatriot Colin Bland.

Playing for South Africa in the Hero Cup, he achieved a one-day international record by taking five catches in an innings against West Indies at Bombay. He analyses the techniques required for good fielding and has become a thoughtful tutor much in demand by students of the game.

VIVIAN RICHARDS

Viv Richards was a genius of a batsman who was able to win matches for the West Indies off his own bat. He played 121 Test matches and 187 one-day internationals. He scored 8540 Test runs at an average of 50.23 which included 24 hundreds.

His dominating presence was felt all over the world by the best bowlers in the world. He was a successful West Indian captain, a brilliant fielder, a useful bowler and above all a joy to watch. In a first-class career for Combined Islands and Leeward Islands, Queensland, Somerset and Glamorgan he hit 114 centuries.

APPENDIX

THE LAWS OF CRICKET

The Laws are the copyright of the Marylebone Cricket Club; they are those of the 1980 Code. Copies of the Laws in pocket size may be obtained from the Secretary, MCC, Lord's Cricket Ground, London, NW8 8QN.

LAW 1   THE PLAYERS

1 Number of Players and Captain
A match is played between two sides each of eleven Players, one of whom shall be Captain. In the event of the Captain not being available at any time a Deputy shall act for him.

2 Nomination of Players
Before the toss for innings, the Captain shall nominate his Players who may not thereafter be changed without the consent of the opposing Captain.

NOTES

(a) More or Less than Eleven Players a Side
A match may be played by agreement between sides of more or less than eleven players but not more than eleven players may field.

LAW 2   SUBSTITUTES AND RUNNERS: BATSMAN OR FIELDSMAN LEAVING THE FIELD: BATSMAN RETIRING: BATSMAN COMMENCING INNINGS

1 Substitutes
In normal circumstances, a Substitute shall be allowed to field only for a player who satisfies the Umpires that he has become injured or become ill during the match. However, in very exceptional circumstances, the Umpires may use their discretion to allow a substitute for a player who has to leave the field or does not take the field for other wholly acceptable reasons, subject to consent being given by the opposing Captain. If a player wishes to change his shirt, boots, etc., he may leave the field to do so (no changing on the field) but no Substitute will be allowed.

2 Objection to Substitutes
The opposing Captain shall have no right of objection to any player acting as Substitute on the field, nor as to where he shall field; however, no Substitute shall act as Wicket-Keeper.

3 Substitute Not to Bat or Bowl
A Substitute shall not be allowed to bat or bowl.

4 A Player for Whom a Substitute has Acted

A player may bat, bowl or field even though a Substitute has acted for him.

5 Runner

A runner shall be allowed for a Batsman who during the match is incapacitated by illness or injury. The player acting as Runner shall be a member of the batting side and shall, if possible, have already batted in that innings.

6 Runner's Equipment

The player acting as Runner for an injured Batsman shall wear the same external protective equipment as the injured Batsman.

7 Transgression of the Laws by an Injured Batsman or Runner

An injured Batsman may be out should his Runner break any one of Laws 33: (Handled the Ball), 37: (Obstructing the Field) or 38: (Run Out). As Striker he remains himself subject to the Laws. Furthermore, should he be out of his ground for any purpose and the wicket at the Wicket-Keeper's end be put down he shall be out under Law 38: (Run Out) or Law 39: (Stumped) irrespective of the position of the other Batsman or the Runner and no runs shall be scored.

When not the Striker, the injured Batsman is out of the game and shall stand where he does not interfere with the play. Should he bring himself into the game in any way then he shall suffer the penalties that any transgression of the Laws demands.

8 Fieldsman Leaving the Field

No Fieldsman shall leave the field or return during a session of play without the consent of the Umpire at the Bowler's end. The Umpire's consent is also necessary if a Substitute is required for a Fieldsman, when his side returns to the field after an interval. If a member of the fielding side leaves the field or fails to return after an interval and is absent from the field for longer than 15 minutes, he shall not be permitted to bowl after his return until he has been on the field for at least that length of playing time for which he was absent. This restriction shall not apply at the start of a new day's play.

9 Batsman Leaving the Field or Retiring

A Batsman may leave the field or retire at any time owing to illness, injury or other unavoidable cause, having previously notified the Umpire at the Bowler's end. He may resume his innings at the fall of a wicket, which for the purposes of this Law shall include the retirement of another Batsman.

If he leaves the field or retires for any other reason he may only resume his innings with the consent of the opposing Captain.

When a Batsman has left the field or retired and is unable to return owing to illness, injury or other unavoidable cause his innings is to be recorded as 'retired, not out'. Otherwise it is to be recorded as 'retired, out'.

10 Commencement of a Batsman's Innings

A Batsman shall be considered to have commenced his innings once he has stepped on to the field of play.

NOTES

(a) Substitutes and Runners
For the purpose of these Laws allowable illnesses or injuries are those which occur at any time after the nomination by the Captains of their teams.

LAW 3   THE UMPIRES

1 Appointment
Before the toss for innings two Umpires shall be appointed, one for each end, to control the game with absolute impartiality as required by the Laws.

2 Change of Umpire
No Umpire shall be changed during a match without the consent of both Captains.

3 Special Conditions
Before the toss for innings, the Umpires shall agree with both Captains on any special conditions affecting the conduct of the match.

4 The Wickets
The Umpires shall satisfy themselves before the start of the match that the wickets are properly pitched.

5 Clock or Watch
The Umpires shall agree between themselves and inform both Captains before the start of the match on the watch or clock to be followed during the match.

6 Conduct and Implements

Before and during a match the Umpires shall ensure that the conduct of the game and the implements used are strictly in accordance with the Laws.

7 Fair and Unfair Play

The Umpires shall be the sole judges of fair and unfair play.

8 Fitness of Ground, Weather and Light

(a) The Umpires shall be the sole judges of the fitness of the ground, weather and light for play.

  (i) However, before deciding to suspend play or not to start play or not to resume play after an interval or stoppage, the Umpires shall establish whether both Captains (the Batsmen at the wicket may deputise for their Captain) wish to commence or to continue in the prevailing conditions; if so, their wishes shall be met.

  (ii) In addition, if during play, the Umpires decide that the light is unfit, only the batting side shall have the option of continuing play. After agreeing to continue to play in unfit light conditions, the Captain of the batting side (or a Batsman at the wicket) may appeal against the light to the Umpires, who shall uphold the appeal only if, in their opinion, the light has deteriorated since the agreement to continue was made.

(b) After any suspension of play, the Umpires, unaccompanied by any of the Players or Officials shall, on their own initiative, carry out an inspection immediately the conditions improve and shall continue to inspect at intervals. Immediately the Umpires decide that play is possible they shall call upon the Players to resume the game.

9 Exceptional Circumstances

In exceptional circumstances, other than those of weather, ground or light, the Umpires may decide to suspend or abandon play. Before making such a decision the Umpires shall establish, if the circumstances allow, whether both Captains (the Batsmen at the wicket may deputise for their Captain) wish to continue in the prevailing conditions: if so their wishes shall be met.

10 Position of Umpires

The Umpires shall stand where they can best see any act upon which their decision may be required.

Subject to this over-riding consideration the Umpire at the Bowler's end shall stand where he does not interfere with either the Bowler's run-up or the Striker's view.

The Umpire at the Striker's end may elect to stand on the off instead of the leg side of the pitch, provided he informs the Captain of the fielding side and the Striker of his intention to do so.

11 Umpires Changing Ends

The Umpires shall change ends after each side has had one innings.

12 Disputes

All disputes shall be determined by the Umpires and if they disagree the actual state of things shall continue.

13 Signals

The following code of signals shall be used by Umpires who will wait until a signal has been answered by a Scorer before allowing the game to proceed.

Boundary	by waving the arm from side to side.
Boundary 6	by raising both arms above the head.
Bye	by raising an open hand above the head.
Dead Ball	by crossing and re-crossing the wrists below the waist.
Leg Bye	by touching a raised knee with the hand.
No Ball	by extending one arm horizontally.
Out	by raising the index finger above the head. If not out the Umpire shall call 'not out'.
Short run	by bending the arm upwards and by touching the nearer shoulder with the tips of the fingers.
Wide	by extending both arms horizontally.

14 Correctness of Scores

The Umpires shall be responsible for satisfying themselves on the correctness of the scores throughout and at the conclusion of the match. See Law 21.6 (Correctness of Result).

NOTES

(a) Attendance of Umpires
The Umpires should be present on the ground and report to the Ground Executive or the equivalent at least 30 minutes before the start of a day's play.

(b) Consultation Between Umpires and Scorers
Consultation between Umpires and Scorers over doubtful points is essential.

(c) Fitness of Ground
The Umpires shall consider the ground as unfit for play when it is so wet or slippery as to deprive the Bowlers of a reasonable foothold, the Fieldsmen, other than the deep-fielders, of the power of free movement, or the Batsmen the ability to play their strokes or to run between the wickets. Play should not be suspended merely because the grass and the ball are wet and slippery.

(d) Fitness of Weather and Light
The Umpires should only suspend play when they consider that the conditions are so bad that it is unreasonable or dangerous to continue.

LAW 4   THE SCORERS

1 Recording Runs
All runs scored shall be recorded by Scorers appointed for the purpose. Where there are two Scorers they shall frequently check to ensure that the score sheets agree.

2 Acknowledging Signals
The Scorers shall accept and immediately acknowledge all instructions and signals given to them by the Umpires.

LAW 5   THE BALL

1 Weight and Size
The ball, when new, shall weigh not less than 5½ ounces/155.9g. nor more than 5¾ ounces/163g.: and shall measure not less than 8¹³⁄₁₆ inches/22.4cm., nor more than 9 inches/22.9cm. in circumference.

2 Approval of Balls
All balls used in matches shall be approved by the Umpires and Captains before the start of the match.

3 New Ball
Subject to agreement to the contrary, having been

made before the toss, either Captain may demand a new ball at the start of each innings.

4 New Ball in Match of 3 or More Days' Duration
In a match of 3 or more days' duration, the Captain of the fielding side may demand a new ball after the prescribed number of overs has been bowled with the old one. The Governing Body for cricket in the country concerned shall decide the number of overs applicable in that country which shall be not less than 75 6-ball overs (55 8-ball overs).

5 Ball Lost or Becoming Unfit for Play
In the event of a ball during play being lost or, in the opinion of the Umpires, becoming unfit for play, the Umpires shall allow it to be replaced by one, that in their opinion, has had a similar amount of wear. If a ball is to be replaced, the Umpires shall inform the Batsmen.

NOTES

(a) Specifications
The specifications as described in 1 above shall apply to top-grade balls only. The following degrees of tolerance will be acceptable for other grades of ball.
  (i) Men's Grades 2–4
   Weight: 5⁵⁄₁₆ ounces/150g. to 5¹³⁄₁₆ ounces/165g.
   Size: 8¹¹⁄₁₆ inches/22.0cm. to 9¹⁄₁₆ inches/23.0cm.
  (ii) Women's
   Weight: 4¹⁵⁄₁₆ ounces/140g. to 5⁵⁄₁₆ ounces/150g.
   Size: 8¼ inches/21.0cm. to 8⅞ inches/22.5cm.
  (iii) Junior
   Weight: 4⁵⁄₁₆ ounces/133g. to 5¹⁄₁₆ ounces/143g.
   Size: 8¹⁄₁₆ inches/20.5cm. to 8¹¹⁄₁₆ inches/22.0cm.

LAW 6   THE BAT

Width and Length
The bat overall shall not be more than 38 inches /96.5cm. in length; the blade of the bat shall be made of wood and shall not exceed 4¼ inches/10.8cm. at the widest part.

NOTES

(a) *The blade of the bat may be covered with material for protection, strengthening or repair. Such material shall not exceed ¹⁄₁₆ inch/1.56mm. in thickness.*

LAW 7   THE PITCH

1 Area of Pitch

The pitch is the area between the bowling creases – see Law 9: (The Bowling and Popping Creases). It shall measure 5 feet/1.52m. in width on either side of a line joining the centre of the middle stumps of the wickets – see Law 8: (The Wickets).

2 Selection and Preparation

Before the toss for innings, the Executive of the Ground shall be responsible for the selection and preparation of the pitch; thereafter the Umpires shall control its use and maintenance.

3 Changing the Pitch

The pitch shall not be changed during a match unless it becomes unfit for play, and then only with the consent of both Captains.

4 Non-Turf Pitches

In the event of a non-turf pitch being used, the following shall apply:
(a) *Length*
    That of the playing surface to a minimum of 58 feet (17.68m.).
(b) *Width*
    That of the playing surface to a minimum of 6 feet (1.83m.).
See Law 10: (Rolling, Sweeping, Mowing, Watering the Pitch and Re-marking of Creases) Note (a).

LAW 8   THE WICKETS

1 Width and Pitching

Two sets of wickets, each 9 inches/22.86cm. wide, and consisting of three wooden stumps with two wooden bails upon the top, shall be pitched opposite and parallel to each other at a distance of 22 yards/20.12m. between the centres of the two middle stumps.

2 Size of Stumps

The stumps shall be of equal and sufficient size to prevent the ball from passing between them. Their tops shall be 28 inches/71.1cm. above the ground, and shall be dome-shaped except for the bail grooves.

3 Size of Bails

The bails shall be each 4⅜ inches/11.1cm. in length and when in position on the top of the stumps shall not project more than ½ inch/1.3cm. above them.

NOTES

(a) Dispensing with Bails
In a high wind the Umpires may decide to dispense with the use of bails.
(b) Junior Cricket
For Junior Cricket, as defined by the local Governing Body, the following measurements for the Wickets shall apply:

Width	*8 inches/20.32cm.*
Pitched	*21 yards/19.20m.*
Height	*27 inches/68.58cm.*
Bails	*each 3⅞ inches/9.84cm. in length and should not project more than ½inch/1.3cm. above them.*

LAW 9   THE BOWLING, POPPING AND RETURN CREASES

1 The Bowling Crease

The bowling crease shall be marked in line with the stumps at each end and shall be 8 feet 8 inches/2.64m. in length, with the stumps in the centre.

2 The Popping Crease

The popping crease, which is the back edge of the crease marking, shall be in front of and parallel with the bowling crease. It shall have the back edge of the crease marking 4 feet/1.22m. from the centre of the stumps and shall extend to a minimum of 6 feet/1.83m. on either side of the line of the wicket.

The popping crease shall be considered to be unlimited in length.

3 The Return Crease

The return crease marking, of which the inside edge is the crease, shall be at each end of the bowling crease and at right angles to it. The return crease shall be marked to a minimum of 4 feet/1.22m. behind the wicket and shall be considered to be unlimited in length. A forward extension shall be marked to the popping crease.

LAW 10   ROLLING, SWEEPING, MOWING, WATERING THE PITCH AND RE-MARKING OF CREASES

1 Rolling

During the match the pitch may be rolled at the

request of the Captain of the batting side, for a period of not more than 7 minutes before the start of each innings, other than the first innings of the match, and before the start of each day's play. In addition, if, after the toss and before the first innings of the match, the start is delayed, the Captain of the batting side may request to have the pitch rolled for not more than 7 minutes. However, if in the opinion of the Umpires, the delay has had no significant effect on the state of the pitch, they shall refuse any request for the rolling of the pitch.

The pitch shall not otherwise be rolled during the match.

The 7 minutes' rolling permitted before the start of a day's play shall take place not earlier than half an hour before the start of play and the Captain of the batting side may delay such rolling until 10 minutes before the start of play should he so desire.

If a Captain declares an innings closed less than 15 minutes before the resumption of play, and the other Captain is thereby prevented from exercising his option of 7 minutes' rolling or if he is so prevented for any other reason, the time for rolling shall be taken out of the normal playing time.

2 Sweeping

Such sweeping of the pitch as is necessary during the match shall be done so that the 7 minutes allowed for rolling the pitch provided for in 1 above, is not affected.

3 Mowing

(a) *Responsibilities of Ground Authority and of Umpires*
All mowings which are carried out before the toss for innings shall be the responsibility of the Ground Authority. Thereafter they shall be carried out under the supervision of the Umpires, see Law 7.2: (Selection and Preparation).

(b) *Initial Mowing*
The pitch shall be mown before play begins on the day the match is scheduled to start or in the case of a delayed start on the day the match is expected to start. See 3(a) above (Responsibilities of Ground Authority and of Umpires).

(c) *Subsequent Mowings in a Match of 2 or More Days' Duration*
In a match of 2 or more days' duration, the pitch shall be mown daily before play begins. Should this mowing not take place because of weather conditions, rest days or other reasons the pitch shall be mown on the first day on which the match is resumed.

(d) *Mowing of the Outfield in a Match of 2 or More Days' Duration*
In order to ensure that conditions are as similar as possible for both sides, the outfield shall normally be mown before the commencement of play on each day of the match if ground and weather conditions allow. See Note (b) to this Law.

4 Watering
The pitch shall not be watered during a match.

5 Re-Marking Creases
Whenever possible the creases shall be re-marked.

6 Maintenance of Foot Holes
In wet weather, the Umpires shall ensure that the holes made by the Bowlers and Batsmen are cleaned out and dried whenever necessary to facilitate play. In matches of 2 or more days' duration, the Umpires shall allow, if necessary, the re-turfing of foot holes made by the Bowler in his delivery stride, or the use of quick-setting fillings for the same purpose, before the start of each day's play.

7 Securing of Footholds and Maintenance of Pitch
During play, the Umpires shall allow either Batsman to beat the pitch with his bat and players to secure their footholds by the use of sawdust, provided that no damage to the pitch is so caused, and Law 42: (Unfair Play) is not contravened.

NOTES

(a) Non-Turf Pitches
The above Law 10 applies to turf pitches.

The game is played on non-turf pitches in many countries at various levels. While the conduct of the game on these surfaces should always be in accordance with the Laws of cricket, it is recognised that it may sometimes be necesssary for Governing Bodies to lay down special playing conditions to suit the type of non-turf pitch used in their country.

In matches played against Touring Teams, any special playing conditions should be agreed in advance by both parties.

(b) Mowing of the Outfield in a Match of 2 or More Days' Duration

If, for reasons other than ground and weather conditions, daily and complete mowing is not possible, the Ground Authority shall notify the Captains and Umpires, before the toss for innings, of the procedure to be adopted for such mowing during the match.

(c) Choice of Roller

If there is more than one roller available the Captain of the batting side shall have a choice.

LAW 11   COVERING THE PITCH

1 Before the Start of a Match
Before the start of a match complete covering of the pitch shall be allowed.

2 During a Match
The pitch shall not be completely covered during a match unless prior arrangement or regulations so provide.

3 Covering Bowlers' Run-up
Whenever possible, the Bowlers' run-up shall be covered, but the covers so used shall not extend further than 4 feet/1.22m. in front of the popping crease.

NOTES

(a) Removal of Covers
The covers should be removed as promptly as possible whenever the weather permits.

LAW 12   INNINGS

1 Number of Innings
A match shall be of one or two innings of each side according to agreement reached before the start of play.

2 Alternate Innings
In a two innings match each side shall take their innings alternately except in the case provided for in Law 13: (The Follow-On).

3 The Toss
The Captains shall toss for the choice of innings on the field of play not later than 15 minutes before the time scheduled for the match to start, or before the time agreed upon for play to start.

4 Choice of Innings
The winner of the toss shall notify his decision to bat or to field to the opposing Captain not later than 10 minutes before the time scheduled for the match to start, or before the time agreed upon for play to start. The decision shall not thereafter be altered.

5 Continuation After One Innings of Each Side
Despite the terms of 1 above, in a one innings match, when a result has been reached on the first innings the Captains may agree to the continuation of play if, in their opinion, there is a prospect of carrying the game to a further issue in the time left. See Law 21: (Result).

NOTES

(a) Limited Innings – One-Innings Match
In a one-innings match, each innings may, by agreement, be limited by a number of overs or by a period of time.
(b) Limited Innings – Two-Innings Match
In a two-innings match, the first innings of each side may, by agreement, be limited to a number of overs or by a period of time.

LAW 13   THE FOLLOW-ON

1 Lead on First Innings
In a two-innings match the side which bats first and leads by 200 runs in a match of five days or more, by 150 runs in a three-day or four-day match, by 100 runs in a two-day match, or by 75 runs in a one-day match, shall have the option of requiring the other side to follow their innings.

2 Day's Play Lost
If no play takes place on the first day of a match of 2 or more days' duration, 1 above shall apply in accordance with the number of days' play remaining from the actual start of the match.

LAW 14   DECLARATIONS

1 Time of Declaration
The Captain of the batting side may declare an innings closed at any time during a match irrespective of its duration.

2 Forfeiture of Second Innings
A Captain may forfeit his second innings, provided his decision to do so is notified to the opposing Captain and Umpires in sufficient time to allow 7 minutes' rolling of the pitch. See Law 10: (Rolling, Sweeping, Mowing, Watering the

Pitch and Re-Marking of Creases). The normal 10 minute interval between innings shall be applied.

LAW 15   START OF PLAY

1 Call of Play

At the start of each innings and of each day's play and on the resumption of play after any interval or interruption the Umpire at the Bowler's end shall call 'play'.

2 Practice on the Field

At no time on any day of the match shall there be any bowling or batting practice on the pitch.

No practice may take place on the field if, in the opinion of the Umpires, it could result in a waste of time.

3 Trial Run-up

No Bowler shall have a trial run-up after 'play' has been called in any session of play, except at the fall of a wicket when an Umpire may allow such a trial run-up if he is satisfied that it will not cause any waste of time.

LAW 16   INTERVALS

1 Length

The Umpire shall allow such intervals as have been agreed upon for meals, and 10 minutes between each innings.

2 Luncheon Interval – Innings Ending or Stoppage Within 10 Minutes of Interval

If an innings ends or there is a stoppage caused by weather or bad light within 10 minutes of the agreed time for the luncheon interval, the interval shall be taken immediately.

The time remaining in the session of play shall be added to the agreed length of the interval but no extra allowance shall be made for the 10 minutes' interval between innings.

3 Tea Interval – Innings Ending or Stoppage Within 30 Minutes of Interval

If an innings ends or there is a stoppage caused by weather or bad light within 30 minutes of the agreed time for the tea interval, the interval shall be taken immediately.

The interval shall be of the agreed length and, if applicable, shall include the 10 minute interval between innings.

4 Tea Interval – Continuation of Play

If at the agreed time for the tea interval, nine wickets are down, play shall continue for a period not exceeding 30 minutes or until the innings is concluded.

5 Tea Interval – Agreement to Forego

At any time during the match, the Captains may agree to forego a tea interval.

6 Intervals for Drinks

If both Captains agree before the start of a match that intervals for drinks may be taken, the option to take such intervals shall be available to either side. These intervals shall be restricted to one per session, shall be kept as short as possible, shall not be taken in the last hour of the match and in any case shall not exceed 5 minutes.

The agreed times for these intervals shall be strictly adhered to except that if a wicket falls within 5 minutes of the agreed time then drinks shall be taken out immediately.

If an innings ends or there is a stoppage caused by weather or bad light within 30 minutes of the agreed time for a drinks interval, there will be no interval for drinks in that session.

At any time during the match the Captains may agree to forego any such drinks interval.

NOTES

(a) Tea Interval – One-day Match
In a one-day match, a specific time for the tea interval need not necessarily be arranged, and it may be agreed to take this interval between the innings of a one-innings match.
(b) Changing the Agreed Time of Intervals
In the event of the ground, weather or light conditions causing a suspension of play, the Umpires, after consultation with the Captains, may decide in the interest of time-saving, to bring forward the time of the luncheon or tea interval.

LAW 17   CESSATION OF PLAY

1 Call of Time

The Umpire at the Bowler's end shall call 'time' on the cessation of play before any interval or interruption of play, at the end of each day's play, and at the conclusion of the match. See Law 27: (Appeals).

2 Removal of Bails

After the call of 'time', the Umpires shall remove the bails from both wickets.

3 Starting a Last Over

The last over before an interval or the close of play shall be started provided the Umpire, after walking at his normal pace, has arrived at his position behind the stumps at the Bowler's end before time has been reached.

4 Completion of the Last Over of a Session

The last over before an interval or the close of play shall be completed unless a Batsman is out or retires during that over within 2 minutes of the interval or the close of play or unless the Players have occasion to leave the field.

5 Completion of the Last Over of a Match

An over in progress at the close of play on the final day of a match shall be completed at the request of either Captain even if a wicket falls after time has been reached.

If during the last over the Players have occasion to leave the field the Umpires shall call 'time' and there shall be no resumption of play and the match shall be at an end.

6 Last Hour of Match – Number of Overs

The Umpires shall indicate when one hour of playing time of the match remains according to the agreed hours of play. The next over after that moment shall be the first of a minimum of 20 6-ball overs (15 8-ball overs), provided a result is not reached earlier, or there is no interval or interruption of play.

7 Last Hour of Match – Intervals Between Innings and Interruptions of Play

If, at the commencement of the last hour of the match, an interval or interruption of play is in progress or if, during the last hour, there is an interval between innings or an interruption of play, the minimum number of overs to be bowled on the resumption of play shall be reduced in proportion to the duration, within the last hour of the match, of any such interval or interruption.

The minimum number of overs to be bowled after a resumption of play shall be calculated as follows:

(a) In the case of an interval or interruption of play being in progress at the commencement of the last hour of the match, or in the case of a first interval or interruption a deduction shall be made from the minimum of 20 6-ball overs (or 15 8-ball overs).

(b) If there is a later interval or interruption a further deduction shall be made from the minimum number of overs which should have been bowled following the last resumption of play.

(c) These deductions shall be based on the following factors:

  (i) the number of overs already bowled in the last hour of the match or, in the case of a later interval or interruption in the last session of play.

  (ii) the number of overs lost as a result of the interval or interruption allowing one 6-ball over for every full three minutes (or one 8-ball over for every full four minutes) of interval or interruption.

  (iii) any over left uncompleted at the end of an innings to be excluded from these calculations.

  (iv) any over of the minimum number to be played which is left uncompleted at the start of an interruption of play shall be completed when play is resumed and to count as one over bowled.

  (v) an interval to start with the end of an innings and to end 10 minutes later; an interruption to start on the call of 'time' and to end on the call of 'play'.

(d) In the event of an innings being completed and a new innings commencing during the last hour of the match, the number of overs to be bowled in the new innings shall be calculated on the basis of one 6-ball over for every three minutes or part thereof remaining for play (or one 8-ball over for every four minutes or part thereof remaining for play); or alternatively on the basis that sufficient overs be bowled to enable the full minimum quota of overs to be completed under circumstances governed by (a), (b) and (c) above. In all such cases the alternative which allows the greater number of overs shall be employed.

8 Bowler Unable to Complete an Over During Last Hour of the Match

If, for any reason, a Bowler is unable to complete an over during the period of play referred to in 6 above, Law 22.7: (Bowler Incapacitated or Suspended during an Over) shall apply.

LAW 18   SCORING

1 A Run

The score shall be reckoned by runs. A run is scored –

(a) So often as the Batsmen, after a hit or at any time while the ball is in play, shall have crossed and made good their ground from end to end.

(b) When a boundary is scored. See Law 19: (Boundaries).

(c) When penalty runs are awarded. See 6 below.

2 Short Runs

(a) If either Batsman runs a short run, the Umpire shall call and signal 'one short' as soon as the ball becomes dead and that run shall not be scored. A run is short if a Batsman fails to make good his ground on turning for a further run.

(b) Although a short run shortens the succeeding one, the latter if completed, shall count.

(c) If either or both Batsmen deliberately run short the Umpire shall, as soon as he sees that the fielding side have no chance of dismissing either Batsman, call and signal 'dead ball' and disallow any runs attempted or previously scored. The Batsmen shall return to their original ends.

(d) If both Batsmen run short in one and the same run, only one run shall be deducted.

(e) Only if 3 or more runs are attempted can more than one be short and then, subject to (c) and (d) above, all runs so called shall be disallowed. If there has been more than one short run the Umpires shall instruct the Scorers as to the number of runs disallowed.

3   Striker Caught

If the Striker is Caught, no run shall be scored.

4   Batsman Run Out

If a Batsman is Run Out, only that run which was being attempted shall not be scored. If, however, an injured Striker himself is run out no runs shall be scored. See Law 2.7: (Transgression of the Laws by an Injured Batsman or Runner).

5   Batsman Obstructing the Field

If a Batsman is out Obstructing the Field, any runs completed before the obstruction occurs shall be scored unless such obstruction prevents a catch being made in which case no runs shall be scored.

6 Runs Scored for Penalties

Runs shall be scored for penalties under Laws 20: (Lost Ball), 24: (No Ball), 25: (Wide Ball), 41.1: (Fielding the Ball) and for boundary allowances under Law 19: (Boundaries).

7 Batsman Returning to Wicket he has Left

If, while the ball is in play, the Batsmen have crossed in running, neither shall return to the wicket he has left even though a short run has been called or no run has been scored as in the case of a catch. Batsmen, however, shall return to the wickets they originally left, in the cases of a boundary and of any disallowance of runs and of an injured Batsman being, himself, run out. See Law 2.7: (Transgression of the Laws by an Injured Batsman or Runner).

NOTES

(a) Short Run

A Striker taking stance in front of his popping crease may run from that point without penalty.

LAW 19   BOUNDARIES

1 The Boundary of the Playing Area

Before the toss for innings, the Umpires shall agree with both Captains on the boundary of the playing area. The boundary shall, if possible, be marked by a white line, a rope laid on the ground, or a fence. If flags or posts only are used to mark a boundary, the imaginary line joining such points shall be regarded as the boundary. An obstacle, or person, within the playing area shall not be regarded as a boundary unless so decided by the Umpires before the toss for innings. Sight-screens within, or partially within, the playing area shall be regarded as the boundary and when the ball strikes or passes within or under or directly over any part of the screen, a boundary shall be scored.

2 Runs Scored for Boundaries

Before the toss for innings, the Umpires shall agree with both Captains the runs to be allowed for boundaries, and in deciding the allowance for them, the Umpires and Captains shall be guided by the prevailing custom of the ground. The allowance for a boundary shall normally be 4 runs, and 6 runs for all hits pitching over and clear of the boundary line or fence, even though the ball has been previously touched by a Fieldsman. 6 runs shall also be scored if a Fieldsman, after catching a ball, carries it over the boundary. See Law 32: (Caught) Note (a). 6 runs shall not be scored when a ball struck by the Striker hits a sight-screen full pitch if the screen is within, or partially within, the playing area, but if the ball is struck directly over a sight-screen so situated, 6 runs shall be scored.

3 A Boundary
A boundary shall be scored and signalled by the Umpire at the Bowler's end whenever, in his opinion –
(a) A ball in play touches or crosses the boundary, however marked.
(b) A Fieldsman with ball in hand touches or grounds any part of his person on or over a boundary line.
(c) A Fieldsman with ball in hand grounds any part of his person over a boundary fence or board. This allows the Fieldsman to touch or lean on or over a boundary fence or board in preventing a boundary.

4 Runs Exceeding Boundary Allowance
The runs completed at the instant the ball reaches the boundary shall count if they exceed the boundary allowance.

5 Overthrows or Wilful Act of a Fieldsman
If the boundary results from an overthrow or from the wilful act of a Fieldsman, any runs already completed and the allowance shall be added to the score. The run in progress shall count provided that the Batsmen have crossed at the instant of the throw or act.

NOTES

(a) Position of Sight-Screens
Sight-screens should, if possible, be positioned wholly outside the playing area, as near as possible to the boundary line.

LAW 20   LOST BALL

1 Runs Scored
If a ball in play cannot be found or recovered any fieldsman may call 'lost ball' when 6 runs shall be added to the score; but if more than 6 have been run before 'lost ball' is called, as many runs as have been completed shall be scored. The run in progress shall count provided that the Batsmen have crossed at the instant of the call of 'lost ball'.

2 How Scored
The runs shall be added to the score of the Striker if the ball has been struck, but otherwise to the score of byes, leg-byes, no-balls or wides as the case may be.

LAW 21   THE RESULT

1 A Win – Two-Innings Matches
The side which has scored a total of runs in excess of that scored by the opposing side in its two completed innings shall be the winners.

2 A Win – One-Innings Matches
(a) One-innings matches, unless played out as in 1 above, shall be decided on the first innings, but see Law 12.5: (Continuation After One Innings of Each Side).
(b) If the Captains agree to continue play after the completion of one innings of each side in accordance with Law 12.5: (Continuation After One Innings of Each Side) and a result is not achieved on the second innings, the first innings result shall stand.

3 Umpires Awarding a Match
(a) A match shall be lost by a side which, during the match,
   (i) refuses to play, or
   (ii) concedes defeat,
and the Umpires shall award the match to the other side.
(b) Should both Batsmen at the wickets or the fielding side leave the field at any time without the agreement of the Umpires, this shall constitute a refusal to play, and, on appeal, the Umpires shall award the match to the other side in accordance with (a) above.

4 A Tie
The result of a match shall be a tie when the scores are equal at the conclusion of play, but only if the side batting last has completed its innings.

If the scores of the completed first innings of a one-day match are equal, it shall be a tie but only if the match has not been played out to a further conclusion.

5 A Draw
A match not determined in any of the ways as in 1, 2, 3 and 4 above shall count as a draw.

6 Correctness of Result

Any decision as to the correctness of the scores shall be the responsibility of the Umpires. See Law 3.14: (Correctness of Scores).

If, after the Umpires and Players have left the field, in the belief that the match has been concluded, the Umpires decide that a mistake in scoring has occurred, which affects the result, and provided time has not been reached, they shall order play to resume and to continue until the agreed finishing time unless a result is reached earlier.

If the Umpires decide that a mistake has occurred and time has been reached, the Umpires shall immediately inform both Captains of the necessary corrections to the scores and, if applicable, to the result.

7 Acceptance of Result

In accepting the scores as notified by the scorers and agreed by the Umpires, the Captains of both sides thereby accept the result.

NOTES

(a) Statement of Results
The result of a finished match is stated as a win by runs, except in the case of a win by the side batting last when it is by the number of wickets still then to fall.
(b) Winning Hit or Extras
As soon as the side has won, see 1 and 2 above, the Umpire shall call 'time', the match is finished, and nothing that happens thereafter other than as a result of a mistake in scoring, see 6 above, shall be regarded as part of the match.

However, if a boundary constitutes the winning hit – or extras – and the boundary allowance exceeds the number of runs required to win the match, such runs scored shall be credited to the side's total and, in the case of a hit, to the Striker's score.

LAW 22   THE OVER

1 Number of Balls
The ball shall be bowled from each wicket alternately in overs of either 6 or 8 balls according to agreement before the match.

2 Call of 'Over'
When the agreed number of balls has been bowled, and as the ball becomes dead or when it becomes clear to the Umpire at the Bowler's end that both the fielding side and the Batsmen at the wicket have ceased to regard the ball as in play, the Umpire shall call 'over' before leaving the wicket.

3 No Ball or Wide Ball
Neither a no ball nor a wide ball shall be reckoned as one of the over.

4 Umpire Miscounting
If an Umpire miscounts the number of balls, the over as counted by the Umpire shall stand.

5 Bowler Changing Ends
A Bowler shall be allowed to change ends as often as desired provided only that he does not bowl two overs consecutively in an innings.

6 The Bowler Finishing an Over
A Bowler shall finish an over in progress unless he be incapacitated or be suspended under Law 42.8: (The Bowling of Fast Short Pitched Balls), 42.9: (The Bowling of Fast High Full Pitches), 42.10: (Time Wasting) and 42.11: (Players Damaging the Pitch). If an over is left incomplete for any reason at the start of an interval or interruption of play, it shall be finished on the resumption of play.

7 Bowler Incapacitated or Suspended During an Over
If, for any reason, a Bowler is incapacitated while running up to bowl the first ball of an over, or is incapacitated or suspended during an over, the Umpire shall call and signal 'dead ball' and another Bowler shall be allowed to bowl or complete the over from the same end, provided only that he shall not bowl two overs, or part thereof, consecutively in one innings.

8 Position of Non-Striker
The Batsman at the Bowler's end shall normally stand on the opposite side of the wicket to that from which the ball is being delivered, unless a request to do otherwise is granted by the Umpire.

LAW 23   DEAD BALL

1   The Ball Becomes Dead, when:
(a) It is finally settled in the hands of the Wicket-Keeper or the Bowler.
(b) It reaches or pitches over the boundary.
(c) A Batsman is out.
(d) Whether played or not, it lodges in the clothing or equipment of a Batsman or the clothing of an Umpire.

(e) A ball lodges in a protective helmet worn by a member of the fielding side.

(f) A penalty is awarded under Law 20: (Lost Ball) or Law 41.1: (Fielding the Ball).

(g) The Umpire calls 'over' or 'time'.

2 Either Umpire Shall Call and Signal 'Dead Ball', when:

(a) He intervenes in a case of unfair play.

(b) A serious injury to a Player or Umpire occurs.

(c) He is satisfied that, for an adequate reason, the Striker is not ready to receive the ball and makes no attempt to play it.

(d) The Bowler drops the ball accidentally before delivery, or the ball does not leave his hand for any reason, other than in an attempt to run out the Non-Striker (see Law 24.5 – Bowler Attempting to Run Out the Non-Striker Before Delivery).

(e) One or both bails fall from the Striker's wicket before he receives delivery.

(f) He leaves his normal position for consultation.

(g) He is required to do so under Law 26.3: (Disallowance of Leg Byes), etc.

3 The Ball Ceases to be Dead, when:

The Bowler starts his run-up or bowling action.

4 The Ball is not Dead, when:

(a) It strikes an Umpire (unless it lodges in his dress).

(b) The wicket is broken or struck down (unless a Batsman is out thereby).

(c) An unsuccessful appeal is made.

(d) The wicket is broken accidentally either by the Bowler during his delivery or by a Batsman in running.

(e) The Umpire has called 'no ball' or 'wide'.

NOTES

(a) Ball Finally Settled

Whether the ball is finally settled or not – see 1(a) above · – must be a question for the Umpires alone to decide.

(b) Action on Call of 'Dead Ball'

(i) *If 'dead ball' is called prior to the Striker receiving a delivery the Bowler shall be allowed an*

additional ball.

(ii) *If 'dead ball' is called after the Striker receives a delivery the Bowler shall not be allowed an additional ball, unless a 'no ball' or 'wide' has been called.*

LAW 24   NO BALL

1 Mode of Delivery

The Umpire shall indicate to the Striker whether the Bowler intends to bowl over or round the wicket, overarm or underarm, right- or left-handed. Failure on the part of the Bowler to indicate in advance a change in his mode of delivery is unfair and the Umpire shall call and signal 'no ball'.

2 Fair Delivery – the Arm

For a delivery to be fair the ball must be bowled not thrown – see Note (a) below. If either Umpire is not entirely satisfied with the absolute fairness of a delivery in this respect he shall call and signal 'no ball' instantly upon delivery.

3 Fair Delivery – the Feet

The Umpire at the bowler's wicket shall call and signal 'no ball' if he is not satisfied that in the delivery stride:

(a) the Bowler's back foot has landed within and not touching the return crease or its forward extension or

(b) some part of the front foot whether grounded or raised was behind the popping crease.

4 Bowler Throwing at Striker's Wicket Before Delivery

If the Bowler, before delivering the ball, throws it at the Striker's wicket in an attempt to run him out, the Umpire shall call and signal 'no ball'. See Law 42.12: (Batsman Unfairly Stealing a Run) and Law 38: (Run Out).

5 Bowler Attempting to Run Out Non-Striker Before Delivery

If the Bowler, before delivering the ball, attempts to run out the non-Striker, any runs which result shall be allowed and shall be scored as no balls. Such an attempt shall not count as a ball in the over. The Umpire shall not call 'no ball'. See Law 42.12: (Batsman Unfairly Stealing a Run).

6 Infringement of Laws by a Wicket-Keeper or a Fieldsman

The Umpire shall call and signal 'no ball' in the event of the Wicket-Keeper infringing Law 40.1: (Position of Wicket-Keeper) or a Fieldsman infringing Law 41.2 : (Limitation of On-side Fields-men) or Law 41.3: (Position of Fieldsmen).

7 Revoking a Call
An Umpire shall revoke the call 'no ball' if the ball does not leave the Bowler's hand for any reason. See Law 23.2: (Either Umpire Shall Call and Signal 'Dead Ball').

8 Penalty
A penalty of one run for a no ball shall be scored if no runs are made otherwise.

9 Runs from a No Ball
The Striker may hit a no ball and whatever runs result shall be added to his score. Runs made otherwise from a no ball shall be scored no balls.

10 Out from a No Ball
The Striker shall be out from a no ball if he breaks Law 34: (Hit the Ball Twice) and either Batsman may be Run Out or shall be given out if either breaks Law 33: (Handled the Ball) or Law 37: (Obstructing the Field).

11 Batsman Given Out off a No Ball
Should a Batsman be given out off a no ball the penalty for bowling it shall stand unless runs are otherwise scored.

NOTES

(a) Definition of a Throw
A ball shall be deemed to have been thrown if, in the opinion of either Umpire, the process of straightening the bowling arm, whether it be partial or complete, takes place during that part of the delivery swing which directly precedes the ball leaving the hand. This definition shall not debar a Bowler from the use of the wrist in the delivery swing.

(b) No Ball not Counting in Over
A no ball shall not be reckoned as one of the over. See Law 22.3: (No Ball or Wide Ball).

LAW 25 WIDE BALL

1 Judging a Wide
If the Bowler bowls the ball so high over or so wide of the wicket that, in the opinion of the Umpire, it passes out of reach of the Striker, standing in a normal guard position, the Umpire shall call and signal 'wide ball' as soon as it has passed the line of the Striker's wicket.

The Umpire shall not adjudge a ball as being a wide if:
(a) The Striker, by moving from his guard position, causes the ball to pass out of his reach.
(b) The Striker moves and thus brings the ball within his reach.

2 Penalty
A penalty of one run for a wide shall be scored if no runs are made otherwise.

3 Ball Coming to Rest in Front of the Striker
If a ball which the Umpire considers to have been delivered comes to rest in front of the line of the Striker's wicket, 'wide' shall not be called. The Striker has a right, without interference from the fielding side, to make one attempt to hit the ball. If the fielding side interfere, the Umpire shall replace the ball where it came to rest and shall order the Fieldsmen to resume the places they occupied in the field before the ball was delivered.

The Umpire shall call and signal 'dead ball' as soon as it is clear that the Striker does not intend to hit the ball, or after the Striker has made one unsuccessful attempt to hit the ball.

4 Revoking a Call
The Umpire shall revoke the call if the Striker hits a ball which has been called 'wide'.

5 Ball not Dead
The ball does not become dead on the call of 'wide ball' – see Law 23.4: (The Ball is Not Dead).

6 Runs Resulting from a Wide
All runs which are run or result from a wide ball which is not a no ball shall be scored wide balls, or if no runs are made one shall be scored.

7 Out from a Wide
The Striker shall be out from a wide ball if he breaks Law 35: (Hit Wicket); or Law 39: (Stumped). Either Batsman may be Run Out and shall be out if he breaks Law 33: (Handled the Ball), or Law 37: (Obstructing the Field).

8 Batsman Given Out Off a Wide
Should a Batsman be given out off a wide, the penalty for bowling it shall stand unless runs are otherwise made.

NOTES

(a) Wide Ball not Counting in Over
A wide ball shall not be reckoned as one of the over – see Law 22.3: (No Ball or Wide Ball).

LAW 26   BYE AND LEG-BYE

1 Byes

If the ball, not having been called 'wide' or 'no ball', passes the Striker without touching his bat or person, and any runs are obtained, the Umpire shall signal 'bye' and the run or runs shall be credited as such to the batting side.

2 Leg-byes

If the ball, not having been called 'wide' or 'no ball', is unintentionally deflected by the Striker's dress or person, except a hand holding the bat, and any runs are obtained the Umpire shall signal 'leg-bye' and the run or runs so scored shall be credited as such to the batting side.

Such leg-byes shall only be scored if, in the opinion of the Umpire, the Striker has:
(a)   attempted to play the ball with his bat, or
(b)   tried to avoid being hit by the ball.

3 Disallowance of Leg-byes

In the case of a deflection by the Striker's person, other than in 2(a) and (b) above, the Umpire shall call and signal 'dead ball' as soon as one run has been completed or when it is clear that a run is not being attempted or the ball has reached the boundary.

On the call and signal of 'dead ball' the Batsmen shall return to their original ends and no runs shall be allowed.

Law 27   APPEALS

1 Time of Appeals

The Umpires shall not give a Batsman out unless appealed to by the other side which shall be done prior to the Bowler beginning his run-up or bowling action to deliver the next ball. Under Law 23.1: (g) (The Ball Becomes Dead) the ball is dead on 'over' being called; this does not, however, invalidate an appeal made prior to the first ball of the following over provided 'time' has not been called. See Law 17.1: (Call of Time).

2 An Appeal 'How's That?'

An appeal 'How's That?' shall cover all ways of being out.

3 Answering Appeals

The Umpire at the Bowler's wicket shall answer appeals before the other Umpire in all cases except those arising out of Law 35: (Hit Wicket) or Law 39: (Stumped) or Law 38: (Run Out) when this occurs at the Striker's wicket.

When either Umpire has given a Batsman not out, the other Umpire shall, within his jurisdiction, answer the appeal or a further appeal, provided it is made in time in accordance with 1 above (Time of Appeals).

4 Consultation by Umpires

An Umpire may consult with the other Umpire on a point of fact which the latter may have been in a better position to see and shall then give his decision. If, after consultation, there is still doubt remaining the decision shall be in favour of the Batsman.

5 Batsman Leaving His Wicket Under a Misapprehension

The Umpires shall intervene if satisfied that a Batsman, not having been given out, has left his wicket under a misapprehension that he has been dismissed.

6 Umpire's Decision

The Umpire's decision is final. He may alter his decision, provided that such alteration is made promptly.

7 Withdrawal of an Appeal

In exceptional circumstances the Captain of the fielding side may seek permission of the Umpire to withdraw an appeal providing the outgoing Batsman has not left the playing area. If this is allowed, the Umpire shall cancel his decision.

LAW 28   THE WICKET IS DOWN

1 Wicket Down

The wicket is down if:
(a)   Either the ball or the Striker's bat or person completely removes either bail from the top of the stumps. A disturbance of a bail, whether temporary or not, shall not constitute a complete removal, but the wicket is down if a bail in falling lodges between two of the stumps.
(b)   Any player completely removes with his hand or arm a bail from the top of the stumps, providing that the ball is held in that hand or in the hand of the arm so used.
(c)   When both bails are off, a stump is struck out of the ground by the ball, or a player strikes

or pulls a stump out of the ground, providing that the ball is held in the hand(s) or in the hand of the arm so used.

2 One Bail Off
If one bail is off, it shall be sufficient for the purpose of putting the wicket down to remove the remaining bail, or to strike or pull any of the three stumps out of the ground in any of the ways stated in 1 above.

3 All the Stumps Out of the Ground
If all the stumps are out of the ground, the fielding side shall be allowed to put back one or more stumps in order to have an opportunity of putting the wicket down.

4 Dispensing With Bails
If owing to the strength of the wind, it has been agreed to dispense with the bails in accordance with Law 8: Note (a) (Dispensing With Bails) the decision as to when the wicket is down is one for the Umpires to decide on the facts before them. In such circumstances and if the Umpires so decide the wicket shall be held to be down even though a stump has not been struck out of the ground.

NOTES

(a) Remaking the Wicket
If the wicket is broken while the ball is in play, it is not the Umpire's duty to remake the wicket until the ball has become dead – see Law 23: (Dead Ball). A member of the fielding side, however, may remake the wicket in such circumstances.

LAW 29   BATSMAN OUT OF HIS GROUND

When Out of His Ground
A Batsman shall be considered to be out of his ground unless some part of his bat in his hand or of his person is grounded behind the line of the popping crease.

LAW 30   BOWLED

Out Bowled
The Striker shall be out bowled if:
(a) His wicket is bowled down, even if the ball first touches his bat or person.
(b) He breaks his wicket by hitting or kicking the ball on to it before the completion of a stroke,

or as a result of attempting to guard his wicket. See Law 34.1: (Out – Hit the Ball Twice).

NOTES

(a) Out bowled – not L.B.W.
The Striker is out Bowled if the ball is deflected on to his wicket even though a decision against him would be justified under Law 36: (Leg Before Wicket).

LAW 31   TIMED OUT

1 Out Timed Out
An incoming Batsman shall be out Timed Out if he wilfully takes more than two minutes to come in – the two minutes being timed from the moment a wicket falls until the new batsman steps on to the field of play.

If this is not complied with and if the Umpire is satisfied that the delay was wilful and if an appeal is made, the new Batsman shall be given out by the Umpire at the Bowler's end.

2 Time to be Added
The time taken by the Umpires to investigate the cause of the delay shall be added at the normal close of play.

NOTES

(a) Entry in Score Book
The correct entry in the score book when a Batsman is given out under this Law is 'timed out', and the Bowler does not get credit for the wicket.
(b) Batsmen Crossing on the Field of Play
It is an essential duty of the Captains to ensure that the in-going Batsman passes the out-going one before the latter leaves the field of play.

LAW 32   CAUGHT

1 Out Caught
The Striker shall be out Caught if the ball touches his bat or if it touches below the wrist his hand or glove, holding the bat, and is subsequently held by a Fieldsman before it touches the ground.

2 A Fair Catch
A catch shall be considered to have been fairly made if:
(a) The Fieldsman is within the field of play throughout the act of making the catch.
   (i) The act of making the catch shall start from the time when the Fieldsman first

handles the ball and shall end when he both retains complete control over the further disposal of the ball and remains within the field of play.

    (ii) In order to be within the field of play, the Fieldsman may not touch or ground any part of his person on or over a boundary line. When the boundary is marked by a fence or board the Fieldsman may not ground any part of his person over the boundary fence or board, but may touch or lean over the boundary fence or board in completing the catch.

(b) The ball is hugged to the body of the catcher or accidentally lodges in his dress or, in the case of the Wicket-Keeper, in his pads. However, a Striker may not be caught if a ball lodges in a protective helmet worn by a Fieldsman, in which case the Umpire shall call and signal 'dead ball'. See Law 23: (Dead Ball).

(c) The ball does not touch the ground even though a hand holding it does so in effecting the catch.

(d) A Fieldsman catches the ball, after it has been lawfully played a second time by the Striker, but only if the ball has not touched the ground since being first struck.

(e) A Fieldsman catches the ball after it has touched an Umpire, another Fieldsman or the other Batsman. However a Striker may not be caught if a ball has touched a protective helmet worn by a Fieldsman.

(f) The ball is caught off an obstruction within the boundary provided it has not previously been agreed to regard the obstruction as a boundary.

3 Scoring of Runs

If a Striker is caught, no runs shall be scored.

NOTES

(a) Scoring from an Attempted Catch
When a Fieldsman carrying the ball touches or grounds any part of his person on or over a boundary marked by a line, 6 runs shall be scored.
(b) Ball Still in Play
If a Fieldsman releases the ball before he crosses the boundary, the ball will be considered to be still in play and it may be caught by another Fieldsman. However, if the original Fieldsman returns to the field of play and handles the ball, a catch may not be made.

LAW 33   HANDLED THE BALL

1 Out Handled the Ball

Either Batsman on appeal shall be out Handled the Ball if he wilfully touches the ball while in play with the hand not holding the bat unless he does so with the consent of the opposite side.

NOTES

(a) Entry in Score Book
The correct entry in the score book when a Batsman is given out under this Law is 'handled the ball'; and the Bowler does not get credit for the wicket.

LAW 34   HIT THE BALL TWICE

1 Out Hit the Ball Twice

The Striker, on appeal, shall be out Hit the Ball Twice if, after the ball is struck or is stopped by any part of his person, he wilfully strikes it again with his bat or person except for the sole purpose of guarding his wicket: this he may do with his bat or any part of his person other than his hands, but see Law 37.2: (Obstructing a Ball from Being Caught).

    For the purpose of this Law, a hand holding the bat shall be regarded as part of the bat.

2 Returning the Ball to a Fieldsman

The Striker, on appeal, shall be out under this Law, if, without the consent of the opposite side, he uses his bat or person to return the ball to any of the fielding side.

3 Runs from Ball Lawfully Struck Twice

No runs except those which result from an overthrow or penalty, see Law 41: (The Fieldsman), shall be scored from a ball lawfully struck twice.

NOTES

(a) Entry in Score Book
The correct entry in the score book when the Striker is given out under this Law is 'hit the ball twice', and the Bowler does not get credit for the wicket.
(b) Runs Credited to the Batsman
Any runs awarded under 3 above as a result of an overthrow or penalty shall be credited to the Striker, provided the ball in the first instance has touched the bat, or, if otherwise, as extras.

LAW 35   HIT WICKET

1 Out Hit Wicket

The Striker shall be out Hit Wicket if, while the ball is in play:

(a) His wicket is broken with any part of his person, dress, or equipment as a result of any action taken by him in preparing to receive or in receiving a delivery, or in setting off for his first run, immediately after playing, or playing at, the ball.

(b) He hits down his wicket whilst lawfully making a second stroke for the purpose of guarding his wicket within the provisions of Law 34.1: (Out Hit the Ball Twice).

NOTES

(a) Not Out Hit Wicket

A Batsman is not out under this Law should his wicket be broken in any of the ways referred to in 1(a) above if:

(i) It occurs while he is in the act of running, other than in setting off for his first run immediately after playing at the ball, or while he is avoiding being run out or stumped.

(ii) The Bowler after starting his run-up or bowling action does not deliver the ball; in which case the Umpire shall immediately call and signal 'dead ball'.

(iii) It occurs whilst he is avoiding, a throw-in at any time.

LAW 36   LEG BEFORE WICKET

1 Out L.B.W.

The Striker shall be out L.B.W. in the circumstances set out below:

(a) *Striker Attempting to Play the Ball*

The Striker shall be out L.B.W. if he first intercepts with any part of his person, dress or equipment a fair ball which would have hit the wicket and which has not previously touched his bat or a hand holding the bat, provided that:

(i) The ball pitched in a straight line between wicket and wicket or on the off side of the Striker's wicket, or was intercepted full pitch, and

(ii) the point of impact is in a straight line between wicket and wicket, even if above the level of the bails.

(b) *Striker Making No Attempt to Play the Ball*

The Striker shall be out L.B.W. even if the ball is intercepted outside the line of the off-stump, if, in the opinion of the Umpire, he has made no genuine attempt to play the ball with his bat, but has intercepted the ball with some part of his person and if the other circumstances set out in (a) above apply.

LAW 37   OBSTRUCTING THE FIELD

1 Wilful Obstruction

Either Batsman, on appeal, shall be out Obstructing the Field if he wilfully obstructs the opposite side by word or action.

2 Obstructing a Ball from Being Caught

The Striker, on appeal, shall be out should wilful obstruction by either Batsman prevent a catch being made.

This shall apply even though the Striker causes the obstruction in lawfully guarding his wicket under the provisions of Law 34. See Law 34.1: (Out Hit the Ball Twice).

NOTES

(a) Accidental Obstruction

The Umpires must decide whether the obstruction was wilful or not. The accidental interception of a throw-in by a Batsman while running does not break this Law.

(b) Entry in Score Book

The correct entry in the score book when a Batsman is given out under this Law is 'obstructing the field', and the bowler does not get credit for the wicket.

LAW 38   RUN OUT

1 Out Run Out

Either Batsman shall be out Run Out if in running or at any time while the ball is in play – except in the circumstances described in Law 39: (Stumped) – he is out of his ground and his wicket is put down by the opposite side. If, however, a Batsman in running makes good his ground he shall not be out Run Out if he subsequently leaves his ground, in order to avoid injury, and the wicket is put down.

2 'No Ball' Called

If a no ball has been called, the Striker shall not be given Run Out unless he attempts to run.

3 Which Batsman is Out

If the Batsmen have crossed in running, he who

runs for the wicket which is put down shall be out; if they have not crossed, he who has left the wicket which is put down shall be out. If a Batsman remains in his ground or returns to his ground and the other Batsman joins him there, the latter shall be out if his wicket is put down.

4 Scoring of Runs

If a Batsman is run out, only that run which is being attempted shall not be scored. If however an injured Striker himself is run out, no runs shall be scored. See Law 2.7: (Transgression of the Laws by Injured Batsman or Runner).

NOTES

(a) Ball Played on to Opposite Wicket
If the ball is played on to the opposite wicket neither Batsman is liable to be Run Out unless the ball has been touched by a Fieldsman before the wicket is broken.
(b) Entry in Score Book
The correct entry in the score book when the Striker is given out under this Law is 'run out', and the Bowler does not get credit for the wicket.
(c) Run Out off a Fieldsman's Helmet
If, having been played by a Batsman, or having come off his person, the ball rebounds directly from a Fieldsman's helmet on to the stumps, with either Batsman out of his ground, the Batsman shall be 'Not Out'.

LAW 39 STUMPED

1 Out Stumped

The Striker shall be out Stumped if, in receiving a ball, not being a no ball, he is out of his ground otherwise than in attempting a run and the wicket is put down by the Wicket-Keeper without the intervention of another Fieldsman.

2 Action by the Wicket-Keeper

The Wicket-Keeper may take the ball in front of the wicket in an attempt to Stump the Striker only if the ball has touched the bat or person of the Striker.

NOTES

(a) Ball Rebounding from Wicket-Keeper's Person
The Striker may be out Stumped if in the circumstances stated in 1. above, the wicket is broken by a ball rebounding from the Wicket-Keeper's person or equipment other than a protective helmet or is kicked or thrown by the Wicket-Keeper on to the wicket.

LAW 40 THE WICKET-KEEPER

1 Position of Wicket-Keeper

The Wicket-Keeper shall remain wholly behind the wicket until a ball delivered by the Bowler touches the bat or person of the Striker, or passes the wicket, or until the Striker attempts a run.

In the event of the Wicket-Keeper contravening this Law, the Umpire at the Striker's end shall call and signal 'no ball' at the instant of delivery or as soon as possible thereafter.

2 Restriction on Actions of the Wicket-Keeper

If the Wicket-Keeper interferes with the Striker's right to play the ball and to guard his wicket, the Striker shall not be out, except under Laws 33: (Handled the Ball), 34: (Hit the Ball Twice), 37: (Obstructing the Field), 38: (Run Out).

3 Interference with the Wicket-Keeper by the Striker

If in the legitimate defence of his wicket, the Striker interferes with the Wicket-Keeper, he shall not be out, except as provided for in Law 37.2: (Obstructing a Ball From Being Caught).

LAW 41 THE FIELDSMAN

1 Fielding the Ball

The Fieldsman may stop the ball with any part of his person, but if he wilfully stops it otherwise, 5 runs shall be added to the run or runs already scored; if no run has been scored 5 penalty runs shall be awarded. The run in progress shall count provided that the Batsmen have crossed at the instant of the act. If the ball has been struck, the penalty shall be added to the score of the Striker, but otherwise to the score of byes, leg-byes, no balls or wides as the case may be.

2 Limitation of On-side Fieldsmen

The number of on-side Fieldsmen behind the popping crease at the instant of the Bowler's delivery shall not exceed two. In the event of infringement by the fielding side the Umpire at the Striker's end shall call and signal 'no ball' at the instant of delivery or as soon as possible thereafter.

3 Position of Fieldsmen

While the ball is in play and until the ball has made contact with the bat or the Striker's person or has passed his bat, no Fieldsman, other than the Bowler, may stand on or have any part of his person extended over the pitch (measuring 22 yards/20.12m. × 10 feet/3.05m.). In the event of a Fieldsman contravening this Law, the Umpire at the Bowler's end shall call and signal 'no ball' at the instant of delivery or as soon as possible thereafter. See Law 40.1: (Position of Wicket-Keeper).

4 Fieldsmen's Protective Helmets

Protective helmets, when not in use by members of the fielding side, shall only be placed, if above the surface, on the ground behind the Wicket-Keeper. In the event of the ball, when in play, striking a helmet whilst in this position, five penalty runs shall be awarded, as laid down in Law 41.1 and Note (a).

NOTES

(a) Batsmen Changing Ends
The 5 runs referred to in 1 above are a penalty and the Batsmen do not change ends solely by reason of this penalty.

LAW 42   UNFAIR PLAY

1 Responsibility of Captains

The Captains are responsible at all times for ensuring that play is conducted within the spirit of the game as well as within the Laws.

2 Responsibility of Umpires

The Umpires are the sole judges of fair and unfair play.

3 Intervention by the Umpire

The Umpires shall intervene without appeal by calling and signalling 'dead ball' in the case of unfair play, but should not otherwise interfere with the progress of the game except as required to do so by the Laws.

4 Lifting the Seam

A Player shall not lift the seam of the ball for any reason. Should this be done, the Umpires shall change the ball for one of similar condition to that in use prior to the contravention. See Note (a)

5 Changing the Condition of the Ball

Any member of the fielding side may polish the ball provided that such polishing wastes no time and that no artificial substance is used. No one shall rub the ball on the ground or use any artificial substance or take any other action to alter the condition of the ball.

In the event of a contravention of this Law, the Umpires, after consultation, shall change the ball for one of similar condition to that in use prior to the contravention.

This Law does not prevent a member of the fielding side from drying a wet ball, or removing mud from the ball. See Note (b).

6 Incommoding the Striker

An Umpire is justified in intervening under this Law and shall call and signal 'dead ball' if, in his opinion, any Player of the fielding side incommodes the Striker by any noise or action while he is receiving the ball.

7 Obstruction of a Batsman in Running

It shall be considered unfair if any Fieldsman wilfully obstructs a Batsman in running. In these circumstances the Umpire shall call and signal 'dead ball' and allow any completed runs and the run in progress or alternatively any boundary scored.

8 The Bowling of Fast Short Pitched Balls

The bowling of fast short pitched balls is unfair if, in the opinion of the Umpire at the Bowler's end, it constitutes an attempt to intimidate the Striker. See Note (d).

Umpires shall consider intimidation to be the deliberate bowling of fast short pitched balls which by their length, height and direction are intended or likely to inflict physical injury on the Striker. The relative skill of the Striker shall also be taken into consideration.

In the event of such unfair bowling, the Umpire at the Bowler's end shall adopt the following procedure:
(a) In the first instance the Umpire shall call and signal 'no ball', caution the Bowler and inform the other Umpire, the Captain of the fielding side and the Batsmen of what has occurred.
(b) If this caution is ineffective, he shall repeat the above procedure and indicate to the Bowler that this is a final warning.
(c) Both the above caution and final warning shall continue to apply even though the Bowler may later change ends.
(d) Should the above warnings prove ineffective the Umpire at the Bowler's end shall:
     (i)   At the first repetition call and signal 'no ball' and when the ball is dead direct the Captain to take the Bowler off forthwith

and to complete the over with another Bowler, provided that the Bowler does not bowl two overs or part thereof consecutively. See Law 22.7: (Bowler Incapacitated or Suspended During an Over).

(ii) Not allow the Bowler, thus taken off, to bowl again in the same innings.

(iii) Report the occurrence to the Captain of the batting side as soon as the Players leave the field for an interval.

(iv) Report the occurrence to the Executive of the fielding side and to any governing body responsible for the match who shall take any further action which is considered to be appropriate against the Bowler concerned.

9 The Bowling of Fast High Full Pitches

The bowling of fast high full pitches is unfair.

A fast high full pitched ball shall be defined as a ball that passes, or would have passed, on the full above waist height of a Batsman standing upright at the crease. Should a Bowler bowl a fast high full pitched ball, either Umpire shall call and signal 'No Ball' and adopt the procedure of caution, final warning, action against the Bowler and reporting as set out in Law 42.8.

10 Time Wasting

Any form of time wasting is unfair.

(a) In the event of the Captain of the fielding side wasting time or allowing any member of his side to waste time, the Umpire at the Bowler's end shall adopt the following procedure:

(i) In the first instance he shall caution the Captain of the fielding side and inform the other Umpire of what has occurred.

(ii) If this caution is ineffective he shall repeat the above procedure and indicate to the Captain that this is a final warning.

(iii) The Umpire shall report the occurrence to the Captain of the batting side as soon as the Players leave the field for an interval.

(iv) Should the above procedure prove ineffective the Umpire shall report the occurrence to the Executive of the fielding side and to any governing body responsible for that match who shall take appropriate action against the Captain and the Players concerned.

(b) In the event of a Bowler taking unnecessarily long to bowl an over the Umpire at the Bowler's end shall adopt the procedures, other than the calling of 'no ball', of caution, final warning, action against the Bowler and reporting as set out in 8. above.

(c) In the event of a Batsman wasting time (see Note (e)) other than in the manner described in Law 31: (Timed Out), the Umpire at the Bowler's end shall adopt the following procedure:

(i) In the first instance he shall caution the Batsman and inform the other Umpire at once, and the Captain of the batting side, as soon as the Players leave the field for an interval, of what has occurred.

(ii) If this proves ineffective, he shall repeat the caution, indicate to the Batsman that this is a final warning and inform the other Umpire.

(iii) The Umpire shall report the occurrence to both Captains as soon as the Players leave the field for an interval.

(iv) Should the above procedure prove ineffective, the Umpire shall report the occurrence to the Executive of the batting side and to any governing body responsible for that match who shall take appropriate action against the Player concerned.

11 Players Damaging the Pitch

The Umpires shall intervene and prevent Players from causing damage to the pitch which may assist the Bowlers of either side. See Note (c).

(a) In the event of any member of the fielding side damaging the pitch the Umpire shall follow the procedure of caution, final warning and reporting as set out in 10 (a) above.

(b) In the event of a Bowler contravening this Law by running down the pitch after delivering the ball, the Umpire at the Bowler's end shall first caution the Bowler. If this caution is ineffective the Umpire shall adopt the procedures, other than the calling of 'no ball', of final warning, action against the Bowler and reporting as set out in 8. above.

(c) In the event of a Batsman damaging the pitch the Umpire at the Bowler's end shall follow the procedures of caution, final warning and reporting as set out in 10 (c) above.

12 Batsmen Unfairly Stealing a Run

Any attempt by the Batsman to steal a run during the Bowler's run-up is unfair. Unless the Bowler attempts to run out either Batsman – see Law 24.4: (Bowler Throwing At Striker's Wicket Before Delivery) and Law 24.5: (Bowler Attempting to Run Out Non-Striker Before Delivery) – the Umpire shall call and signal 'dead ball' as soon as the Batsmen cross in any such attempt to run. The Batsmen shall then return to their original wickets.

13 Player's Conduct

In the event of a Player failing to comply with the instructions of an Umpire, criticising his decisions by word or action, or showing dissent, or generally behaving in a manner which might bring the game into disrepute, the Umpire concerned shall in the first place report the matter to the other Umpire and to the Player's Captain requesting the latter to take action. If this proves ineffective, the Umpire shall report the incident as soon as possible to the Executive of the Player's team and to any Governing Body responsible for the match, who shall take any further action which is considered appropriate against the Player or Players concerned.

NOTES

(a) The Condition of the Ball

Umpires shall make frequent and irregular inspections of the condition of the ball.

(b) Drying of a Wet Ball

A wet ball may be dried on a towel or with sawdust.

(c) Danger Area

The danger area on the pitch, which must be protected from damage by a Bowler, shall be regarded by the Umpires as the area contained by an imaginary line 4 feet/1.22m. from the popping crease, and parallel to it, and within two imaginary and parallel lines drawn down the pitch from points on that line 1 foot/30.48cm. on either side of the middle stump.

(d) Fast Short Pitched Balls

As a guide, a fast short pitched ball is one which pitches short and passes, or would have passed, above the shoulder height of the Striker standing in a normal batting stance at the crease.

(e) Time Wasting by Batsmen

Other than in exceptional circumstances, the Batsman should always be ready to take strike when the Bowler is ready to start his run-up.